ANDREW JOHNSON

Also by Eric L. McKitrick

Andrew Johnson and Reconstruction

Slavery Defended: The Views of the Old South

Andrew Johnson

A PROFILE

EDITED BY

ERIC L. McKITRICK

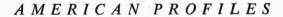

AMERICAN PROFILES

General Editor: Aïda DiPace Donald

HILL AND WANG : NEW YORK

Contents

Introduction   **vii**

Brief Biography of Andrew Johnson   **xxiii**

Runaway Apprentice   **1**
   ROBERT W. WINSTON

The Tailor-Politician   **13**
   GEORGE F. MILTON

Impressions of Andrew Johnson   **42**
   OLIVER P. TEMPLE

Andrew Johnson as Military Governor of Tennessee   **54**
   CLIFTON R. HALL

Andrew Johnson, Outsider   **68**
   ERIC L. MCKITRICK

Johnson and His Policy   **78**
   HOWARD K. BEALE

v

Andrew Johnson: The Last Jacksonian   112
    KENNETH M. STAMPP

Johnson and the Negro   139
    LaWANDA COX and JOHN H. COX

Afterthought: Why Impeachment?   164
    ERIC L. MCKITRICK

The Tennessee Epilogue   193
    GEORGE F. MILTON

Bibliographical Note   219

Contributors   223

Introduction

No truly satisfactory biography of Andrew Johnson has ever been written, and conceivably a great contribution might result if some highly able person were to undertake such a work. And yet there may be reason to doubt whether a new biography of Johnson— fully up to scale, as biographies of prominent figures deserve to be—is at present urgently needed, or that the lack of one represents a serious gap in our knowledge. The problem of Andrew Johnson's Presidency has received considerable attention in recent years; by contrast, the remainder of Johnson's career does not make more than a modest claim on our interest, and there seem to be few compelling reasons why it should. Such a contrast is, of course, to some extent inherent in the career of anyone who becomes President of the United States. But with Johnson the contrast is extreme. Many a public man who did not achieve that office has nevertheless received extensive and loving biographic treatment, whereas in Andrew Johnson's case, were it not for his somewhat fortuitous nomination as Lincoln's running mate in 1864, there is serious question whether anyone would have wanted to write a book about him at all, loving or otherwise. His pre-Presidential career is virtually without distinction. Even as an individual, he cannot rank among the most attractive American figures.

With few exceptions, the entire tone of what has been written about Andrew Johnson has been inspired and governed throughout by the authors' view of a single subject, Reconstruction. On no other important public issue did Johnson exert significant influence. On this one, for good or ill, his influence was profound. Consequently, most men writing of Johnson have really been writing of Reconstruction, directly or indirectly, and oftener than not, directly. Even their treatment of Johnson the man, their assessments of his early life, and their judgments of the personality traits that emerged from the influences of his Tennessee environment and carried over into his Presidency have been shaped by their approval or disapproval of the course he took with regard to Reconstruction. The man himself has always been secondary; his character, attainments, and personal stature have tended to alter with the fluctuations of the larger argument. The most sympathetic biographies of Johnson—indeed, the only ones worthy of being called "biographies" at all—were conceived in the 1920's at the very high tide of reaction against Radical Reconstruction, which Johnson bitterly opposed, and nearly every word in them is heavy with judgment upon what their authors felt was one of the most degraded episodes of American history. Their value as biography, therefore, must depend to more than the usual degree on how well their authors' judgments on history have held up over time. For that matter, in virtually all the writing on Andrew Johnson that has been done from the beginning of the present century, the line between biography and the history of public affairs could hardly be said to exist. Historians and biographers, though their functions are always and everywhere on the point of merging, are in Johnson's case almost impossible to distinguish.

Andrew Johnson's historical reputation has thus been inversely related to that of Radical Reconstruction. As the latter declined, the former—after a few years' lag—rose.

Probably the most important historical writing on the Johnson era prior to the beginning of the twentieth century was done by men who had themselves taken some part in the history that Johnson helped to make. Henry Wilson was a Senator from Massachusetts during the Johnson administration and Vice-President under Grant; James G. Blaine was a Representative from

Maine, Speaker of the House, a Senator, candidate for the Presidency, and Secretary of State under Garfield and Harrison; George Boutwell was a Representative and later a Senator from Massachusetts, one of the Managers of Impeachment at Johnson's trial, and Secretary of the Treasury under Grant; and Carl Schurz was a Senator from Missouri, Secretary of the Interior under Hayes, and a long-time advocate of reform in the tariff and civil service. All were Republicans, all had supported Radical Reconstruction, all wrote historical reminiscences, and all wrote withering condemnations of Andrew Johnson. Johnson's public policy, in opposing the Congressional program of Reconstruction, was wicked and foolish; his personal qualities—his narrowness, egotism, and want of tact —made him unfit to occupy high public office.

By the turn of the century, however, Radical Reconstruction had been dead for a generation, and most of the sentiments that had originally brought it about were now in disrepute. The political and social fortunes of the American Negro, steadily declining since the mid-seventies, were reaching a new low. The movement in the Southern states to disfranchise and segregate their Negroes was brought to completion during the early years of the so-called Progressive Era, unopposed either by Northern public opinion or by the legislative or judicial processes of the federal government. Indeed, Southern practices in this regard were reflected to a considerable extent in Northern attitudes and practices as well. Thus Reconstruction, insofar as it had conferred rights and privileges upon the Negro that a new generation of white Americans no longer wanted him to exercise, had apparently been a mistake. All this was reflected not only at every level of public opinion but in the refined realm of historical scholarship, now coming professionally into its own. Scholars turning their attention to Reconstruction in the early 1900's were not prepared to find much that was praiseworthy in it. All took as their starting-point the assumption that Reconstruction was unwise, unjust, and unnatural. In their work, moreover, were to be found the first signs that the low reputation of Andrew Johnson might eventually be revised.

The leading figures of the new scholarship were James Ford Rhodes and William Archibald Dunning, both of whom published major statements in 1907, the fortieth anniversary year of the passage of the Reconstruction Acts. Each disapproved of Reconstruction, and neither believed in Negro equality. Neither, however, was as yet prepared to go very far in praising Johnson. Rhodes, indeed, thought it "difficult to conceive of one so ill-fitted" for the delicate work of Reconstruction as was Andrew Johnson. "Born in the midst of degrading influences . . . , brought up in the misery of the poor white class, he had no chance for breeding, none for book education, none for that half-conscious betterment which comes from association with cultivated and morally excellent people." Dunning was somewhat more mild about the President. Though he thought Johnson "was not a statesman of national size," and that his speeches—"offensive" and "abounding in self-praise"—were "disastrous and . . . inexcusable," he gave the President credit for "integrity of purpose, force of will, and rude intellectual force." Both Dunning and Rhodes believed that a policy of leniency and early readmission of the former Confederate states would have been the correct one if tactfully pursued, but that Johnson's stubborn refusal to concede to Congress a share in the work of Reconstruction alienated moderate Republicans and threw away any chances of success which the Presidential plan may have had. "Johnson stood for some correct principles," according to Rhodes, "but he had the knack of doing even right things in the wrong way."

This sort of ambivalence toward Johnson and his policy—right things done in the wrong way—characterized much of the writing on Reconstruction done in the pre–World War era. Though such an ambivalence persisted in some form for a number of years, the balance nevertheless tended to shift steadily in Johnson's favor. More and more of the once-maligned President's virtues were discovered as an ever more massive case was built up for the horrors of carpetbag Reconstruction. The many studies of Reconstruction in the various Southern states, pursued under Dunning's inspiration and often under his direct guidance at Columbia University, were not directly concerned with national politics. But they were cumulative in their effect, and they formed an indispensable base for all subsequent thought on the subject as a whole.

A number of these studies, it ought to be noted, had considerable merit, and some—James W. Garner's on Mississippi and C. Mildred Thompson's on Georgia being outstanding examples— are, for their time, models of scholarly objectivity. They represent a generation thinking a subject through for the first time, and there is somewhat less dogmatism in them, and rather more balance, than one might expect in view of the reactionary tone in which Reconstruction later came to be discussed in the 1920's. Nonetheless, that same "progressive" generation was one which was consumed with the problem of civic corruption as well as that of racial purity, and what its scholars saw, or thought they saw, in Reconstruction added up to a composite picture whose implications seemed overwhelming. It was the picture, soon stereotyped in the thinking of North and South alike, of irresponsible rule by ignorant Negroes, unprincipled scalawags, and corrupt carpetbaggers, mercifully brought to an end at long last by the resolute action of a united white community. As the evidence thus seemed to pile up, it was sooner or later bound to occur to someone that the man who first foresaw and tried to prevent this degraded state of affairs, Andrew Johnson, should at last be given some positive and ungrudging recognition.

James Schouler said as much in 1912. Schouler, who had been writing history since 1880, predicted in a magazine article that Johnson would "be held in kinder regard by posterity than he was by fellow-countrymen during his lifetime." In 1913 he published his own *History of the Reconstruction Period,* wherein he praised Johnson's "broad statesmanship," his "patriotism, energy, and courage," and the understanding of Southern conditions which "made him of invaluable service for reunion." Schouler had not been the first to urge such a view. Two of Johnson's own cabinet officers, Hugh McCulloch and Gideon Welles, had already published reminiscences in which much was made of the President's firmness and high principles. David DeWitt's *Impeachment and Trial of Andrew Johnson,* which appeared in 1903, had argued not only that the impeachment was an unjust and unwarranted proceeding (on that point, public opinion had long been agreed), but

also that Johnson's policy as a whole was wise and sound. But now
Schouler's was a major voice, coming from a historian of repute,
and the note he sounded would in time be echoed by a majority.

There continued to be reservations—Schouler himself expressed
some—regarding Johnson's political tact. Such reservations appeared in works published by Benjamin B. Kendrick, Clifton R.
Hall, and Ellis P. Oberholtzer in 1914, 1916, and 1917 respectively, but the note of criticism was for the most part muted in
approval of Johnson's broad purposes. Indeed, J. G. de Roulhac
Hamilton wrote in 1915, "The time has come for Americans to see
him as he was; to hold up his noble qualities for the admiration
and emulation of the generations of coming Americans." And in
that same year Lawrence H. Gipson declared of Johnson, "it is to
be doubted if there was a man living at that time who possessed a
saner insight into the more vital of the national problems."

By the mid-1920's the basic work on Reconstruction had been
done, and historical thought on the subject had hardened into
dogma. Whatever balance had once prevailed was now gone, and it
was in this setting that the image of Andrew Johnson underwent a
purification that would have astonished his contemporaries. To the
reaction against Reconstruction, by this time complete, was now
added another kind of reaction, inherited from World War I,
against "war hatred," together with immensely exaggerated no-
tions about the power of "propaganda." Johnson, like Lincoln
desiring only to bind up the nation's wounds, had been crucified by
a vindictive phalanx of Radical Republicans. These men, bent on
perpetuating their party in power, proceeded under the malignant
leadership of Thaddeus Stevens and Charles Sumner to churn out
venomous streams of propaganda, prolonging the bitterness of
wartime, slandering the President, and preparing the North for the
notorious Reconstruction Acts of 1867 which shackled the South
under Negro and carpetbag domination. Andrew Johnson, standing virtually alone as all about him succumbed to hysteria, was
now ready to take on heroic proportions.

And yet it is a curious phenomenon of any polemical writing,
history being no exception, that it tends to embrace the same
categories, and to take on the same tone, as that which it under-

takes to combat. Likewise the literature on Johnson and Reconstruction produced during this period is streaked with the same
venom that was supposed to have been the chief characteristic of
Johnson's radical pursuers. Sometimes the very titles reflect this.
Don C. Seitz's *Dreadful Decade,* published in 1926, exhibited a
faultless Johnson; it was, at the same time, an extended snarl
against Thaddeus Stevens and Charles Sumner. Much the same
can be said of Claude Bowers' *Tragic Era,* which appeared three
years later. Bowers was sure that "the Southern people literally
were put to the torture," and he wanted, as he said, "to recreate
the black and bloody drama of those years" and "to picture the
moving masses . . . surging crazily under the influence of the
poisonous propaganda on which they were fed." He was convinced, moreover, that "Andrew Johnson, who fought the bravest
battle for constitutional liberty and the preservation of our institutions ever waged by an Executive, until recently was left in the
pillory to which unscrupulous gamblers for power consigned him,
because the unvarnished truth that vindicates him makes so many
statues in public squares and parks seem a bit grotesque." Never,
he declared, had public men "been so brutal, hypocritical, and
corrupt."

Perhaps this is not the only sort of atmosphere in which a
favorable biography of Andrew Johnson might be written, but it is
hard to imagine a more auspicious one. In 1928, 1929, and 1930
three such biographies appeared, and none of a serious sort has
been attempted since. They were Robert W. Winston's *Andrew
Johnson, Plebeian and Patriot,* Lloyd Paul Stryker's *Andrew Johnson, A Study in Courage,* and George F. Milton's *The Age of
Hate: Andrew Johnson and the Radicals.* Winston was a North
Carolina judge whose father had served in the administration of
Jonathan Worth, the first post-bellum Governor elected in that
state; Stryker was a celebrated New York trial lawyer; and Milton
was editor of the Chattanooga *News.* In the works of all three, the
figure of Johnson achieves full grandeur.

Judge Winston seems to have been a somewhat mellow elderly
gentleman, hopelessly steeped in the racial prejudices of his time,
and his sense of history—in terms both of sequence and of cause

and effect—was amiably chaotic. ("If Johnson had favored the Fourteenth and Fifteenth Amendments in 1866," he wrote, "civil war would have resulted.") And yet Winston's very amateurishness—his being only casually in touch with the current research and polemics—may have preserved for his book a certain detachment. The mentality at work in it seems more akin to that of a border-state Unionist of Civil War time than of a twentieth-century historian: Winston is less concerned with damning radicals (though he never doubts their profound wrongness) than with simply exhibiting the intrepidity and rugged virtues of a man whose type he himself had known, through personal experience and family tradition.

Stryker was neither temperate nor scholarly. In a work popping with exclamation points, he deals with Johnson and his enemies with the same broad extravagance he might have used in addressing a trial jury on behalf of an accused felon. He seems to have believed that his case was not worth much unless he could show that his client had been framed by a conspiracy of monsters. Thaddeus Stevens was "like some cold-bellied snake with poison-fangs fitfully darting"; Charles Sumner was a "pedant" and "prig" ("serene, bland, cold, can't you see him?") who consorted with "lying hypocrites." Ben Butler, with his "squat figure" and "the minatory manners of the cheap police court tout," pours forth "brackish torrents of abuse." James Ashley is "one of Stevens' wharf rats."

Playing upon his jury's prejudices, Stryker sighs for the graces of the old South—the "charm and courage of her women, the stately poise and valor of her men"—and proceeds to show the extent of the South's postwar humiliation by painting scenes of buffoonery at the Reconstruction conventions, ridiculing the Negro members and mimicking their speech. "It was to prevent the enactment of such scenes as these that Andrew Johnson sat in Washington suffering the assaults of those who had conspired to make them possible." The beleaguered but heroic Johnson, with his veto of the Reconstruction Act, handed down "one of the great documents of American history."

Milton's book is in a number of ways strikingly different from the other two biographies. Much longer, more comprehensive, richer in matters of detail, and finer in texture, it is clearly the work of a better mind. Milton's scholarship is highly scrupulous, and may still be depended upon to a degree well surpassing that of either of his predecessors. Nevertheless, *The Age of Hate* is anchored in its time. Though it contains an element always indispensable to good history and biography—a closely circumstantial narrative of events—the hard line of the doctrinaire runs all through it, and the author's judgment differs hardly at all from that which had by then become orthodox on Johnson, on the radicals, and on the entire subject of Reconstruction. As with the others, no small share of the emotion in *The Age of Hate* is the author's own, all directed toward Johnson's radical tormentors. Charles Sumner is the "eerie, evil genius," "spinning tenuous spider-webs of far-fetched theory about negro equality." The "double-faced" Edwin Stanton is another "evil genius," and Thaddeus Stevens, the "Caliban" of Reconstruction, "had hatred stamped upon his brows." Senator Samuel Pomeroy is simply "a Radical scoundrel." To these are contrasted the attributes of Johnson, "a man of distinction and of impressiveness," "calm and reversed," "scrupulously clean," with a "dazzling, tender beautiful smile." And of the enormity of the Reconstruction Act, a solemn exegesis of Johnson's veto message leaves no doubt.

Another book on Andrew Johnson appeared in 1930, one which may now be seen as a clear transition between what had preceded it and much of what was to follow. This was Howard K. Beale's *The Critical Year: A Study of Andrew Johnson and Reconstruction*. In it, the admiration for Johnson which had by that time become standard, the heavy distaste for radicals and radicalism, the disapproval of Reconstruction and its "vindictiveness"—all this was as much in evidence as ever. But there was also something new. Beale's work contained an element that would, ironically enough, do much to protect the reputation of Andrew Johnson throughout the greater part of an entire new generation, even in the face of that generation's growing liberalism in matters of race. This was Beale's strategy of tying Reconstruction to that view of American history which Charles Beard had made so compelling in

An Economic Interpretation of the Constitution and *The Rise of American Civilization*: that the moving force of history must be sought in the clash of opposing economic interests. Just as Beard had discovered that the "real" power behind the movement toward civil war was not the issue of slavery as such, but rather the gathering momentum of Northern capitalism insistent on taking control of the federal government from the agrarian South, so Beale saw behind the triumph of radicalism over Andrew Johnson the final stroke that opened the way for the Era of Big Business. In a campaign of vituperation and appeal to war hatreds as a cover for their real designs, business interests successfully worked to exclude the South for the time being from federal representation in order to consolidate their policies on finance, currency, tariffs, and the protection of monopolies. "On the great economic questions of the day," Beale announced, "the 'Radicals' were in general conservative, and the opponents of their reconstruction policy tended toward radicalism of an agrarian type." The real "radicalism," in short, was now represented by none other than Andrew Johnson: hater of aristocracy, friend of the common man, "an enemy of bondholders, national banks, monopolies, and a protective tariff."

By thus turning Johnson into something of a pre-Populist, a man who instinctively resisted the heartless exploitations of Big Business, Beale kept him within the pale not only for writers such as James G. Randall who would continue to think of Reconstruction much as their predecessors had, but also for younger men whose interests were to turn more and more to the economic aspects of the subject. For the next twenty-five or thirty years it did not seem that anything new needed to be said about Andrew Johnson, and virtually nothing was. Beale's image of him proved to be remarkably serviceable; meanwhile the man's actual narrowness, his lack of imagination, and his bitter racial bigotry all remained somehow protected from the direct scrutiny of new historians whose attention now lay elsewhere. Symptomatic of this was an essay by T. Harry Williams published in 1946, which surveyed a number of the viewpoints on Reconstruction then current. In it, Williams gave both prominence and approval to the "Beale thesis" on the economic motives of the Republican reconstructionists. He did not, however, so much as mention the name of Beale's central character, Andrew Johnson.

Beale's influence, then, had a very important and indeed salutary latent function for younger historians of the late 1930's and 1940's. He had invited them, in effect, to rethink the subject of Reconstruction, and had done it in such a way that the re-examination might proceed piecemeal. Without being pressed to change their minds all at once, students of the subject found themselves turning away from the exclusively political dimensions of Reconstruction that had preoccupied their predecessors for so long, in order to investigate a range of economic problems that had never before been adequately studied. Changes in the patterns of landholding, taxation, public finance, transportation, and industry in the Southern states during Reconstruction provided the focus for a number of essays and monographs, and among the discoveries made was that the men associated with these interests did not always behave in ways that accorded with the older, schematic political accounts of the subject. Meanwhile a second new concern was gradually coming to the fore. That the interests of the Southern Negro in Reconstruction might themselves constitute an item entitled to consideration and analysis was now occurring to more and more persons writing about the post-Civil War era. This new turn made a real difference, and it was, appropriately, Howard Beale himself who first called general attention to it. In an essay published in 1940, just a decade after his *Critical Year,* Beale issued another call—this time clear, detailed, and explicit—for the "rewriting of Reconstruction history." Perhaps, he said, Reconstruction need not be regarded as an episode of such unrelieved badness after all: it may have been one of achievement as well as destruction. Everything and everyone connected with it—radicals, Negroes, scalawags, carpetbaggers, Bourbon restorationists, businessmen—ought to be reconsidered and re-examined. Beale's own views were in the process of change, and his own hero of ten years before, Andrew Johnson, now received no more than casual mention.

An interesting foretaste of what might conceivably happen to the image of Andrew Johnson should the fortunes of the Negro ever become a major historical concern had already been afforded by two Marxist studies of Reconstruction published in the 1930's. One was W. E. B. Du Bois' *Black Reconstruction in America,* which appeared in 1935, and the other was James S. Allen's *Reconstruction: The Battle for Democracy,* published two years later. Both are flawed by the somewhat mechanical schemes of organization imposed upon them, and the shape and quality of actual events are often unduly altered to fit the model that a Marxist explanation required. Yet in contrast to the tentative, uneven, and frequently confused efforts of the community of liberal white historians in the early stages of thinking their way from one position to another on Reconstruction, there is an element in the work of both Du Bois and Allen that shows a striking clarity of aim. Each gives the Negro a central role in what each describes without hesitation as a revolutionary movement, and it then becomes automatically obvious to both that the chief enemy of the revolution was Andrew Johnson. For Du Bois, Johnson was "a poor white, steeped in the limitations, prejudices, and ambitions of his social class," from whom the Negro could expect nothing. "Because he could not conceive of Negroes as men, he refused to advocate universal democracy, of which, in his young manhood, he had been the fiercest advocate, and made strong alliance with those who would restore slavery under another name." Allen was not concerned with Johnson's personal qualities at all (Du Bois was at least interested in his origins); for him, Johnson was simply the instrument of a reactionary Bourbon fragment of the bourgeoisie, for whom "there could be no more appropriate nickname" than "Jefferson Davis Johnson." The work of Du Bois and Allen never quite got into the main stream of American historical thought— Allen's in particular having little in the way of scholarship to sustain it—and neither has ever been taken with more than partial seriousness. But at the very least, each sounded a sharp note of warning that with regard to the man who acted as President of the United States at the inception of Reconstruction, the last word had not by any means been spoken.

By the mid-1950's several streams of thought had begun to coalesce in such a way that it could hardly be more than a matter of time before a full re-evaluation of Andrew Johnson would occur. A majority of scholars no longer took for granted that the Reconstruction Acts and their consequences were automatically to be regarded as a lurid nightmare. The interests of three and a half million newly emancipated slaves had at last been generally recognized—symbolically assisted by the 1954 Supreme Court decision on segregation—as a legitimate object of historical attention. And finally, a reaction against Beardian modes of historical analysis, under way since the late 1940's, had given energy and authority once more to the study of political forces and political behavior. And it once more became clear, as it had been clear to men writing seventy years before, that Reconstruction was essentially a political decision, made under conditions of extreme political uncertainty and disruption, and that the key figure in creating those conditions had been Andrew Johnson.

The opening statement on this note was made in 1956 by David Donald. In an article bluntly entitled "Why They Impeached Andrew Johnson," the author asserted in effect that the much-maligned seventeenth President had been maligned for good and sufficient reasons. "Johnson's defenders," he wrote,

have pictured Radical Reconstruction as the work of a fanatical minority, led by Sumner and Stevens, who drove their reluctant colleagues into adopting coercive measures against the South. In fact, every major piece of Radical legislation was adopted by the nearly unanimous vote of the entire Republican membership of Congress. Andrew Johnson had left them no other choice.

In the illusion that he could act as President without also acting as party leader, by his haste to rush the former Confederate states back into the Union without proper safeguards for the rights of freedmen and in the face of strong public opinion and party sentiment, Johnson left himself open to many, if not most, of the things that were charged against him in his time. As for the "high crimes and misdemeanors" for which he was impeached, it might well be, Donald concluded, that "before the bar of history itself Andrew Johnson must be impeached with an even graver charge—

that through political ineptitude he threw away a magnificent opportunity."

Statements to a similar effect, and in considerable profusion of detail, would shortly come in a rush. My own *Andrew Johnson and Reconstruction* was published in the summer of 1960; others had been in preparation well before and appeared soon thereafter. In the fall of 1960 Harold Hyman's article, "Johnson, Stanton, and Grant: A Reconsideration of the Army's Role in the Events Leading to Impeachment," gave a foretaste of the book he completed for the late Benjamin Thomas, *Stanton: The Life and Times of Lincoln's Secretary of War* (1962). In 1963 came LaWanda and John Cox's *Politics, Principle, and Prejudice, 1865–1866* and William R. Brock's *An American Crisis: Congress and Reconstruction, 1865–1867.* Kenneth Stampp published his *Era of Reconstruction, 1865–77* in 1965. In all these studies, despite the variations in focus, Andrew Johnson's refusal to cooperate with Congress is held fully responsible for the federal government's failure to work out an orderly program of Reconstruction.

As of the present writing, it does not appear likely that the personal stature of Andrew Johnson will undergo dramatic upward fluctuations in any way comparable to those it has undergone in the past, so long as his reputation remains tied to his Presidency and to historical judgments on Reconstruction. When, for example, the extent of Johnson's interference with the work of the Freedmen's Bureau is fully perceived, as it is in a new study of that subject by William McFeely, his reputation may be depressed even further. Harold Hyman's disclosures of Johnson's interference with the Army in its efforts to enforce the Reconstruction Acts accomplished a similar result a few years ago. The emphasis in my own study rested on the way in which any creative and durable settlement on Reconstruction—to the extent that such a possibility existed—was doomed without Presidential support. Brock, on the other hand, made an excellent case that even the limited benefits accorded to the Negro during this era would not have been achieved but for the united effort that was required to overcome Presidential vetoes. And yet, whatever the final merits of the respective cases, the judgments on the President himself come out about the same. It will probably never again be possible for a historian to make a really admirable chief executive out of Andrew Johnson.

All this, however, has brought us a long way from the point at which this essay began, that of Andrew Johnson as a subject of biography. Will it ever be possible for a biographer to write about this man with humanity and justice, and on a scale which renders judgments on performance perhaps not superfluous but at least secondary? It has, to be sure, never been done yet. But by the same token, the last and most authoritative word has quite obviously not been said. If, then, there is to be a next word, what might it be like?

At least one omen is now on the horizon, from which a tentative projection might be ventured. The first volume of *The Papers of Andrew Johnson,* under the editorship of Leroy P. Graf and Ralph W. Haskins, was issued in 1967. This undertaking, with its meticulous editorial apparatus and concern for absolute accuracy, is the most recent in what has now become established as a separate genre, whose distinguished standards have already emerged in similar projects on Jefferson, Hamilton, Madison, and Franklin. The standards are those of completeness, precision, and neutrality. This is, of course, no guarantee that the next biography of Johnson, when written, will be characterized by those same virtues. Still, such a bellwether exercises beneficent coercions on all biography. The standards are at hand, and the materials eventually will be, upon which may be erected something of permanent usefulness: a broad and inclusive view not simply of a public official—slanted and colored by the way that official acted at a particular point in the national life—but of a career.

As a representative political career in the America of his time, Andrew Johnson's story, if properly located amid the conditions that created it, *would* have a kind of meaning. It is a career which has its inception at the very outset of the Jacksonian era—one of the critical breakpoints in American history. The true setting of that career is not the national capital but the state of Tennessee, and its chronological center is not the Reconstruction era but that of the 1830's and 1840's. The man's whole life depended on politics: what were the conditions, and what was the nature of the society in which such a man could rise from the mudsill to become a power in his time? Could this have been managed in the previous generation, or in another part of the country? What were the values that he represented, and what were the texture, the quality, the meaning of political life in the ante-bellum Southern borderland? Andrew Johnson's "swing around the circle" in 1866 represented a culture-clash of two worlds, that of isolated rural Tennessee and a newer world of mass media and urban life. The two never quite communicated. At every stop on that disastrous tour, Andrew Johnson vainly shouted that he had risen from a tailor's bench to become alderman, mayor, legislator, Representative, Governor, Senator, and President of the United States—as though he somehow sensed that his audiences were not quite willing to believe it. It *was* incredible, and still is. We would still welcome the full account of exactly how it was done.

ERIC L. MCKITRICK

Northampton, Massachusetts
Summer, 1968

Andrew Johnson, 1808–1875

Andrew Johnson, born December 29, 1808, at Raleigh, North Carolina, had an early life of virtually unrelieved poverty. His father, a handyman and porter at the local tavern, died when the boy was three; his mother, who did sewing and washing, had all she could do to support him until he was old enough, at fourteen, to be apprenticed to a tailor. Three years later the family trekked across the mountains into East Tennessee and in September, 1826, settled in Greeneville. Andrew opened a tailor shop there, and at nineteen married Eliza McCardle, an orphan girl two years his junior. Andrew had had no schooling but had somehow picked up the rudiments of reading; Eliza taught him to write and cipher. Business prospered, and in a few years the Johnsons found themselves in tolerably comfortable circumstances.

Andrew Johnson, preoccupied with self-improvement, joined local debating societies, practiced oratory in his shop, and began to nourish political ambitions. He was elected town alderman in 1829, the very year his idol, Old Hickory, entered the White House. At twenty-two he was elected mayor, and in 1835 he went to the legislature. He appears to have been one of the organizers of the Democratic party in Greene County. He became a State Senator in 1841 and a member of Congress in 1843. Ten years later, he was Governor of Tennessee.

Aside from the Homestead legislation he advocated in Congress and his efforts as Governor to raise the school tax, Johnson did not take a very positive view of the functions of government. Politics for him was largely a drama of personal hostilities: the overcoming of conspiracies of "parasites" to engross public offices and appropriate public funds, of "aristocrats" bent on oppressing the people, and of enemies of every sort conspiring to persecute him. He pictured himself as the champion of the common man, insisting always on his plebeian origins and remaining at the same time morbidly sensitive about them. President Polk noted in his diary after a talk with Johnson that "it was manifest from the tenor of it that he wished to play the demagogue at home, and to assume that the administration intended to attack him and make a victim of him." He was a tireless worker, though not noted for either flexibility or imagination. Jefferson Davis commented, not unkindly: "His habits were marked by temperance, industry, courage, and unswerving perseverance; also by inveterate prejudices or preconceptions on certain points, and these no arguments could change." Johnson was elected to the Senate in 1857, and was there when Tennessee seceded from the Union in 1861.

With the coming of the Civil War, Andrew Johnson, whose physical courage no one could question, emerged at his best. A staunch Unionist, he toured Tennessee during the secession crisis, vainly imploring the people of his state to remain loyal. When the last hope was gone, he returned to Washington and stayed at his post in the Senate until early in 1862, when parts of Tennessee including the capital were brought under federal military control. President Lincoln thereupon asked Johnson to go to Nashville as Military Governor. He went, and amid many dangers remained there until late in February, 1865. Johnson's Unionism, perseverance, and courageous work in Tennessee had earned him the nomination as Lincoln's running mate the previous June, and when he left Nashville, it was to assume his new duties as Vice-President of the United States.

The most familiar phase of Johnson's career is, of course, that which began on April 15, 1865, the day of Lincoln's death, when he took the oath of office as President. Though Johnson uttered harsh words about punishing the South's "traitorous aristocrats," he was shortly to launch a program of restoring the former Confederate states to Congressional representation, and to assume that the entire problem of Reconstruction—or "restoration," as he insisted on calling it—was exclusively a Presidential function. For what was seen as undue haste in restoring all the South's former rights without proper safeguards either for the newly emancipated Negroes or for the Southerners' own future loyalty, Johnson alienated the Republican majority in Congress and a considerable sector of Northern public opinion. He vetoed bills on civil rights and other matters with a regularity that soon brought the executive and legislative branches of government to the point of impasse, and at length convinced Congress that it had no choice but to take the question of Reconstruction wholly into its own hands. The result was the Reconstruction Acts of March, 1867, which placed the Southern states under military government. Allegedly for violating the Tenure of Office Act, but actually for having totally exhausted Congress' patience, Johnson was impeached in February, 1868. He was acquitted by the margin of one vote. He served out the remainder of his term, but absented himself from the inauguration of his successor, Ulysses S. Grant.

Back in Tennessee, Johnson longed to vindicate himself with a return to public life, and ran for Congress unsuccessfully in 1872. In 1875, however, after a bitter fight and more than fifty ballots, the legislature elected him once again to the United States Senate. He attended the three-week session in March and made one speech, a blistering denunciation of General Grant. It was his last. On a visit to his daughter at Carter's Station, Tennessee, he suffered a stroke and died on July 31, 1875.

Johnson's widow, Eliza McCardle Johnson (October 4, 1810–January 15, 1876), survived him less than six months. A sufferer from consumption, she had been an invalid for many years. They had five children: Martha Johnson Patterson (October 25, 1828–July 10, 1901); Charles (February 19, 1830–April 4, 1863), killed in a fall while riding; Mary Johnson Stover (Brown) (May 8, 1832–April 19, 1883); Robert (February 22, 1834–April 22,

1869), whose alcoholism blighted most of his adulthood; and Andrew, Jr. (August 5, 1852–March 12, 1879), known as "Frank."*

E. L. McK.

* I am indebted to the generosity of Patricia P. Clark, Assistant Editor of the Andrew Johnson Papers, Knoxville, Tennessee, for supplying the birth and death dates of Johnson's family.

ANDREW JOHNSON

ROBERT W. WINSTON

✪

Runaway Apprentice

At the beginning of the last century, there stood in the town of Raleigh, North Carolina, a spacious, ramshackle building called Casso's Inn. Within the hotel yard a small cottage for the use of employees of the establishment had been provided, and there, on December 29, 1808, Andrew, second son of Jacob Johnson and Mary McDonough his wife, was born.[1]

This inn was a noted place in its day. Located on two highways, one running north and south and the other east and west, and just across the street from the State House, it boasted of "a stable equal to any on the continent, sufficient to contain from thirty to forty head of horses," and of a bar unexcelled for its brands of foreign and domestic liquors. During festive occasions the towns-people would come together at Casso's and celebrate with round dances and the cotillion, with bountiful feasts, and with the ever-flowing bowl. And Peter Casso, the landlord, was well fitted for the position of host. Having been a soldier in the Revolutionary War, he was a man of the world; his wife was received into the best circles, and their daughter, "pretty Peggy," as Colonel William Polk once named her in a gracious toast, was a general favorite. But the popularity of the inn was not more due to the Casso family than to their porter, Jacob Johnson, and to "Polly," his faithful wife.[2]

[1] R. H. Battle, *Library Southern Literature,* VI, 2719.
[2] David L. Swain, *Early Times in Raleigh* (1867) and *Memorial Address on Jacob Johnson.*

Now the occasion of Andy Johnson's birth is well remembered. That particular night, it being Christmas week, with seven days of frolic and merrymaking, a ball was going on at the inn. Soon after the ball, it became known that a son had been born to the Johnson family, and pretty Peggy tripped down to the cottage to lend a hand. "What are you going to name the boy?" she asked. Mrs. Johnson invited suggestions. "Andrew Jackson Johnson," was the reply. And so, with the middle name omitted for the sake of brevity, Andrew Johnson set out on his earthly pilgrimage.[3]

The community into which this young chap was thus unceremoniously ushered was typically Southern. Though the little town, of less than a thousand souls, could not claim to be as aristocratic as Richmond and Charleston, it was not without a slaveholding aristocracy.[4] During the hunting season, Governor Turner, Treasurer Haywood, General Beverly Daniel, and other notables, "mounted on well-bred horses, accoutered with shot-pouch and horn and followed by a pack of yelping hounds, could be seen driving the deer or chasing the fox." Evening teas at the homes of the Devereaux, the Mordecais, Hoggs, Hills, Camerons, and Polks were presided over by Mrs. Gales, mother of the editor of the *National Intelligencer,* and "other intellectual ladies, who graciously mingled with the young and the beautiful of the village." Fishing parties on Crab Tree Creek were frequent, "winding up with a dance at the paper mills"; and, on the first of May, "beautiful ceremonies honored the Queen" of that historic day.

Jacob Johnson's relationship to the aristocratic people of Raleigh was a peculiar one. Socially, he had no recognition at all—he was simply "a poor white." Yet in the position of a dependent, with the requisites of "vigor, docility and fidelity," he was the best-loved person in town. Belonging to that class which Hammond, the scholarly Senator from South Carolina, dubbed the "mudsills of society and political government," he could not, without great effort, have risen in the social or political scale; but

---

[3] K. P. Battle, "Early History of Raleigh," *Centennial Address.* Johnson's relatives think he was named for his mother's brother, but Dr. Battle gives the account in the text.

[4] S. A. Ashe, *Biographical History of North Carolina,* IV, 228–241.

he did not wish to rise; the likeable fellow craved no more than he had. His cottage, situated on Main Street only a few steps from the Capitol, was in the heart of things, and there was work a plenty, menial though it might be.[5] "Mudsills" the Johnsons were born, and mudsills they died. As their son in afterdays rather proudly declared, they belonged to that class called "plebeians." In fact, so little impression did Jacob and his wife make on the community, no one has taken the pains to remember or record the parentage of either. Their pedigree, lost in obscurity as Mr. Lincoln said of his, was short and sweet like the annals of the poor. This much however is known of Jacob Johnson, no man in the community "bore a more blameless character," and no woman was more deserving of respect than Mary McDonough, his Scotch wife.

And it would be a mistake to conclude that Jacob Johnson was a person of no consequence. In the cardinal virtues, such as honesty and bravery, no one stood higher than Jacob. When Colonel Polk, cousin of President James K. Polk, opened the first state bank at Raleigh he appointed Jacob Johnson its porter. At one time he was captain of Muster Division No. 20 of the Town of Raleigh, with sundry citizen-soldiers under him. Occasionally he filled the position of sexton to the Presbyterian Church and had the privilege of ringing the only bell in town. As this bell hung at Casso's corner, the inn had a great advantage over the rival hotel called the Eagle, which had no such distinguishing appurtenance.[6]

Standing under the spreading oaks which give the name of "The City of Oaks" to Raleigh, Jacob Johnson would pull away at the bell rope, ringing for weddings, for fires, or for funerals. And Jacob had other accomplishments; he was an excellent caterer, and could barbecue and baste the young pig to a nicety; he was also a huntsman, a fisherman, and an all-round good fellow. In a word, no man of his class was more esteemed than Jacob Johnson. Mrs. Polly Johnson, too, was indispensable, not only serving Mrs. Casso but being her friend. Such Fourth of July dinners they spread—

[5] W. H. Wheeler, *Reminiscences,* p. 435. The cottage is now located in Raleigh's public park; it then stood about 200 feet north of the present Masonic Temple.

[6] Swain, *Memorial Address.*

roasting ears, Brunswick stew, barbecued pig, and hard cider—
while the noisy patriots, crowding the four-acre square across the
street, drank "as many standing toasts as there were states in the
Union."

In the midst of rich and powerful friends one might think Jacob
would have accumulated property, but he did not. The acquisitive
instinct he did not possess. Though Dr. William G. Hill, the town
physician, Colonel Thomas Henderson, editor of the Raleigh *Star,*
Colonel William Polk, and other influential men were his friends,
nothing came of their friendship. At birth as at death, poverty was
Jacob's portion, and how could it have been otherwise? In the
Southern life of that day, based on pedigree and slavery and
looking down on manual labor, it must be said there was no
influential middle class. A race had been developed unsurpassed
for elegance of manner, for bravery, for loyalty, and for other
attributes of manhood, but of a substantial yeomanry there was
none—from master to slave there was no halfway ground. The
caste system forbade it.

With these conditions Jacob Johnson and his wife were not
dissatisfied. One looks in vain for traces of that galling of the spirit
which marked their second-born son. Since there was no work
Jacob Johnson could engage in but menial labor, he cheerfully
went about his daily task. Uneducated and without family connections, he could not, had he desired, have entered a learned profession. Poor, he could not purchase a farm or operate a mercantile
business. Raleigh being a rural village, without factories or other
industries, and the uplands of that section well-nigh exhausted by
unscientific agriculture, opportunities for making a living were few
and far between.

As Jacob's patrons and friends were the owners of rich river
bottoms on the Cape Fear, the Neuse, the Roanoke, and the Tar,
he might have been an overseer and lived on one of these
plantations; but a life in town he preferred to a life in the country.
His genial, social disposition craved the companionship of the city,
where the legislature met, state and United States courts sat, where
there were occasional circuses and minstrel shows, and where
Peter Casso's fine bar was in easy reach. Not that he drank to

excess, for he did not; Colonel Polk, his employer, would not have stood for that. But country life to such a happy-go-lucky fellow would have been simply unbearable. The days of "come-easy, go-easy" were soon to end. Fate had something sterner in store than barbecues and fish frys for the little family.

One December day in 1811, a merry party had gathered at Hunter's Mill, on Walnut Creek, a few miles from town. In the midst of the revelry—no doubt dancing, cockfighting, gander-pulling, and general carousal—Colonel Tom Henderson and two other hilarious individuals pushed off from the shore in a canoe and were soon amidstream and in ten-foot water. One of the number rocked the boat and over it turned. There were loud cries for help. The Colonel and one of the men, who could not swim, were sinking beneath the waves for the third and last time, when, rushing to the gunwale, and "heedless of his own life," Jacob Johnson sprang into the icy stream. Diving and struggling, he succeeded, "with great effort," in fishing up his friend the Colonel, to whose coat the other drowning man was clinging. In a word, he saved the lives of two human beings, but lost his own. Exposure and exhaustion proved too much for him. Shortly afterward Jacob Johnson, father of the seventeenth President of the United States, died a martyr and a hero.

The Raleigh *Star* of January 12, 1812, announcing his death, called attention to his useful life, to his "honesty, sobriety, industry and humane friendly disposition." "No one laments his death more than the editor of this paper," Colonel Henderson wrote, "for he owes his life to the boldness and humanity of Johnson." Fifty years after this heroic act a monument was erected to the memory of Jacob Johnson, as a testimonial to his courage and self-sacrifice and as the appreciation of a grateful community. On this tablet one may read:

In memory of Jacob Johnson. An honest man, loved and respected by all who knew him.

Little Andy was now three years old, and William, his older brother, afterward turning out to be a ne'er-do-well, was eight. The mother, left penniless, with two small children dependent upon her, was almost an object of charity. But with brave heart she secured a hand loom and set up the business of weaving and spinning cloth. By industry and enterprise, she soon acquired such a reputation she was known as "Polly, the Weaver." The burden of supporting the family was too heavy for her, however, and on August 14, 1814, she disposed of Bill by apprenticing him to Colonel Thomas Henderson, her husband's friend. About this time, Mrs. Johnson entered upon a second matrimonial venture. This second husband, a fellow named Turner Dougherty, was more impecunious, if possible, than herself and bad matters were made worse.

In a year or so, Colonel Henderson died and Bill's apprenticeship came to an end. He was then bound to J. J. Selby, the town tailor. Andy had grown to be fourteen years old at that time and he too was apprenticed to the same tailor. By the terms of the indenture, the boys were to serve Selby till they arrived at age. The master bound himself to furnish them with victuals and clothes and "to instruct them in the trade of a tailor." At this point historians have gone somewhat astray as to a certain date; they assert that Andy was ten years old when he became a "bound-boy," whereas, he was fourteen years of age. As witness the following record:

State of North Carolina ⎫
Wake County   ⎭

At a court of Pleas and Quarterly Sessions begun and held at the Court House in Raleigh on the 3rd Monday of February, 1822 being the forty-sixth year of American Independence (and the 18th day of February).

The Worshipful ⎫   CHARLES L. HINTON
Present   ⎬   NATHANIEL RAND
                ⎭   MERRITT DILLARD

Ordered that A. Johnson, an orphan boy and the son of Jacob Johnson, deceased, 14 years of age, be bound to Jas. J. Selby till he arrive at lawful age to learn the trade of a Tailor.

Andy, only three years old when his father died, could have remembered little or nothing of him or of his cordial intercourse with the men who ran the town. But as the child grew and looked about and saw other children at play or at school, living in comfortable homes with gardens of roses, honeysuckle, and bamboo, or watched the well-to-do people as they rode here and there "in coaches drawn by dapple grays" and driven by Negro coachmen, while he, a bound-boy, was penned indoors or after the day's grind trudged afoot, could he do less than contrast his lot with theirs? Who, indeed, can say how much those days at Selby's shop, and before, fixed the child's mind, making him resentful of any reflection on the laboring man, and the champion of his rights.

However this may be, at Selby's the sturdy chap never flinched or repined. Among the lads of the town he "always led the crowd." "Somehow or other Andy would have things his own way." "If he said 'go a-hunting,' the boys went hunting; if he said 'let's go swimming,' they went swimming." A small piercing black eye, a will to do or die, a spirit that never quailed—these set the lad above his surroundings.[7] And he was always courteous and attentive to business. When a rich patron on horseback would come to the shop Andy would run out and hold his mount, graciously accepting the tip and listening to many a word of cheer and advice.

At this time the foreman of the tailor shop was an educated man named Litchford, who took a fancy to the chap. As Litchford describes Andy, he was "a wild, harum-scarum boy with no unhonorable traits, however."[8] On holidays, or during summer afternoons, the apprentice boy, with his playmates, would roam the forests, climb the trees for bird nests, go seining in the creeks, and often return home with clothing dripping wet or torn to shreds. The exasperated Mrs. Selby scolded in vain; finally she made a coarse, heavy, homespun shirt, and, stripping Andy to the skin, clothed him in this nontearable "whole undergarment."

It was Mr. Litchford and Dr. Hill who taught the boy his A B C's. As there was no public school in Raleigh at that time, and his mother could not read or write, the only education the lad received was at the hands of these two men. Dr. Hill occasionally would drop into Selby's tailor shop and instruct him, or, while he was

[7] John Savage, *Life of Johnson,* Chap. 1.
[8] *Loc. cit.*

plying his needle and shoving his hot goose, read from *Enfield's Speaker,* or from the newspapers of the day.[9] Once Dr. Hill read a paragraph from an essay on elocution. This essay gives the rules for successful oratory. First and most important one must speak slowly. "Almost all persons who have not studied the art of speaking," so the book runs, "have a habit of uttering their words so rapidly that the exercise of reading aloud, slowly and deliberately, ought to be made use of for a considerable time. Aim at nothing higher, till you can read distinctly and deliberately.

> Learn to speak slow, all other graces
> Will follow in their proper places.[10]

By following these directions—speaking slowly and deliberately —Andrew Johnson's voice was well trained; it would "carry further than a city block." As an encouragement to the little fellow and a reward for his desire to educate himself, Dr. Hill presented him with the collection of speeches and essays. Unfortunately, when Johnson's home at Greeneville, Tennessee, was seized by the Confederate government, the little keepsake, dog-eared and well worn, was destroyed.[11]

And so the days of Andy Johnson's apprenticeship grew into weeks, the weeks into months. Many hours a day, shut out from fresh air, crouched down over needle and thread, deprived of the joys of childhood, the lad bent to his task; the inside of a schoolhouse he never saw. Finally, after two years of apprenticeship, an incident happened that changed the course of his life—he ran away from his master. One account of this event is that Selby insulted the lad "and was soundly thrashed"; but Litchford gives another account. At that time in Raleigh there was living an old woman named Wells, and Andy Johnson and three other bound-

[9] Jacob Johnson, not being able to write, made his cross mark to the bond he was required to give at marriage.

[10] This book is referred to as the *United States Speaker;* the *Standard Speaker;* the *Columbia Speaker.* I have chosen *Enfield's Speaker* because copies of it are at the University of North Carolina, near Johnson's native place. Cf. *Harper's Young People,* September 30, 1890.

[11] Savage, p. 22.

boys "rocked" this old lady's house—precisely why is not recorded. Anyway, she threatened to "persecute" the boys and off they skipped. However this may be, on June 24, 1824, the citizens of Raleigh read in the Raleigh *Gazette* the following notice:

TEN DOLLARS REWARD

Ran away from the Subscribed, on the night of the 15th instant, two apprentice boys, legally bound, named WILLIAM and ANDREW JOHNSON. The former is of a dark complexion, black hair, eyes, and habits. They are much of a height, about 5 feet 4 or 5 inches. The latter is very fleshy, freckled face, light hair, and fair complexion. They went off with two other apprentices, advertised by Messrs. Wm. & Chas. Fowler. When they went away, they were well clad—blue cloth coats, light colored homespun coats, and new hats; the maker's name in the crown of the hats, is Theodore Clark. I will pay the above Reward to any person who will deliver said apprentices to me in Raleigh, or I will give the above Reward for Andrew Johnson alone.

All persons are cautioned against harboring or employing said apprentices on pain of being prosecuted.

JAMES J. SELBY, *Tailor.*

Raleigh, S.C., June 24, 1824.

Now Selby was in such a dudgeon when he wrote this notice he described Bill for Andy and Andy for Bill, Andy having the black hair and black eyes and Bill the light hair and freckled face. At all events the reward brought no tangible results.

After a flight of several days, the runaways hauled up at the town of Carthage, about seventy-five miles from Raleigh; and there they made a halt and remained several months. Renting a shack, Andy opened a tailor shop of his own and advertised for business. Business came pouring in. Specimens of Andy's handicraft are still preserved in that section, and a monument commemorates the occasion of his residence in Carthage.

But Carthage was too near Raleigh. Memories of Selby still haunting Andy, he took to his heels again, arriving at Laurens, South Carolina, sometime during the winter of 1824. At Laurens the usual love affair of a youngster of sixteen took place. Andy fell in love with a "beautiful" young woman named Sarah Word, by whom the tender passion was reciprocated. Unhappily for the course of true love, the parents objected. A boy with no equipment but a kit of tailor's tools was surely no match for a promising South Carolina beauty. The dutiful maiden, therefore, "sighing like a lover but obeying like a child," broke the affair up and the romance ended. Andy's connection with this love scrape and his failure to press his suit and marry Sarah, over the heads of her parents, added to the esteem in which he was held by the people of Laurens.[12]

After a year or so in South Carolina, Andy and his brother Bill worked their way back to Raleigh. Andy was determined to serve out his apprenticeship with Selby. But Selby had given up his shop in Raleigh and moved twenty miles away in the country. On the boy trudged to make apology and take up his dog's life again. Selby wanted security, however. This Andy would not give and master and servant parted company forever.

As Andrew Johnson, penniless and out of a job, walked the streets of Raleigh or hung around Casso's Inn during those dismal days of 1826, the game of life seemed blocked against him. Though his old friend Litchford had opened a shop of his own, he was afraid to employ an advertised runaway. And then there was Selby—at any moment he might "put the law" to Andy for jumping his contract of indenture. In fact, the jails were full of debtors who could not pay their debts. The upshot of the business was that Andy resolved to leave North Carolina and to go west where there were fertile, unappropriated lands, and where he thought the laws were respecters of persons as well as of property. Why not Tennessee? Tennessee had already enticed from North Carolina her ablest sons: James Robertson, "the father of Tennessee," John Haywood, her greatest judge, Andrew Jackson, Hugh L. White, and James K. Polk.

The little Johnson family, therefore, put their heads together, resolving that matters might be improved by a move. They certainly could not be made worse. One August day in 1826, dumping their earthly belongings into a two-wheeled cart, without cover against rain or shine, they set out for their new home. No covered

---

[12] Greeneville *Sentinel,* February 10, 1910; *National Magazine,* VI, 63.

wagon, no barking, prancing dog, no romance. One hour Turner Dougherty and Polly would ride and the boys would walk; then, turn and turn about, the boys would ride and the old folks walk. "Ride and tie," this arrangement is called by the poorer Southern countryfolk when making a long journey with an overcrowded vehicle. At the end of the first day the little caravan had made nearly thirty miles, hauling up at Chapel Hill, the seat of the University of North Carolina. Here a family named Craig gave them shelter for the night.[13] Leaving Chapel Hill, they moved westward, fording rivers, climbing mountains, camping by the wayside. The Eno, the Haw, the Yadkin, the Catawba, the Swannanoa, the French Broad, the Pigeon, the Nolichucky, and their tributaries, many of these streams without bridges, all lay between them and their journey's end. Following the Daniel Boone trail, they scaled the Blue Ridge where Andrew Jackson crossed half a century before and—tradition says—met "old Hickory" on horseback.[14] Here they camped for the night and Bill and Andy went forth and killed a mountain bear. Next day, they passed down the French Broad River and along the Allen Stand Road, until they came into the Nolichucky country.[15]

A wonderful sight now caught their eye. To the west lay the Cumberland Mountains, to the north and east the Blue Ridge, between, a fertile valley. Here their journey ended, and on a certain Saturday evening in September, 1826, the weary little band pitched their tent for the last time, camping at the "Gum Spring" in the town of Greeneville, Tennessee. Unharnessing the weary pony, Andy walked up the hillside and got a bundle of fodder while his mother was busy with supper. W. R. Brown, an old resident, let him have the provender, and took such a fancy to the boy that a long friendship began. Next day Andy visited the tailor shop and procured work. In a short time, however, he moved on to Rutledge in the adjoining county, resolved to possess and run a

[13] Forty years after, President Johnson and Secretary Seward arrived in this village to be invested with academic honors and fêted as befitted their station.
[14] Thompson, *Southern Hero Tales,* p. 66.
[15] Johnson Mss. Greenville.

shop in his own name. At Rutledge, and at other places in Tennessee, he worked at his trade for several months. But in March, 1827, when he heard that the Greeneville tailor had quit business, he rejoined his mother and opened up a shop of his own—the "A. Johnson Tailor Shop," renowned in song and story.

GEORGE F. MILTON

✪

The Tailor-Politician

In 1829, Andrew Johnson was elected alderman, his first step in a lifelong career in politics. This initial plunge was a result of the affection of the young men of the town who frequented his tailor-shop debating society. For the little twelve-by-twelve log cabin had become the loafing place of the young men of Greeneville. Their conversations were accompanied by much boisterous merriment, but this did not disturb their tailor host at all.

"Andy, however, neither lost his temper nor suspended his twofold employment of reading and sewing," one of them relates.[1] "The moment the needle passed through the cloth, his eye would return to the book, and anon to the needle again; and so, enter when you would, it was ever the same determined read and sew, and sew and read. His sober industry and intelligence won the favor of the grave and sedate, and his genial tolerance of the jovial groups which frequented his shop secured him unbounded popularity with the young men of the place."

[1] G. W. Bacon, *Life of Andrew Johnson* (London, n.d. [apparently 1866]), pp. 6, 7, quoting statement to him of Alexander Hawthorne. Hawthorne's account does not comport with the traditional story that, in order to be elected, Johnson made a bitter campaign against the town aristocrats. Cf. Winston, pp. 23–24; James S. Jones, *Andrew Johnson* (Greeneville, Tenn., 1901), p. 20; John Savage, *Life of Andrew Johnson* (New York, 1866), p. 19.

13

They were so impressed with the tailor that they determined to give him a substantial proof of their admiration by electing him to the town council. Accordingly, on the Saturday night preceding the Monday town election, a dozen of his admirers gathered to make up their slate at the counting room where Alexander Hawthorne, a ringleader in the plan, was employed. "The first name we put down for alderman," Hawthorne tells us, "was Andy Johnson, the rest were soon selected, and as there was no printing office in the place, we wrote out the ballots. We resolved to keep everything secret until Monday morning. Then we went to the polls and worked for our candidates. Our whole ticket was elected by a sweeping majority."

The tally sheet of this election, which has been preserved, shows that while Johnson was elected, his vote of eighteen was the smallest received by any of the seven successful candidates. Interestingly enough, not alone Andrew Johnson, a tailor, but also Blackstone McDannel, a plasterer, and Mordecai Lincoln, a tanner, were elected. The success of these three plebeians gives strength to the story that the artisans waged a campaign against the aristocrats of the little town.[2]

In any event, the "best people" of the town were astounded at the idea of a tailor's election to the council. But Andy filled his office to the people's satisfaction. He took pride in his humble origin and, whenever occasion arose, battled for the rights of the mechanics and artisans of the town. They responded loyally to his championship. In 1830 he was re-elected to the council; the next year he was chosen mayor, holding that post for three successive terms. In 1832 the county court made him a trustee of the Rhea Academy, no small honor for a twenty-three-year-old tailor who had never gone to school a day in his life.

Johnson next turned his thoughts to the legislature. In those days modes of candidature were informal. It was in the decade

[2] This tally sheet is in the possession of Mrs. S. A. LaRue, of Greeneville, Tennessee, a great-granddaughter of Blackstone McDannel. There were twenty-seven candidates voted upon. The successful ones were: J. W. Harold, 31 votes; 'Squire Mordecai Lincoln (the same who married Johnson and Eliza McCardle), 26; McDannel, 26; D. Alexander, 25; A. Brown and J. Lister, 19 each; and Johnson, 18 votes.

when King Caucus was dying and King Convention was not yet crowned. The young tailor's nomination to represent Washington and Greene counties in the legislature was achieved with ease and informality. The coming canvass had been thoroughly discussed in his tailor-shop debating society, and Andy's ambition had been fired. One Saturday night in the spring of 1835, the usual crowd gathered in Jones's store, smoking, chewing, and "swapping lies." They began discussing the men who had entered the race.[3] After listening to this talk a few minutes, Andy sprang from his seat to say: "I, too, am in the fight."[4]

At the time he was but twenty-seven years old; his friends feared he would be no match for his opponent, Major Matthew Stephenson, a wealthy citizen of character and social position.[5] But as soon as Andy "went after him," the aristocratic Major cut a sorry figure. An appeal to the common people against the aristocrats elected Johnson to the legislature. He "hacked and arraigned" Stephenson until the latter's friends pitied him, and Andy was elected by a small plurality.[6]

Johnson's service in the Tennessee House was not conspicuous. That body's Journal records that he opposed a motion to invite the ministers of the gospel at the capital to open the daily sessions with prayer. He opposed the chartering of the Hiwassee Railroad Company on the ground that railroad charters were unconstitutional, being monopolies and perpetuities. As a strict constructionist, Johnson was against the state's undertaking a great scheme of building macadamized turnpikes, a program very popular in mountain-bound East Tennessee;[7] and his consequent defeat in the legislative race of 1837 by Brookins Campbell, who stood for internal improvement, is not surprising.

[3] Winston, pp. 29–30.
[4] Jones, p. 21.
[5] Oliver P. Temple, *Notable Men of Tennessee, from 1833 to 1875* (New York, 1912), p. 363.
[6] Temple, never a friendly critic of Johnson, claims that in this first campaign Johnson exhibited a "disposition to pander to the prejudice of the people," that "he was almost brutal in his assaults," and that "all the kindly amenities of high debate between gentlemen were wanting" (*loc. cit.*).
[7] Jones, pp. 22–23.

Two years later Johnson had another battle with Campbell and defeated him. In this canvass the Greeneville tailor was a very advanced states'-rights Democrat, almost a follower of Calhoun, but this phase was not lasting. From 1840 onward, "Old Hickory" was Andrew Johnson's political pilot, the model of his conduct and the idol of his heart.[8]

When Johnson first took the leap from village politics to those of state and nation, the Democracy of Greene County was in a plastic, almost a chaotic state.[9] Almost its only fixed principle was an immutable faith in Andrew Jackson. In the nation at large politics was almost as chaotic as in East Tennessee. The period from 1830 to 1850 in American politics was marked by party flux. The Whig party had been born with little to cement its membership save a common opposition to Andrew Jackson and Jacksonism. It attracted the rich and the aristocratic and had "no reason for existence other than its devotion to things that were passed."[10] The fact that the Whigs were bound together by their hatred of Jacksonism caused true Democrats everywhere to make the person and principles of Old Hickory their guiding star. The constancy with which Johnson preached Andrew Jackson to his Greene County neighbors was not empty demagogism, and his tactics proved him a master of political stagecraft.

A record of this process shows that in the winter or spring of 1840, Johnson called the Greene County Democracy in mass meeting at Greeneville. It proved so successful that it became the model for the Jackson-Johnson Democratic rally in Greeneville every year. Loyal partisans poured forth from the Democratic

[8] Temple contends that in 1835 Johnson was a Whig, that in 1836 he supported Hugh Lawson White for President, and that he did not become a Democrat until after his defeat of Campbell in 1839 (pp. 366 ff.). Inasmuch as Senator White was a Tennessean, the idol of East Tennessee, and inasmuch further as the dividing lines between Whig and Democrat had not yet been so clearly drawn as later, Johnson's 1836 position is not impossible to reconcile with that he later took.

[9] Temple has an unusually illuminating tribute to Johnson's popular leadership (pp. 371 ff.).

[10] Edward Channing, *History of the United States* (New York, 1926), VI, 124.

strongholds until there was scarcely an able-bodied man left at home. Afoot, on horseback, or in wagons, they came, without banners or music, but "in the strength and simple power of an irresistible outpouring."[11] A few empty boxes set up against the courthouse wall formed Andrew Johnson's rostrum. Between ten and eleven in the morning the speaker ascended the impromptu stand. Immediately George Foute, clerk of the Greene County court, a lieutenant of Johnson, came forward to read in a clear, sonorous voice resolutions which Johnson himself had prepared.

These resolutions ran the gamut of American political history. They flayed Hamilton, the father of Federalism, and lauded Jefferson, the founder of Democracy. John Adams and his Alien and Sedition Laws were excoriated. Henry Clay and the "corrupt bargain" of the 1824 election were denounced, and Andrew Jackson, the second savior of the country, the conqueror of the octopus of the United States Bank, held final place.

After Foute, who always acted as chairman, had read these resolutions, Andrew Johnson spoke for two or three hours. It was not an oration, but a speech, all the more effective because he did not rant. Even in 1840, Andy was a compelling public speaker, and his power to move the minds of men grew steadily for the next twenty years. He would begin in a low, soft tone, which grew stronger as he warmed up. It was no turgid outpouring, yet there was no hesitation, no groping after words. An excellent judge of the temper of a crowd, at the outset of his career Johnson interlarded his speech with wit and humor and anecdote; in the sixties he did so much less often. He did not seek for oratorical effect, but his voice rang out and was heard for a great distance; contemporaries thought it particularly adapted to the open air. His tones were loud but not unmusical, his articulation was amazingly clear, his choice of words appropriate and simple. Temple was struck by "the exact language coming to his lips to express the idea in his mind."[12]

The Democracy of Greene County came to believe that Andrew Johnson was the reincarnation of Andrew Jackson, and that he too

[11] Temple, p. 372.
[12] *Ibid.*, p. 373.

was destined to be President of the United States. On the firm foundation of the confidence of his home folks, the tailor-politician built his political career. He never forgot or grew cold toward this Greene County Democracy. At least once every year, until the Civil War, this scene was repeated. The meeting would begin with the reading of these resolutions, which George Foute carefully preserved from year to year and read with great oratorical effect. On Andrew Johnson's great days, Richard M. Woods, for many years Greene County's high sheriff, would be present "to preserve order"—and more especially to give to the crowd a sign, by a smile or a nod, when to laugh and when to shout.

At the perorations on these occasions—when Johnson would inform his auditors that "eternal vigilance is the price of liberty," and that "power is always stealing from the many to give to the few"—the individuals in the crowd would furtively glance around them to see if anyone was trying to steal from them. Johnson had one rhetorical figure especially dear to the hearts of Greene County's Democracy. It was an impassioned appeal to the party to stand together, "hand in hand, shoulder to shoulder, foot to foot, and to make a long pull, a strong pull, and a pull together." This delicate reference to the time-honored custom among the wagoners of the day of helping one another out always set the old wagoners in the crowd wild with delight, and their war whoops could be heard for miles. After the speaking had ended, Greene County Democracy would take the homeward road. Often it would be late in the afternoon when Johnson finished, and some of the wilder of his partisans would visit Greeneville's grogshops and make their way home much later, ready to fight at the drop of the hat any man who doubted that Andrew Johnson was the greatest man in the United States.

Such was the testing block upon which the ambitious young politician tried out his rapidly forming theories of national affairs. It was not long before he had a chance to use them in a larger arena than that of the General Assembly of the state. In 1840, he was chosen one of the Democratic electors from the state at large. It was a distinct honor. In picking him, such men as James K. Polk, A. O. P. Nicholson, Aaron V. Brown, and Felix Grundy were passed over. In 1841 Johnson was elected State Senator, and in 1843 he ran for Congress in a strong Whig district and carried his fight.[13] His opponent was Colonel John A. Aiken of Jonesboro, a lawyer of repute and a forceful orator.[14] The campaign centered about the United States Bank, with Johnson defending Old Hickory's views in opposing the bank.

In the forties, Congressional customs of punctilio were pronounced, and the new Solon must tread cautiously lest he commit some blunder which might mar his career. Andrew Johnson did tread with caution and was well regarded during his first term. While Congress was in session, Washington was alive with parties, receptions, routs, levees, and balls, only to languish like a stricken city during the long recess. Johnson had little aptitude or heart for society. He constantly borrowed books from the Congressional Library and devoted himself to mastering the details of public affairs. He was attentive to his committee assignments and was always eager to respond to the wants and wishes of his friends back home. With his devoted friend, George W. Jones of Tennessee, Johnson impressed the country with the way in which he, "a sentinel at the doors of the Treasury," used his voice and recorded his vote against jobs and grabs of all description.[15]

Johnson was painfully scrupulous about taking pay from the government. He had been named a member on a committee to investigate a contested election, the type of *per diem* assignment most Congressmen were eager to get because of the extra pay. Not so Johnson. He caused to be entered in the account book of the Sergeant at Arms of the House of Representatives: "I have no doubt of the legality of the charge of $768.00, but I doubt my

[13] Temple claims that while Johnson was in the State Senate, he had passed a redistricting bill, adding to the hitherto strongly Whig First Congressional District enough Democratic counties to insure his own election to Congress the next year (pp. 216–217).

[14] Jones, p. 32.

[15] Thurlow Weed, in *New York Tribune,* January 29, 1875.

moral right to more than pay for the days actually engaged in the service, and accordingly decline to receive the balance."[16]

His maiden speech warmed the hearts of the Greene County Democracy. It was a defense of Andrew Jackson, made in connection with a resolution Johnson had offered to refund to the aged hero the fine imposed on him for having declared martial law in New Orleans in 1815.[17] In Johnson's first term, an increased tariff was urged; he placed himself squarely against such increases, terming the tariff "an oppressive and nefarious system of plundering the great masses of the people for the benefit of the few." The Texas question was soon injected by John C. Calhoun, and Johnson was a staunch annexationist.

In 1845, William G. Brownlow, a young Methodist preacher and spitfire Whig editor of Jonesboro, entered the lists against Andy. The Parson knew he was no match for Johnson on the stump, and did not attempt to meet him there; but he employed the columns of his paper, the Jonesboro *Whig,* to blast his opponent's reputation. Of these efforts the most amusing to a modern reader is Brownlow's scathing card, *"Ten Reasons For Believing Andrew Johnson To Be An Atheist."*[18] The Parson's *Whig* "extra" of June 25, 1845, took note of his opponent's denunciation of him in a speech at the courthouse as a "hyena," a "devil," a "coward," and "a man of no character," and replied: "Andrew Johnson is a VILE CALUMNIATOR, AN INFAMOUS DEMAGOGUE, A COMMON AND PUBLIC LIAR, AN IMPIOUS INFIDEL, AND AN UNMITIGATED VILLAIN. . . . Mr. Johnson knows where to find me, at all times."

A few issues later, the Whig Parson printed two columns of excited brevier charging Andrew Johnson with having hired a

---

16 Johnson Mss., I, No. 94; true copy of p. 121, ledger of Sergeant at Arms. In 1860, he counseled his son Robert, then a member of the Tennessee legislature: "I would in the receipt of my *per diem* be very careful not to take pay for any more time than I was employed as legislator. . . . It will be worth more to you in the future than it is now."

17 Jones, p. 34. It is to be noted that the resolution passed, and Old Hickory was repaid.

18 Jonesboro *Whig,* July 4, 1845. On July 23, Brownlow charges that Johnson is, among other things, an abolitionist! I am indebted to the late Selden Nelson, of Knoxville, Tennessee, for these rare and racy issues.

rapscallion brother of Brownlow's to assassinate him. Politics was politics, indeed, in those days in East Tennessee. Another charge was that Johnson was not the son of Jacob Johnson at all, but a "by-blow" of John Haywood, in 1808 Judge of a North Carolina Superior Court; "the very spit of the Judge's nephew." This aspersion raised Johnson's temper to the boiling point and he denounced it.

Johnson's indignation at the insinuation about his birth was slow to cool, and shortly before the election, after a trip to Raleigh to seek testimony on the matter, he issued an open letter to the public. "These vandals and hyenas," he wrote, "would dig up the grave of Jacob Johnson, my father, and charge my mother with bastardy." He then cited numerous affidavits to disprove the charge. "As for my religion," he added, "it is the doctrines of the Bible, as taught and practiced by Jesus Christ."[19] Brownlow's canards did not carry the election, for Johnson registered a triumph.

Johnson's second term coincided with the Presidency of James K. Polk, a fellow Tennessean and fellow Democrat. But Polk was an aristocrat, Andy a plebeian, and their relations soon became strained. The Congressman quarreled with Polk over patronage and his avoidance of the White House became conspicuous. After "a frank conversation" of an hour's length between the two, the President committed to his diary his belief that Johnson "wished to

[19] The late John Trotwood Moore, *Saturday Evening Post,* April 1929. Mrs. Moore has kindly furnished me with a copy of the full text of Mr. Moore's article, which was printed only in part by the *Post.* According to Moore, in his inquiries at Raleigh, Johnson "thoroughly disproved the slander," and secured numerous affidavits of good people still living to disprove the charge. No Raleigh paper of the day contained any reference to Johnson's visits. In a letter to Josephus Daniels, Moore claimed, in May 1929, that Johnson had issued a pamphlet on the subject. This pamphlet is unknown to Johnson collectors. One fable about Johnson's recognition of illegitimacy is destroyed by Pulaski Cowper, late private secretary to Governor Bragg of North Carolina. In 1867, Cowper heard Johnson's oration over the monument to his father, and says that Johnson referred to "the reputed grave of my father," rather than to "the grave of my reputed father." For this information I am indebted to Mr. Josephus Daniels of Raleigh, in a letter of May 11, 1929.

play the demagogue. . . . I would almost prefer to have two Whigs here. . . ."[20]

On the very next day, Johnson wrote a friend in Tennessee that Polk, "very deficient in moral courage," was not thought "competent to lead a great party," had acted "with great duplicity to the party," and was not "respected as a man." "Polk's appointments, all in all," he added, "are the most damnable set that was ever made by any President since the government was organized. . . . He has a set of interested *parasites* about him, who flatter him until he does not know himself. He seems to be acting upon the principle of hanging an old friend for the purpose of making two new ones. . . . There is one thing I will say . . . *I never betrayed a friend or [was] guilty of the black sin of ingratitude.* I fear Mr. Polk cannot say as much."[21]

Johnson was sorely depressed by the general disfavor with which his home folks viewed his feud with Polk. On January 10, 1847, he wrote to Blackstone McDannel, at Greeneville, addressing him as "My dear friend—*if there is one left that I can call my friend.*" It was a letter of despair. "When I reflect upon my past life and that of my family," he wrote, "when I sum up the many taunts, the jeers, the gotten-up and intended slights to me and mine, . . . I wish from the bottom of my heart that we were all blotted out of existence, and even the remembrance of things that were." He had even come to doubt Sam Milligan's loyalty to him, and as for Greeneville, he was sick of the "backbiting, Sunday-praying scoundrels of the town. I never want to own another foot of dirt in the damned town while I live."

On February 2, 1847, Johnson made a speech destined to plague him in Tennessee for several years. "I wish to Almighty God," he said, "that the whole American people could be assembled in one vast amphitheater in Washington, so that the veil that now conceals from their view the many abuses could be drawn aside," to disclose to them "the secret springs of the entire proceedings of things in this government, of all the intriguings of

[20] *Diary of James K. Polk* (Chicago, 1910), II, 36–41.
[21] Johnson Mss., I, No. 33.

officials in authority, from the highest to the lowest. . . ."[22]
Toward the close of his term, Polk claimed to be unaware if he
had ever given Johnson cause for offense, but lamented that the
latter had been "politically, though not personally, hostile to me
during my whole term. He is very vindictive and perverse in his
temper and conduct. . . ."[23] However, the Congressman from
East Tennessee had more to occupy him than quarrels with the
White House over patronage. He warmly supported Polk's Mexican War policy; as to Oregon, at first he insisted upon the 54° 40'
line, tweaking the Lion's tail as he did so, and then supported
Polk's compromise.

On March 27, 1846, Johnson first introduced his Homestead
Bill, a measure particularly designed to aid the landless whites, the
"mudsills" whence Johnson himself had sprung.

His most noteworthy legislative service prior to secession was
his unflagging advocacy of Homestead legislation. The problem of
the disposition of government land was particularly important to
the people of the trans-Appalachian states. Thomas H. Benton—
the famous "Old Bullion"—had early advocated Homestead legislation. Indeed, the technical excuse for the historic debate between
Hayne and Webster was a resolution of a Connecticut Senator
concerning public lands. Southern members of Congress had been
actively antagonistic to Homestead legislation in the thirties. But
in the next decade, as nine new territories grew up and knocked at
the portals seeking statehood, Southern politicians were aghast.
They feared that these new states in the West, settled by free men
and offering free state constitutions, would unbalance the South's
federal control.

Nor were the Southerners the only enemies of such a Homestead
law as Johnson urged. The Know-Nothings feared that Catholic
immigrants would monopolize the free lands; railroad promoters
wanted them for themselves as a governmental bonus for road
building; and the advocates of a high tariff feared that large

[22] Temple, p. 219.
[23] Polk, IV, 265.

government revenues from land sales would eliminate the need for tariff revenue and thus cause a cut in tariff duties.[24]

The Tennessee Congressman's plan was simple. His object was not to swell federal revenues but to put settlers on the land. He wanted the government's Western holdings to be divided into homesteads to be given without cost to real settlers. Each head of a family, if an American citizen, should be given a quarter-section, if he would settle and cultivate it for a certain number of years.

The House was slow in warming up to this farsighted project. Representatives of such alien interests as Thad Stevens and Jefferson Davis united in crushing it, but by 1850 Johnson was gaining more support. On May 12, 1852, he succeeded in passing his bill in the House. But the Senate stood out against it.

Johnson's advocacy of a Homestead Bill attracted attention to him in the North. He had many invitations to speak to labor and land reform organizations, and in a labor convention he even received votes for nomination as a labor candidate for President. In his own Southland, Johnson was the target of sneers and abuse. "It was an infamous and a nefarious scheme," said the Raleigh *Register*. The Richmond *Whig* called him "the greatest of national humbugs."

During these years of the Homestead fight in the House, Johnson was in a delicate position. Himself a representative of a slave state, an owner of slaves, and a believer in slavery, he had to march in step with his Southern colleagues in the great slavery fights. But he undoubtedly recognized that the ultimate effect of the adoption of the Homestead plan would be to strike a body blow at the future of the entire slave system. To reconcile these two divergent forces was no easy task. While Johnson's attitude on slavery in the forties and early fifties was orthodox enough from the Southern point of view, it was mainly due to his recognition of the necessities of his political situation—"compulsory," Winston terms it. But as a "mudsill" himself, "free land for free labor," the underlying idea of the Homestead Bill, stirred him to the core. The results of Johnson's Homestead campaign in the House were only

[24] Winston has an excellent summary of the Homestead situation when Johnson started his fight (pp. 130 ff.).

educational, but in 1857, when he entered the Senate, he resumed the battle for free land and for free labor.

Johnson's speech of February 2, 1847, against Polk, played a large part in his next contest. It had been the general expectation of the district that Landon C. Haynes, an eloquent and ambitious Democrat, would run against Johnson at the next election; had this occurred, the latter's speech would have won him general Whig support. But Haynes belatedly decided not to run and toward the end of the summer, Oliver P. Temple, a young Whig, entered the fight. Temple made much capital of such Johnsonian phrases as "the intriguings of officials in authority, from the highest to the lowest"; and the Democrats, indignant at Andy, voted for Temple by the hundreds. On election night, when it seemed that Temple had won, Johnson "shed tears, and almost broke down with emotion."[25] The next day the last returns from two distant counties gave Johnson the election by 314 votes.

He made no more anti-Polk speeches.[26] Indeed, in 1848, he delivered a powerful address in defense of the Presidential right of veto—a defense of Polk which has unusual significance in view of Johnson's later career. The veto was a "constructive" thing, one which "enables the people, through their tribunician officer, the President, to arrest or suspend unconstitutional, hasty or improvident legislation, until the people . . . have time and opportunity to consider of its propriety. . . ." In 1849, Andy was re-elected over Nathaniel G. Taylor, the Whig candidate, by a majority quite as great as those of his first two campaigns.

Finally, in 1851, Landon C. Haynes measured his strength against Johnson in a bitter personal campaign. Haynes and Johnson bandied epithets and exchanged accusations "for six hours each day" throughout the long canvass. Haynes denounced Johnson's Homestead plan as bearing fraud and robbery upon its face and having its origin in the hotbed of Jacobinism in France. Johnson's newspaper supporters made much capital out of this,

---

[25] Temple, p. 230.
[26] Polk says (January 1, 1849): "If he had the manliness or independence to manifest his opposition openly, he knows he could not again be elected by his constituents" (IV, 265).

and it contributed to Haynes's defeat.[27] Although an eloquent speaker, the Democrat-aristocrat was "glittering rather than solid," and Johnson's superior ability, courage, and tact triumphed. "In truth," wrote a reminiscent Whig, "eloquence never availed much against the irresistible logical facts always dexterously used by this artful man. No rhetoric, no amount of word painting, could withstand the trenchant blows he struck."

It is little wonder that, in January, 1852, a Tennessee friend wrote Franklin Pierce, who was even then hoping for the Democratic Presidential nomination, without expecting it, that "the great man of this district is the Hon. Andrew Johnson, our representative. His stronghold is with the people, and he can command more votes in the district than any man."[28]

Back in Washington, Johnson was disgusted at the Congress, "the poorest . . . I ever saw," he wrote Milligan, "it deserves the curse of every honest man." Already, Johnson saw "breakers ahead." In the debate over the Compromise of 1850, he gravely reprehended the slavery agitation in Congress and appealed "to the North and to the South, to the East and to the West—to Whigs and to Democrats—to all—to come forward and join in one fraternal band and make one solemn resolve that we will stand by the Constitution . . . as our only ark of safety."

The Whigs now took counsel as to how to bring the tailor's political career to a close. As they controlled the new Tennessee legislature, they redistricted the state, Gustavus A. Henry introducing the bill by which Greene County, Johnson's political bulwark, was cut off from the First District and attached to one overwhelmingly Whig.

The tailor-statesman made up his mind "to bid adieu to political life," a decision which he made with less unwillingness in view of his forebodings over the prospect of Franklin Pierce's Presidency. The latter's "transit has been too sudden," Johnson wrote Sam Milligan; Pierce lacked "that political preparation so necessary to

[27] Greeneville *Spy*, April 17, 1851.
[28] Temple, p. 378; I. A. Graham to Franklin Pierce, Jonesboro, Tennessee, January 24, 1852 (Pierce Photostats, Library of Congress, Washington).

prepare *ordinary* men" for Presidential responsibilities. In addition, the Democratic party now seemed bound together only by the "cohesivity of public plunder."[29] Ill health increased Johnson's willingness to abandon a political career.

A little later, however, he seems to have improved in political and bodily health, for he began to write Tennessee friends that, "under a proper set of circumstances," he would run for Governor.[30] In his swan song in the House, he said that the General Assembly "had parted my garments, and for my vesture are casting lots," adding warmly, "but there is much in the future."[31]

The outcome of the gerrymander was to prove discomfiting to these clever political engineers. William B. Campbell, Governor of the state, and Tennessee's outstanding Whig, refused to seek a third term, thus depriving his party of its strongest candidate. The Whigs fell back on Gustavus A. Henry, a politician familiarly known as the "Eagle Orator." The Democratic county conventions urged many local figures,[32] but Andrew Johnson, indorsed by more counties than all the rest combined, was hailed as "a man of the people, and the people's man."[33]

When the state convention met in Nashville in April, jealous leaders sought to prevent the favorite's choice. At a secret caucus on the night before the convention, three test votes were taken and each time Johnson had a majority. But the leaders nevertheless determined to offer Andrew Ewing of Nashville as the choice of the caucus.

When this was announced the next day, turmoil ensued. Several speakers denounced the caucus, demanding that Johnson be voted on. Finally Ewing withdrew in Johnson's behalf. Then an opposi-

[29] Letter to Sam Milligan, July 20, 1852 (Mss. Pennsylvania Historical Society, Philadelphia).

[30] Letter to Sam Milligan, Washington, December 28, 1852 (Mss. Pennsylvania Historical Society, Philadelphia).

[31] House Journal, Tennessee Legislature, 1851–1852, p. 75.

[32] Among these were Isham G. Harris, Joseph Conn Guild, J. G. Pickett, and Edwin Polk.

[33] W. M. Caskey, "First Administration of Governor Andrew Johnson," *East Tennessee Historical Society Publications,* I (Knoxville, 1929), 45–46. Caskey found that of the 39 counties reported, 12 gave Johnson as first choice, to only 6 for Isham G. Harris, the next man.

tion leader announced capitulation, saying, "It seems that Johnson is strong enough to run all the Democrats out of the convention, and can run Henry out of the State." The Greeneville man was unanimously nominated.

It was charged that Johnson, taking advantage of a casual promise Ewing made several months before, had craftily written to Ewing to commit him and that a keen sense of personal honor had caused Ewing to sacrifice a nomination practically his, to keep a faith which Johnson did not deserve. But the facts as to Ewing's pledge and Johnson's letter disclose no self-abnegation on Ewing's part.[34]

He attended the preconvention caucus, at which Johnson's majority had been unmistakable; yet he shared in the plot to have himself nominated by acclamation. Until it was obvious that the convention would not nominate him, Ewing made no move. His withdrawal arose from his fear "to have the roll called when no names were before the convention except his own and that of his 'friend' Johnson."[35]

Henry, the Eagle Orator, proved no match for Johnson on the stump.[36] The two made a joint canvass of the state, from the Mountains to the Mississippi. Johnson told the voters that he had been not gerrymandered, but "Henry-mandered," out of Congress, and made great headway with this charge. This spirited canvass occasioned an enormous vote and Johnson was elected, with 63,413 votes to Henry's 61,163.

Johnson's inauguration as Governor took place on October 17, 1853. In the Inaugural Address, he struck some popular notes, particularly in emphasizing the crying need for the general education of the people and for better economic treatment of the

[34] According to George W. Jones, *Memorial Address*, Greeneville, June 5, 1878, Johnson's letter had requested Ewing "to withdraw his [Johnson's] name from before the convention in the event he should think it necessary to do so in order to harmonize the convention" (p. 9).

[35] Caskey, p. 48.

[36] Henry did, however, have the satisfaction of a biting retort. At one debate, Johnson had ridiculed the "Eagle Orator," and said the eagle had not left any marks on him. "No," Henry replied, "the eagle is a noble bird, and will not feed on carrion."

laboring classes. The Inaugural became known as the "Jacob's Ladder" speech, because of the Governor's ingenuous declaration: "Democracy and religion are handmaidens to each other. They are two converging lines extending from earth to heaven, where they unite in theocracy." This remark was severely censured, not alone by the "conservative statesmen of this country, but by the aristocratic press of England and France," though the Western Democrats thought it a magnificent philosophy.[37]

The new Governor devoted two months to a penetrating study of state conditions before he sent in his first message, a state paper of high rank. He analyzed the state's debt and made recommendations for alleviating it. He proposed a road-building tax. He wanted the state to get out of the banking business and gradually to liquidate the Bank of Tennessee. He criticized the competition of products of prison labor with those of free labor. He demanded a thoroughgoing reform of the judiciary.

A striking feature was Johnson's insistence on aid for education. "The time has surely arrived," he said, "when the legislature and the people should lay hold of this important question with a strong and unfaltering hand. Tennessee ranks last, except one. The difficulty is that there is not enough funds, and there is no way except to levy and collect a tax from the people of the whole State. . . ." Millions were being spent for internal improvements. "Can there be nothing done to advance the great cause of education?"[38]

Although the House was Whig and the Senate Democratic, Johnson's first term was marked by progressive legislation. A Bureau of Agriculture was established. The Assembly heeded Johnson's urgent appeal for education and passed an act levying heavier taxes for schools than any theretofore. Its internal improvement bill increased state aid in railroad construction. The Iron Horse went galloping over Tennessee at state expense.

Johnson was Tennessee's first Governor to give nearly all his time to his public duties. During this term he rarely discussed national affairs. He paid no attention to the rise of the Know-

[37] Savage, p. 46.
[38] House Journal, Tennessee Legislature, 1853–1854, p. 297.

Nothings and had little to say about the much discussed Kansas-Nebraska Act. When he had a task to do, he stuck to his last.[39]

He was one of the first of the Progressives, in the modern sense of the word. As a disciple of Jefferson and an apostle of Jackson, he thought democracy must be something more than an empty word. He believed the comman man was the cornerstone of the republic and that the people, voting directly, should elect their officials. Thus, in his first message Johnson submitted several proposals for amendments to the federal Constitution. One provided for the election of the President and the Vice-President by the people of the states, rather than by the fictitious electoral college. A second made the tenure of judges of United States courts twelve years, instead of for life. A third sought to have the United States Senators elected by direct vote of the people. The tailor-statesman never lost his enthusiasm for these reforms.

In the fifties, passions were hot and bowie knife and pistol often supplemented verbal argument. A man could not be Governor of Tennessee without being physically as well as politically brave. Johnson well met this test. One morning a placard was posted in Nashville, announcing that the Governor was to be shot "on sight." His friends went to his house to serve as a bodyguard to escort him to the Capitol. "No, gentlemen," he replied, "if I am to be shot at, I want no man to be in the way of the bullet." And he walked alone and with his usual deliberation from his home to Capitol Hill![40]

Thoroughly alarmed by Johnson's achievements, the Whigs determined to put him down at all costs. Consequently they entered into an alliance with the Know-Nothings, that mushroom political growth then sweeping South and nation. Bottomed on anti-Catholicism and similar proscriptions, it had already gained a hundred thousand members in Tennessee.[41] Soon after their party

---

[39] Caskey, p. 58.

[40] Savage, p. 49.

[41] Temple, p. 383. The growth of the Know-Nothings was so sudden and the affiliation of the secret order with the Whigs was so general that Democratic leaders of the North and the South had been much perplexed to know how to handle it. Stephen A. Douglas was among the first to denounce it, in a heated speech at Philadelphia on the Fourth of July, 1854. He called upon all Democrats to stand together against the "allied forces of Aboli-

merger, the Whigs began advocating that both parties dispense with state conventions to select candidates for Governor. Indeed there was no occasion for the Whigs to do so, for the secret conclaves of the Know-Nothings had already determined upon Meredith P. Gentry, "the best natural orator in Congress," as their candidate. And so, on February 12, Gentry issued a card to the papers of the state, referring to "the generous sentiments expressed for me" and adding, "I deem it my duty to respond by respectfully announcing that I am a candidate for the office of Governor of Tennessee, at the next election."

The Democrats, however, were unwilling thus informally to launch their campaign. Their papers insisted on a meeting so they could organize "and fight the fight on religious and political freedom." Governor Johnson was indorsed by nearly every Democratic county, and the delegates to the state convention met in Nashville on March 27 in a fighting mood. Not only was the Governor renominated by acclamation, but resolutions were adopted reprehending Know-Nothingism in the strongest terms.

The two candidates met, agreed on sixty joint meetings, beginning at Murfreesboro on May 1, and ending at Chattanooga on August 1.[42]

Temperance likewise was destined to play a part in the context. Maine's abolition of the liquor traffic had aroused interest and support in the South as well as in the North. In February, 1855, a state-wide temperance convention appointed a committee to ask Johnson where he stood. The committee wrote him, bluntly: "Are you in favor of a law prohibiting the sale of intoxicating liquors as a beverage? Will you, if elected, recommend to the Legislature the passage of such a law . . . ?"[43]

---

tionism, Whigism, Nativism, and religious intolerance, under whatever name or on whatever field they may present themselves" (see Beveridge, *Lincoln,* II, 227). Henry A. Wise made a campaign in Virginia for Governor, attacking the Know-Nothings, just about the time Johnson made his Tennessee onslaught.

[42] Caskey, "Second Administration of Governor Andrew Johnson," *East Tennessee Historical Society Publications,* II, 34 ff.

[43] Gentry, who had been similarly questioned, evaded a direct answer. Late in the campaign, however, the temperance forces gave him their support.

He responded with equal bluntness. He believed "some of the leading provisions of that law are incompatible with the rights and privileges of freemen," and in conflict with the spirit, "if not the very letter of the Constitution of the State." If elected Governor, he could not recommend such a law. He added: "I hope that I have succeeded in making myself understood."[44]

In the opening debate at Murfreesboro, Johnson carried the way into Africa. He arraigned the secret party for "its signs, grips and passwords, its oaths and secret conclaves, its midnight gatherings, its narrowness, littleness and proscriptiveness." In joining the order, he charged, its members "swore to tell a lie." There came a sudden stillness over the audience, full of Know-Nothings, as Johnson, weighing his words, exclaimed: "Show me a Know-Nothing, and I will show you a loathsome reptile, on whose neck every honest man should put his foot."

Under this terrible denunciation, the crowd became "pale with rage" and "still as death." Upon his declaration that the order was "no better than John A. Murrell's clan of outlaws," many voices burst out, "It's a lie, it's a lie!" The sound of cocking pistols was heard from many quarters, and men ceased to breathe. But Johnson looked on, grim, unmoved, and undaunted. Pausing a moment, he resumed his speech. There was no outbreak. His next appointment to speak was in another Know-Nothing stronghold, and a committee of Democrats waited on him, urging him to omit the speech. "I'll make that speech tomorrow," he answered, "if it blows the Democratic Party to hell."[45]

The two candidates canvassed the state from Sullivan to Shelby in a campaign of great bitterness. Many threats were made against Johnson. Word was sent him that if he appeared in a certain Know-Nothing stronghold, he would not leave the hall alive. At the appointed hour, the Governor advanced to the desk, and laid his pistol upon it.

[44] Nashville *True Whig,* April 27, 1855.

[45] Temple, pp. 385–386; Kenneth Rayner, *Andrew Johnson* (New York, 1866), pp. 50–51; Savage, p. 46. The Kansas-Nebraska Bill was the next most important issue in the campaign, Johnson pressing and Gentry evading taking a position upon it. Cf. also John Trotwood Moore Ms., p. 18.

"It is proper," he began, "when free men assemble for the discussion of important public interests that everything should be done decently and in order. I have been informed that part of the business to be transacted on the present occasion is the assassination of the individual who now has the honor of addressing you. . . . Therefore, if any man has come here tonight for the purpose indicated, I do not say to him, let him speak, but, let him shoot."

Thereupon he placed his right hand on his pistol, with the other held open his coat, and looked blandly at the crowd. After a half minute's pause, he announced that it was apparent he had been misinformed, and proceeded with his speech.[46] The boldness of the attack on the Know-Nothings set the state on end. Gentry devoted his best platform oratory to a defense of the secret order, but his words were wasted. Johnson was re-elected, thanks to the heavily increased majorities he received in rural Protestant counties, and thenceforth Know-Nothingism was impotent in the state.

The keynote of his Inaugural was his declaration that "the people have never deserted me; and, God being willing, I will never desert them." His second term was largely given over to continuation of the policies of the first. A new touch was his recommendation that the state sell its stocks and turnpikes, railroads and banks, and liquidate as much as possible of the state debt. He announced with pride that the state had purchased the Hermitage, home and tomb of Andrew Jackson.[47]

When the Democratic state convention met in Nashville on January 8, 1856, Johnson made a short talk, the keynote of which was his statement that "slavery exists. It is black in the South, and

---

[46] Savage, p. 49.

[47] It cost the state $48,000. Tennessee tendered the property to the federal government for use as a site for a Southern branch of the military academy at West Point. The Military Affairs Committee of the House reported favorably, but Congress adjourned without action. Johnson suggested that if Congress continued to ignore the proffer, the Hermitage should be used as a home for future Governors of Tennessee (Jones, pp. 58–59). In January 1857, Governor Johnson went to Washington to urge President Pierce to accept the Tennessee offer. He was unsuccessful. On his way home, his train jumped the track near Chattanooga. Johnson's right arm was broken, and he was in poor health for months. As a result of this accident, his handwriting thenceforward was crabbed and awkward.

white in the North, and it will continue to exist." Anxious to put
Johnson forward as the state's favorite son, the convention resolved "that Andrew Johnson, as a statesman and patriot, has no
superior; that he is our first preference, and we would delight to
honor him with the highest office in the gift of the American
people."

After the Cincinnati convention, Johnson loyally accepted the
Buchanan nomination, and was soon drafted for a speaking campaign throughout Tennessee. He opened in Nashville on July 25
with three hours of closely reasoned argument, the speech evoking
unbounded satisfaction from both friends and foes, so much so
that the Governor was forced to repeat it throughout the state.
Although the "Black Republicans" had not put out an electoral
ticket in Tennessee, Johnson contended that Millard Fillmore, the
Know-Nothing candidate, was a greater abolitionist than Frémont.
After pillorying Fillmore as a compromiser, Johnson said: "My
own opinion is that the South has been engaged in compromises,
as they are termed, long enough. We have been engaged first in one
compromise and then another, until our rights have been all com-
promised away. It is now time to stop. For me, I have nothing to
conceal in reference to my political sentiments; and when I say I
am no compromiser, I think there are many who agree with me."

Lest this be misunderstood as a veiled secession threat, he
added these significant statements, containing a germ of his later
stand in 1861: "I am no alarmist, but I speak what I think. This
Union shall be preserved. Our Southern institutions depend upon
the continuance of the Union, and upon noninterference."[48]

The Tennessee Democrats registered a notable triumph at the
polls, carrying the state for their Presidential nominee for the first
time since Andrew Jackson's day. Not only did the Buchanan
electors receive a majority of 7,500 votes, but also the two Houses
of the state legislature were safely Democratic, and thus Johnson's
election to the United States Senate, should he desire that preferment, was assured.

Johnson did not aspire to a third term as Governor. "If I make a
move for the Senate," he wrote Milligan in December, 1856, "now

[48] Caskey, II, 46–54.

is the time to do it while public opinion is setting in that direction."[49] His friends promptly set to work and early in 1857, the Tennessee legislature sent him there. He was chosen not by the leaders, but by the Democratic masses, whose wish was so manifest that the leaders did not dare say them nay. He always spoke with contempt of the aristocratic leaders and humiliated them whenever chance presented. "Old Andy" was the idol of the Democratic rank and file. He trusted them and they trusted and honored him. "In robust strength," says a contemporary, "Johnson stood alone in his party. His reign at this time was absolute."

From the time he entered the Senate, Johnson verged more and more away from the leaders of the slave states. There was little sympathy between him and the Davis, Cobb, Toombs contingent. They generally considered him a plebeian upstart and he hated what they represented. He was likewise quite unimpressed with Buchanan. "I fear his administration will be a failure," Johnson wrote his son Robert on January 23, 1858. "It is too timid to venture upon anything new or risk much upon anything old." He predicted that there would be much "grannyism" in the conduct of affairs and, as to "Old Buck" himself, "to hear him talk, one would think that he was quite bold and decided, but in practice he is timid and hesitating."

The Tennessean's first address to the Senate, directed against an increase in the regular army, gave him "rank among the first debaters."[50] In 1858 he protested against the federal government's fixing the qualification of voters in Minnesota, then seeking statehood, and denied "that this government has power to go inside a sovereign state and prescribe the qualifications of her voters at the ballot box."

In this same year, Johnson had an untimely altercation with John Bell, his Whig Senatorial colleague from Tennessee. In 1854 Bell had been one of the few Southerners to vote against the Kansas-Nebraska Bill. In his speech he had expressed the view that a Senator whose opinions were "in direct opposition to the settled sense of his constituents" should resign. The Tennessee

[49] Letter to Sam Milligan, December 10, 1856 (Mss. Pennsylvania Historical Society, Philadelphia).
[50] Rayner, p. 53.

legislature, which favored the Kansas-Nebraska Bill, promptly passed a resolution calling on Bell to resign. When Bell sought to answer these resolutions in the Senate, he excoriated some of Johnson's friends in the General Assembly at home. The tailor-statesman felt called upon to defend the legislature. In doing so, he incidentally referred to Bell as "a competitor." Bell resented the reference and replied that Johnson was neither big enough nor good enough to be so classed.

The latter, now thoroughly angry, almost made a scene in the Senate. He told Bell he had had competitors "worthy of my steel, men who recognized me as such." He added that a gentleman, "a well-bred man, will respect me; all others I will make do it." He knew his rights and the right of the state he represented, and would maintain these "at all hazards and to the last extremity." It looked for a while as if the Tennesseans might meet on a dueling ground, but next day both apologized, and though they never became friendly again, formal relations were resumed.[51]

Johnson's main attention was now given to his Homestead Bill. As soon as he reached the Senate, he reintroduced it, and pressed it with all the force he had. With very few exceptions, the Southern Senators opposed it with every parliamentary device at their command. On May 20, 1858, when he had finally managed to have his favorite project made the special order of the day, Johnson made one of his greatest efforts, taking up the cudgels for the free farmer.

Not long before, Senator Hammond of South Carolina had told the Senate that the working classes were "the very mudsills of society," and had compared the "slaves" of North and South. This provoked Johnson, who scorned the idea that the free workers of the North were slaves because they had to earn their daily bread with the sweat of their brows. Such a comparison as the South Carolinian had made would make a slave of every man who was

[51] Possibly this unfortunate affair between Johnson and Bell kept the former from supporting the Bell-Everett ticket in 1860. The fact that Johnson was so staunchly battling for the Union in the winter and spring of 1861 quite probably slaked Bell's Union fervor and caused him to support secession in April 1861. Had Bell joined hands with Johnson, probably Tennessee would not have left the Union.

not a slaveholder. He concluded with a peroration in support of his Homestead plan.[52] Even so mild a rebuke as this did not suit the Senators of the slave states. Mason of Virginia called Johnson "almost an abolitionist." The Homestead Bill failed again.

Johnson brought in his bill again in the first session of the Thirty-sixth Congress, and on April 11 made another powerful appeal for its passage, in the course of which he engaged in several sharp colloquies. When the measure came to final roll call, most of the Southern Senators who had interposed parliamentary obstacles to its passage did not dare to vote against it, and it was passed by forty-four to eight, the yeas including Chestnut and Hammond of South Carolina, Clay and Fitzpatrick of Alabama, Jefferson Davis of Mississippi, Hemphill of Texas, Sebastian of Arkansas, Slidell of Louisiana, and Yulee of Florida! The House quickly passed the measure with amendments, a compromise was agreed on in conference, and on June 20 it was presented to Buchanan for his signature. On June 23, despite what Johnson had deemed the President's commitment to the Homestead Bill, Old Buck returned it with an argumentative veto.

Johnson suspected that most of the Southern slavery phalanx which had voted for his measure had done so after a secret understanding with the President that he would veto it and they would then sustain his negative. When the ultra Southern Democrats, who were Buchanan's main bulwark of support, forced his hand, Johnson believed he quickly forgot his promise and returned the desired veto. And so it proved. A number of Southerners sufficient to keep the bill from repassing changed their votes, in spite of Johnson's despairing efforts.

Early in 1859, Senator Johnson said he did not believe "all the factionists of this government can pull it to pieces." In that December, when John Brown [was hanged for] his raid on Harpers Ferry, Johnson displayed a moderation and good temper in striking contrast to the bitterness and acrimony of the Senatorial extremists of South and North. He made an earnest defense of the constitutional rights of the slave states, without the usual threat of

[52] Savage, pp. 60–71.

secession. "I am no disunionist," he announced. "Because we cannot get our constitutional rights, I do not intend to be one of those who will violate the Constitution. . . . I intend to place myself on the Constitution which I have sworn to support, and to stand there and battle for all its guarantees."[53]

Early in 1860, Johnson's Tennessee advisers thought they saw a real chance for him to become the beneficiary of the war between Douglas and Buchanan, and, by playing a shrewd game, to win the Democratic nomination. They were in doubt as to his wishes, however, and had to send many messages to Washington before gaining his consent. At that, it seems to have been the necessity of the local factional situation rather than any real nomination hopes which induced Johnson to countenance the enterprise. The Tennessee convention met in Nashville on January 17. The Douglas men quickly discovered the impossibility of their securing the delegation, and perforce joined the Johnson party; the next day the convention formally instructed its delegation to the coming Charleston convention to present Andrew Johnson's name. But he felt there was little or no hope of his securing the nomination,[54] and looked with anxiety upon the prospect. "The whole Senate," he wrote, were aspirants, and Jefferson Davis, "burning up with ambition, is nearer consumed by an internal heat than any man I ever saw. . . . What Jeff will do if he is not nominated, *God* only knows." The Tennessee Senator could see little ahead save the division and destruction of the party.[55]

Johnson understood the grim determination of the Western Democrats to nominate the "Little Giant." "Sentiment is almost universal and determined in favor of Douglas," A. Ten Eyck wrote Johnson from Detroit in February. "The gentlemen of position and influence in the South should not shut their eyes to the fact that if Mr. Douglas is not the nominee of the Charleston convention, Mr. Seward is almost certain to be elected. With any other candidate

53 Rayner, pp. 76–77.
54 Letter to Robert Johnson, April 8, 1860 (Johnson Mss., II, No. 250). But he added, "If you and Milligan will go [to Charleston], I will pay the expense of both."
55 Letter to George W. Jones, Washington, March 13, 1860 (Mss. Pennsylvania Historical Society, Philadelphia).

than Mr. Douglas, we cannot hope to carry a single Northern State, except perhaps Illinois. . . . Accept at Charleston the Cincinnati platform intact, without note or comment, if you please. Give us Douglas for our candidate."[56] Thus, while Johnson wanted to pay the expenses of his son Robert and Sam Milligan at the coming convention, he seems to have entertained no serious hope of nomination. His anticipations were well founded.

Throughout the Charleston deadlock the Tennessee delegation stood loyally by the tailor-statesman, but without any real hopes of success. True, Milligan convinced himself that Douglas' friends were Johnson's friends, and believed that when Douglas withdrew, his forces would turn to the Tennessean. But the convention tension became so great that the Douglas men were too angry to compromise or change.

During the platform debates, threats of a bolt by Gulf State delegations greatly disturbed the Tennesseans. On April 29, W. C. Whitthorne, the delegation's chairman, telegraphed from Charleston: "Have you declared for Douglas in the event of the adoption of the minority report? Six or more States will withdraw. What ought Tennessee to do?" Johnson answered promptly and firmly, "I recommend and acquiesce in the nomination, Nicholson, Wright, and Avery concurring." Later that same day, he telegraphed again: "I would hold out; acquiesce in the nomination." These telegrams gave Milligan, Whitthorne, and Andrew Ewing the added force they needed to restrain the delegation hotheads, and to prevent Tennessee's joining the Gulf States bolt.

On May 2, after the bolt, Douglas reached a majority, Johnson was temporarily withdrawn, and a delegate telegraphed him: "We have withdrawn you. Douglas has majority. Ought we support him?" The Senator answered immediately: "The delegates present with all the facts before them are better prepared to determine what course to pursue than I am."[57]

[56] A. Ten Eyck to Andrew Johnson, Detroit, February 20, 1860 (Johnson Mss. Greeneville).
[57] W. C. Whitthorne to Johnson, Charleston, April 29, 1860, and Johnson's reply; W. H. Carroll to Johnson, Charleston, May 2, 1860, and Johnson's reply (Johnson Mss. Greeneville).

But regardless of Johnson's views, the Tennessee delegation was unwilling to go to Douglas. They felt that a Douglas victory "by a purely sectional vote would of itself, more effectively than the secession of the Gulf States, denationalize the party." As soon as the Illinois man seemed to have a chance of nomination under a loose construction of the two-thirds rule, the Tennesseans joined Virginia, Maryland, North Carolina, and Kentucky in insisting upon such a strict construction that Douglas could not possibly win.

Despite the turmoil between the Charleston adjournment and the Baltimore opening, Sam Milligan continued to nurse hopes that Johnson still had a chance. "Your friends lie in the North and Northwest," he wrote the Senator, "and I do believe, by a little concert of action with Mr. Douglas and the conservative men of those States, your nomination at Baltimore is by no means improbable." But he felt, as did Whitthorne, that "the election is lost in any event, and the Extreme South is responsible for it." But the Senator had no delusions, and instructed Milligan not to let his name be presented. In an hour of serious apprehension for the future of the government, Johnson felt it incumbent on all to secure harmony, that "the Union, with the blessings, guarantees and protection of its Constitution be perpetuated forever." He therefore wished the Tennessee delegation to be free to vote for others, and thus to help avert any more deadlocks or bolts. But Milligan's hopes would not be downed; on June 22, he telegraphed Johnson, from Baltimore: "If the withdrawing delegates from the Moderate States North and South should recommend your name for the presidency, would you object?" Johnson would, and the Tennesseans remained with the main convention, stubbornly voting for Andrew Johnson until the thirty-sixth ballot.[58]

After the Democratic split, Johnson supported the Southern Democratic ticket of Breckinridge and Lane. He could not believe that there was any real danger of secession in the event of Lincoln's election, and thought the talk of the Rhetts and Yanceys and Toombses empty campaign bluff. Following the election, when the

[58] Sam Milligan to Andrew Johnson, Greeneville, May 10, 1860 and Baltimore, June 22, 1860 (Johnson Mss. Greeneville); Jones, pp. 64–65.

Cotton South started its secession, Johnson was shocked and indignant. He was himself a states'-rights man and owned a few slaves. But first of all, he was an Andrew Jackson Democrat.

A good epitome of Johnson the Senator was offered by Jefferson Davis in 1865, while a prisoner of state in Fortress Monroe, held for trial on the grave charge of high treason. One day Dr. Craven, the prison physician, fell into conversation with him about the antebellum Senate and Senators. The doctor asked the head of the late Confederate states for his opinion of President Johnson. Davis replied that he knew only what the papers told him of President Johnson. But of Mr. Johnson, when in the Senate, he could speak. Johnson's position with his associates from the South had never been pleasant. In the midst of associates, many of whom pretended to aristocracy, Johnson seemed to keep ever present with him his own plebeian origin as a bar to warm social relations. Davis charged him with having an "almost morbidly sensitive" pride— "the pride of having no pride."

The other Senators, said Davis, respected Johnson's "ability, integrity, and great original forces of character. . . . He was an immense worker and student, but always in the practicalities of life. His habits were marked by temperance, industry, courage, and unswerving perseverance; also by inveterate prejudices or preconceptions on certain points, and these no arguments could change. His faith in the judgment of the people was unlimited, and to their decision he was always ready to submit. One of the people by birth, he remained so by conviction."

Johnson's honesty of character, justice, kindliness, and generosity were notable. "He was eminently faithful to his word," said his imprisoned foeman, "and possessed a courage which took the form of angry resistance if urged to do or not to do anything which might clash with his convictions of duty. He was indifferent to money, and careless of praise or censure, when satisfied on the necessity of any line of action."[59]

[59] John J. Craven, *Prison Life of Jefferson Davis* (New York, 1866), pp. 261 ff.

✪

Impressions of Andrew Johnson

To describe Mr. Johnson as he really was about 1832 or 1833, when I first became old enough to know him, is no easy matter, though few men of this day so impressed themselves upon my young mind. From the beginning he was no ordinary man. At his first appearance in public life, his speeches were strong and sensational. His facts were presented in a bold and vigorous manner. There was in them that salt of bitterness, that impressive personality, which characterized him in so marked a degree in afterlife. Even then he gained victories over every antagonist. His delivery, if not elegant, was at least easy, natural, and pleasing. His flow of language was wonderful considering he was uneducated and inexperienced as a speaker. There was nothing violent or spasmodic in his manner. His voice was good and pleasant. In the course of time it became one of great compass and power.

Mr. Johnson was about 5 feet 10 inches in height, and weighed near 175 pounds. His limbs were strong and muscular, his movements active, indicating superior physical strength. His power of endurance was exceptionally great. His shoulders were large, his head massive, round and broad, his neck short and stout. His forehead was not exceptionally high, but very wide and perpendicular. Above his eyes, at the point where the phrenologists locate the reasoning faculties (causality) were two remarkable bumps or

Reprinted from *Notable Men of Tennessee, from 1833 to 1875: Their Times and Their Contemporaries* by Oliver P. Temple (New York: Cosmopolitan Press, 1912), pp. 451–467.

protuberances swelling out from his brow. His complexion was dark, his eyes black and piercing; his countenance, when in repose, gloomy; when lighted up by a smile, it became attractive. In ordinary conversation his voice was low and soft. His action, while not stately, was easy and rather graceful. In appearance he was far from being rustic. On the whole, nature stamped him as a remarkable man.

Johnson seldom came upon the streets of the village. When he did, it was with a quick, elastic step, giving evidence of the energetic and restless spirit within.

While following his trade, he did most of his work himself. He was a fashionable and a good tailor. From my earliest recollection his shop was the same one which is now, or was until recently, shown to strangers. On the signboard there were the words: A. JOHNSON, TAILOR.

While at work Mr. Johnson discussed with those who came in such questions as were agitating his own mind. He delighted in argument and controversy. Naturally he was belligerent and pugnacious. Besides, he was cautious and suspicious. Everything that did not originate with him was viewed with distrust. No man's opinions were adopted by him on faith. Everything was sifted in his own analytical mind. He was more or less envious of those above him. There was a deep-seated, burning hatred of all men who stood in his way. The passion of his life was the desire of power. It was a consuming one. Nothing, not even its highest fulfillment, could satisfy it.

Ordinarily he did not seem excessively vain, and yet he clung with extreme tenacity to his own opinions. For forty years no man in his own party, in Greene County, dared to oppose or question his plans or policy. He was an absolute autocrat in this respect.

When engaged in a canvass, Johnson could be seen frequently on the streets. He generally gathered a little crowd around him and talked as if making a speech. He was always a hero in the estimation of his friends. In his intercourse with the body of the people there was at all times more or less reserve in the expression of opinions. The Democratic masses followed him blindly and enthusiastically, with the homage always paid by inferiors to superior talents. . . .

The marked deficiencies of Mr. Johnson were language and information—elegant language, exact and precise, in which to present his ideas, and wide range of knowledge for argument and reflection, for adornment and illustration. He was sadly lacking in discipline of mind—the ability to discriminate, to compare, to analyze—which early and continuous education give. He was without the graceful expression, nice taste, acquired by association from infancy with scholarly people. He had ideas, but no vehicle for making them effective. No one, however superior his natural mechanical talents, could construct a delicate watch without the necessary training and tools. Give him these, and how easy the task and how perfect the accomplishment! In an unusual degree Mr. Johnson was without the discipline, the material necessary for high intellectual achievement. That he accomplished what he did, that he was able to rise to such eminence, under such unfavorable conditions, among competitors of such conspicuous talents, is indeed cause of profound amazement. He was far above Charles Sumner, and could never have resembled him.

It is a fact—but by no means a remarkable one—that few uneducated men rise to greatness. It should rather excite surprise that any at all do. General Jackson and Mr. Lincoln are the most notable examples in our history of greatness achieved with deficient early education. They were, however, exceptional in natural ability, as they were in all respects. They were the favored sons of heaven. But they were not entirely without education. Jackson early had the advantages of association with able lawyers, and of refined society, while Lincoln was from boyhood a diligent student, educating himself. Both were admitted when young to the bar— the best school for mental discipline furnished by the age, outside of the university.

Nothing quickens the mind like close conflict with an astute lawyer, in the discussion of profound legal questions. The highest faculties of the intellect are called forth and sharpened by opposition, as steel sharpens steel. No fancy, no declamation, no loose use of words avails, but exactness, concentration, and logic are demanded. Johnson missed the advantage of these intellectual encounters and the daily association with members of the bar. Instead he had the drudgery of earning a living in a calling giving no leisure. He was not only the sole President, but the only great man in our country who never attended school a day in his life.

Mr. Johnson has never received the credit for ability he deserves. There are several obvious reasons why he has always been underrated.

He would have ranked higher had it not been for his habit of pandering to the passions of the people. This lowered him in the opinion of all the better-educated classes of all parties. Grant that he was the friend of the masses; that did not make it necessary for him to foster hatred between the poor and the rich. That was no reason for arraying one class against another. Mr. Lincoln always proved himself, by his acts, very much more than by his professions, a friend of the people. In this respect, however, Mr. Johnson only did what many prominent politicians of both the leading parties are doing today.[1]

Johnson lost much by lack of the amenities of life. He was sadly wanting in sympathy and in kindliness of manner. The refined and cultivated he apparently disliked. These reminded him of his own deficiencies, and in the depths of his heart he detested them. In fact, he hated everything superior to himself. He was conscious of the gulf which separated him from the more refined class of society. On all occasions his speeches tended to divide society, to array the poor and ignorant against the wealthy and intelligent. He was a natural leveler. All his theories and appeals were based on the supposed gullibility of the masses. He never appealed to the broad, enlightened intelligence of the world. Any public man who excites the contempt or the derision of his fellow-men is sure to be undervalued.

That Mr. Johnson was naturally cynical and morose was only too evident from his gloomy countenance. This feeling, no doubt, was increased by his poverty. He plainly saw the advantage that wealth and culture gave. That thought filled his ambitious soul with rage. He disliked the possessor of these things. This natural

[1] He seems to have been the pioneer "insurgent."

tendency was increased by a difficulty with one of his rich neighbors, which probably gave more or less coloring to Johnson's
feeling throughout his whole life.

After Mr. Johnson became President, he improved in outward
manner, and became much more agreeable. When he chose he
could be delightful, but it was hard to undo the habits of forty
years. It was impossible to change his own disposition. There was
little that was gentle about him. Toward his enemies he was
implacable and unforgiving. He had few intimates.

In the solitariness of his own thoughts he seemed to revel; his
mind was active, and forever revolving something new. For society
or idle pleasures he had no taste, and in the common everyday
affairs he took no interest. One absorbing passion consumed his
life. His caution was excessive. When a new political question
arose, or one of grave expediency, he would deliberate long and
anxiously over it. The difficulty would not be as to its justice, but
as to its party effect, or perhaps as to its effect upon his own
personal fortunes. He would discuss the question with friends,
would state hypothetical cases and argue them; he would invite
criticism and then he would answer it. He would thus call out all
the arguments for or against a measure.

He was in a high degree unsociable, preferring solitude. Occasionally he wanted, indeed seemed to require, a friend, a solitary
person. But it was a hearer he needed, someone to listen while he
discanted on some new idea. It was not personal but mental
sociability he desired, food for the mind, not for the heart.

There were two apparent exceptions to the statement that he
had no intimate friends. He did have two. These were Samuel
Milligan and John Jones, both of his county. The former was a
lawyer of Greeneville, and became, in 1865, one of the Supreme
Judges of Tennessee, and afterward a member of the Court of
Claims at Washington.

Judge Milligan was a college graduate. In his mental operations
he was slow, cautious, and logical. Give him time and he was sure
to reach a correct conclusion. He was remarkably free from
prejudice and passion, and honest above all men I ever knew. At

an early day Johnson took him into his confidence, and no safer, truer, or more worthy confidant could have been found.

John Jones was also college-bred, and had studied law, but never followed it as a profession. In dress, habits, and appearance he was the most rural of men. He was almost an anchorite. While he was a farmer, he cared little about farming, or anything else except reading and thinking. His mind was clear, penetrating, and original—indeed, intellectually he was remarkable. Withal he was perfectly honest and candid. This was the man Johnson needed, and he early made him his friend and adviser. When any new question arose, demanding thought and thorough investigation, he would send to the country for Jones, and take him to his house, where the latter would stay for days in consultation with Johnson. Hence Johnson was enabled to appear on the stump, in all his canvasses, thoroughly prepared at every point both for attack and defense.

The world will never know, can never know, how much the political fortunes of Mr. Johnson were helped and shaped by the advice of these two men. Hardly anything shows his sound judgment more clearly than the fact that he kept near him two such strong, honest advisers. The three had served in the legislature together in 1841 and became friends for life. Jones was not a social companion of Mr. Johnson; he was a helper and counselor. Milligan was more than this; he was an intimate friend.

Mr. Johnson was always true to his trusted friends. He held fast to those once admitted to his confidence. His devotion to Judge Milligan and the honors he bestowed on him prove the truth of this. Other examples might be given to the same effect. Indeed, individually he was not false in dealing with men. The virtue of candor he possessed in a much higher degree than most public men. There was no deceit in him. It was always well known what he thought of those around him. If he was an enemy, he was too independent and too bitter to conceal the fact. I am not aware of a single instance in which he promised a favor which he failed to bestow. True, whenever it would promote his personal ambition, he did not hesitate to set aside a debt of gratitude, or to bury the deepest hatreds and become reconciled to his worst enemy. Still he was not, as a rule, either a false, a deceitful, or an untruthful man. Excepting the case of the unfortunate question of veracity between him and General Grant, and the instance already referred to in another chapter, I have no recollection of his veracity ever being seriously called in question.

Johnson was not a great, or a polished orator, yet he was effective and powerful on the stump, and an able and adroit debater. In a long series of debates I am not sure that he ever met his match. Certainly Gustavus A. Henry was not his equal, and, on the whole, he had the advantage over Mr. Gentry.

There was in some respects a striking similarity between Johnson and Stephen A. Douglas. Both were strong on the stump, both were bold and aggressive, both were more or less unscrupulous about the means used to accomplish their ends, and both pandered to the prejudices of the people. Johnson's strength was on the stump, and not in the Senate. He was always interesting on this stage. Men listened to him because he talked about himself and talked about others. This might not please some, but it did please the majority. He made himself felt by his boldness and sometimes by his offensiveness. He had the faculty of impressing his facts on the minds of his hearers as few could do. This arose in part from the earnestness of his manner, the novelty of his matter, and the pungency of his words. Take Gustavus Henry for a comparison. After his discussion with Johnson, men went away remembering him as a handsome, graceful orator, and but little else. As to Johnson, they recalled and could repeat his facts, his arguments, his striking points, and his terrible denunciations. No public speaker in the state has ever left his ideas so deeply impressed on the public mind. Whether men approved or condemned his views, they were certain to remember them.

Johnson had great faith in the efficacy of popular speaking. Indeed, in his earlier days, this was the only direct mode of reaching a rural population, newspapers, which nowadays go everywhere, not circulating much among them. Johnson had accomplished everything by speaking. He could not write. No one cared to read his speeches. But people would listen to the delivery of his bitter harangues. These were plentifully seasoned with salt, vinegar, and red pepper, and served steaming hot. They had a decidedly pungent taste that most men liked.

In his younger days, when Johnson wished to impress a new idea on the people, on an appointed day he would call the people together and would deliver to them one of his long harangues. When as Military Governor of Tennessee, and afterward when he became Vice-President, he wished to deliver a pronunciamento against his fellow-citizens in arms against the government, he would be opportunely serenaded (of course he did not himself arrange it beforehand) and would then give relief to his burdened mind. When he wished to arouse the people to the dangerous designs of Congress, he chartered a train and traveled over the country making speeches at every station from New York to St. Louis, and as Petroleum V. Nasby said, "distributing to the people copies of the Constitution." He preached a crusade against Congress, as Peter the Hermit, many centuries before, preached a crusade against the Mohammedans of the Holy Land; with this difference, however: Peter set all Christendom ablaze with martial ardor; Johnson set all this country aroar with laughter.

In the Senate Johnson was far from being great. His speeches were not remarkable for logic, statesmanship, or learning. They often abounded in personalities and in unworthy appeals to prejudice. There were no splendid passages that will live in political history, to be quoted by coming generations. Indeed, narrowness and partisanship completely obscured all breadth and elevation of view. The only possible exception to this statement was his speeches in East Tennessee, in the spring of 1861, when the dangers which confronted the country seemed to give him a dignity, a fervor of eloquence, an intensity of patriotism unknown in him previously.

It is true that his eighteenth and nineteenth of December speech, in the Senate of 1860, produced perhaps the most profound impression of any speech ever made in the country, but that was not because of its eloquence but because of its startling unexpectedness, its daring positions, its noble patriotism, and the breathless anxiety with which the North was listening—waiting, indeed—for a word of hope from the South. It was the spirit of the speech, the golden opportunity seized and well used, and not the words, that gave permanence to that effort. It inspired the bewildered, despairing North with new hope. It was a vivid light suddenly flashed upon the profoundest darkness.

In canvassing with competitors, Johnson went just as far in personal remarks as it was safe to go. He studied the disposition of his adversary, and ascertained how much personal indignity he would endure. In his debate there was seldom any exhibition of manly courtesy. A kind act or word on his part toward an opposing party was almost unknown. He seemed to be too bitter ever to feel the elevation that inspires noble sentiments.[2] Another peculiarity of his was that in any given case no man could count on what he would do, except that he was sure to do something unexpected, and very likely something disagreeable.

Johnson never went into society in his own town. Before he became President he lived in his own home in almost exclusive retirement, never attending social gatherings. He had one somewhat remarkable habit, considering his desire for popularity, his constant custom of pandering to the prejudices of the people, and that was he always dressed well. He wore the finest material, and when he appeared was always faultlessly neat. I never saw him shabbily attired. He thought, correctly, that to secure the respect of the people and have them look up to him as superior to themselves, he must make the most of his personal appearance. There is very much more in this than demagogues often think. People are never flattered by having a favorite appear before them in mean garb. . . .

Of the personal character and habits of Andrew Johnson, already much has been given, but something yet remains to be said. I doubt if his true character will ever be known by the public as it was by those immediately around him. He was so extreme in his views and utterances, and so angular in outline, that it is difficult

[2] The following incident will illustrate what I have been saying: When he and Gustavus A. Henry, who was the very soul of courtesy, were canvassing for Governor in 1853, soon after the canvass opened Johnson asked a friend if Henry would fight. The reply was that Mr. Henry was very amiable and peaceable, and would avoid a personal difficulty unless the insults were very gross and offensive. "Then," said Johnson, "I will give him hell today."

to describe him as he was. It is hard for those who knew his fierce nature and indomitable will to treat of his virtues and failings with the calm judgment necessary for a just and clear appreciation of the man. By his wonderful personality he stamped himself indelibly on the public mind, and became a part of the history as well as the rightful property of the country. His character, therefore, is open to public criticism. It will be observed that I have in this sketch carefully avoided the sanctity of the domestic circle, and dealing with facts too sacred for the public eye; these do not concern my narrative.

While in many respects Mr. Johnson can be held up as a model for the young men of the country, in others, he cannot be. All men must pay homage to the indomitable will, energy, and courage which enabled him to overcome the most adverse conditions in life, and to rise by his own strength to the most exalted positions of honor. I bow with profound admiration to the statesman or the soldier who successfully cuts his way through obstacles that appall ordinary men, and firmly plants his feet on the highest round of power. Such was the career of Mr. Johnson. While he thus rose and conquered all opposition and filled the land with his name and fame, he was at all times for himself. Personal ambition controlled his life. In the earlier part of his career, if not in the latter part, he strove to rise by working on the baser passions of men, sowing broadcast the seeds of hate and bitterness between classes. An appeal to prejudice was his most effective argument. While able, he was narrow and harsh. In his life as a private citizen he manifested much of that same supreme regard for self only that he did as a public man. If he ever took any active interest in the welfare of the community in which he lived, and which honored him for forty years; if he ever proposed, advocated, or helped any measures tending toward the amelioration of society or the public around him—anything for the promotion of education, art, science, temperance, morality, manufactures, or general progress—anything for the benefit of the toiling masses, for the unfortunate and the helpless, tending to lift them up and make them better and happier, I have never heard of it.

What constitutes a good citizen? It certainly is not one whose life is entirely selfish. A man may be moral in conduct, and honest in his dealings, and yet live so entirely for himself, and so little for others, that he may be no blessing, but the contrary, to the community. Rather is he a good citizen whose life and example are such that they do something, however humble his sphere, toward increasing the happiness of mankind, and in promoting the welfare of his fellow-citizens. He whose acts are just, whose conduct is kind and helpful, who is an inspiration to others to do better, that man is a good citizen. These are not the criteria by which men are usually judged, but they ought to be the test of good citizenship. . . .

Johnson, on the contrary, spent his last years hunting office, quarreling with his enemies, and trying to punish them for some long gone-by wrong. The evening of his life was, as its morning and its noon had been, stormy and tempestuous. There was no mellow sunset gilding the horizon with its soft light.

As said once before, Johnson had few of the gentle amenities of life. It was possibly unfortunate that he had no love for society. Until he became President he avoided its attractions entirely. In outward conduct he was apparently cold and disdainful. He denounced aristocrats, yet imitated them, and if not one at heart himself, he had all their worst ways. His life was exclusive. He stirred up the bad passions of the lower classes. Men who had large property, though earned by honest toil, if they belonged to the opposite party, were denounced as the enemies of the people. He flattered the people—many of them ignorant and degraded— with the most fulsome words. . . .

Johnson's life was full of stormy passions. It had no rest, and but little sunshine in it. He was strong and self-willed; had excessive confidence in his own power, was obstinate and dogmatic, and had little respect for the opinion of others.

Mr. Seward may have flattered himself, while in his Cabinet, that he was influencing him, and shaping his (Johnson's) policy. Never was there a greater mistake. That strong man was master. He was doubtless deferential toward Mr. Seward, but it was in order to use him. Seward with all his ability was in Johnson's hands only as clay in the hands of the potter. And yet with all his imperiousness Johnson, when he desired, could be gracious and winning. . . .

Mr. Johnson's life was one intense, unceasing, desperate, upward struggle. Never was a human breast fired by a more restless, inextinguishable love of power. His ambition was boundless. To it he sacrificed everything—society, pleasure, and ease. None of these had allurements sufficient to draw him from his purpose. The hope of power was the all-controlling object of life. In all the wide universe he worshiped no deity but that of ambition—the ambition to rise, to become great, to have his name sounded abroad, and to bestride the world.

Johnson was a man of the coolest and most unquestioned courage. When he was assailed on account of his loyalty by a mob of ruffians, in Lynchburg, Virginia, on his way home from Washington, in the spring of 1861, and one of them attempted to pull his nose, he drew his revolver, and kept the whole pack at bay.

When he made his great speech in Knoxville, in April, 1861, I had been in the habit of hearing him speak for well-nigh thirty years. I had never seen him so cool, so determined, so eloquent and so impressive in bearing, as on that day. For once, at least, he seemed to have the full stature and the lofty thoughts of a statesman. Whatever his motive may have been, in espousing the cause of the Union there was certainly that day the appearance on his part of absolute sincerity. As he appeared before that large assemblage of earnest, expectant listeners, and appealed with burning words for the preservation of the Union, my heart—all hearts —turned toward him as never before. It seemed as if his lips had been touched by a live coal off the very altar of patriotism. But one such opportunity occurs to a public man in a lifetime. Deeply conscious of the awfulness of the crisis, with thick clouds around him, he arose to the full height of the great occasion. A disinterested love of country seemed to glow in his heart, flame out in his countenance, and burn on his tongue. As with outstretched arms and melting voice he stood that day pleading so persuasively, so kindly, so powerfully for his distracted country, he rose to the very heights of splendid eloquence, and called to mind the fiery spirit and noble thoughts of Demosthenes before the Athenian people.

✪

Andrew Johnson
as Military Governor of Tennessee

The conclusion reached [about the reorganization of the government in Tennessee] will be . . . a condemnation or justification of Johnson's career as Governor; for one cannot read the records of these three critical years without realizing that the essential features of the work were peculiarly his own. Contemporaries fully appreciated this; it was at the Governor personally that their attacks were directed. Only recently, a distinguished participant in those stirring events, Mr. Oliver P. Temple, in an unsparing criticism, has thrust upon his shoulders a heavy burden of blame and reproach.[1]

The first serious charge laid at Johnson's door is that he purposely delayed Reconstruction. This accusation was freely circulated at the time. Mr. Temple says: "The work of reorganizing the state and of revising the constitution might have been and should have been accomplished in a regular, decent way one year, and possibly two, earlier than it was, and the state admitted back into the Union. The last of the Confederate armies was driven out of

[1] Oliver P. Temple, *Notable Men of Tennessee, from 1833 to 1875: Their Times and Their Contemporaries* (New York: Cosmopolitan Press, 1912), pp. 416 ff.

Reprinted with permission from *Andrew Johnson, Military Governor of Tennessee* by Clifton R. Hall (Princeton: Princeton University Press, 1916), pp. 210–223.

Middle and Western Tennessee in the summer of 1863, and out of the greater part of East Tennessee in September of the same year."

Only with the greatest diffidence may the conclusions of one so intimately identified as Mr. Temple with the episodes of which he treats be called in question; but my study of the records, without the advantage of the personal viewpoint of Mr. Temple and others who have expressed opinions similar to his, has forced me to believe that they have been hardly just to Johnson. If my account of the war in Tennessee establishes anything, it is that at no time previous to the end of December, 1864, was a fair, dignified, and representative election possible.

It is true that the successes of June and July, 1863, placed most of the state temporarily in the control of the government. Johnson promptly pronounced for an election in October, if conditions continued favorable. But nothing really decisive had occurred; neither of the Confederate armies in Tennessee had been beaten in a pitched battle; Rosecrans' advance was attended with serious difficulties and might be checked at any time. The Union Army had been just as favorably situated a year previously, only to be maneuvered out of all its advantages, and those who had ventured to celebrate its triumphs had reason to regret their premature enthusiasm. The people were not disposed again to rally around the administration, until they received substantial assurances that the Union domination was permanent. From every point of view, it was desirable that a victory over Bragg should stimulate popular confidence, and there is every reason to believe that Johnson only awaited this to clear the way for the restoration of a civil government with the prestige of victory behind it.

All such hopes were dispelled by the disaster at Chickamauga (September 20). Now, more than ever before, before even a beginning in reorganization could be made, it was absolutely necessary that the Army recover its shattered prestige. The fall and early winter had passed before this was done. More important still, East Tennessee, the citadel of Unionism, was in the grip of Longstreet, whose army hung on desperately in the northeast, even after the siege of Knoxville was raised.

Until January, then, there was no reasonable pretext for an

appeal to the distracted people. On the contrary, many Union men begged Johnson to spare himself and them the mortification of certain failure in an impossible task. Nevertheless, before the end of the month, he had returned to the work, provided the public with a complete program for restoring the state, and arranged for county elections in March, allowing for the "decent" interval which Mr. Temple says was desirable. That Reconstruction in the counties should precede the action of the state as a whole was a wise and provident decision. It would supply the judicial and other machinery most essential for immediate local needs, and, at the same time, would furnish a criterion of the popular attitude toward the government in the various sections, by which the result of a general election could be accurately foretold.

The outcome of the March elections was eminently discouraging. They were commonly designated as farcical, and Johnson's most trusted supporters advised against again inviting so painful a humiliation. In fact, whether the Unionists or the Confederates happened to be at any time temporarily dominant in the state was beside the point. Nothing worthwhile could be done while the army of the Cumberland had a resolute, efficient enemy in its front and cavalry and guerrillas operating in its rear. This situation appertained throughout the summer and fall of 1864. The people of Tennessee awaited the certainty of the permanent control of their state by one side or the other. While the issue was doubtful, their only hope of security lay in judicious inaction; so much, experience had soundly taught them.

During all this period, Johnson appears ready and willing to take forward steps in Reconstruction upon even slight encouragement, while it is the bulk of the Union party who hang back. The East Tennessee convention displays the most extreme anxiety to adjourn without action. The May convention at Nashville declares for an election only when the state can be represented from all its parts. Johnson's correspondence teems with letters urging waiting and watching. From West Tennessee comes the assurance that no vote can be taken there. In July, the municipal government of Memphis is suspended. In August, Forrest enters Memphis. In

September, Gillem is routed in East Tennessee. Everywhere guerrillas abound and refugees flee before them.

One is constrained to believe that Johnson was dealing only with unimpeachable facts when he declared that, under such conditions, an election was impossible.[2] Nevertheless, he never ceased to assert that, whenever a considerable number of citizens manifested their desire to reconstruct the government, he was ready actively to cooperate with them. Indeed, he seems to have driven rather than followed the convention of the fifth of September; all its recommendations were promptly embodied in his proclamations, and every assistance given to forward its designs. Never do we find the Governor opposing a restoration movement by the people; on the contrary, his energies are always devoted to encouraging them. The election of November, held under his auspices, was another fiasco; but he lent his sanction to the call for a convention in December. The work would have been accomplished then, but the invasion of Hood and Breckinridge intervened and the convention could not assemble. At last, on the sixteenth of December, the battle of Nashville created the situation for which he had yearned so long. The Confederate Army was not only beaten, but crushed. Tennessee was positively won for the Union. Never before could this have been said. For the first time, the administration could hope for an unrestrained expression of whatever Union feeling existed in the state. The Governor acted with the utmost possible energy. The Reconstruction convention met on the ninth of January, and he was its guiding spirit. The whole weight of his influence was exerted in favor of immediate, decisive measures. Obstructionists were overruled, slow methods of procedure were discountenanced, and in two months the work was done.

Mr. Temple asks: Was not this long delay in calling a convention due to Johnson's desire to hold his position of Military Governor until he could step into a higher place in March? "His ambi-

---

[2] However, General Thomas and General S. P. Carter, the Provost Marshal General at Nashville, declared in January 1864 that civil authority could and should be restored then. *Official Records,* Series 1, XXXII, Part II, 64; Nashville *Union,* February 16, 1864.

tion was to carry to Washington his own state as a reconstructed member of the Union, and present it as a rich jewel to the nation. It would give him new prestige and éclat. Hence his sudden haste just at the close of his service as military governor."

In response, it may be inquired what advantage could possibly come to Johnson from Reconstruction in March, 1865, which would not have been greatly enhanced by Reconstruction in June, 1864, when he was a candidate for national preferment and mentioned by many for the first place on the ticket; or by Reconstruction in November, 1864, when he was seeking the vote of the people. In either case, his advancement would have been helped immeasurably, and the prestige thus gained would surely have lasted until March. But neither in June nor in November was Reconstruction practicable. As it was, he was compelled, much against his will, to leave the work unfinished and come to Washington without the perfect "jewel" with which he might have courted favors for himself.

If we absolve Johnson from blame for unnecessary delay in the performance of his duty, there remains the charge that the method he adopted was arbitrary, unconstitutional, and permanently injurious in its results. Two other feasible plans were suggested. A legislature might be chosen by popular vote and might inaugurate the desired amendments in the manner prescribed by the constitution itself; or the people might be called upon to elect a second convention for the express purpose of changing the fundamental law. The first alternative, however, was open to the objection that a strict compliance with the constitutional provision for amendment would require a period of several years, which, in such a crisis, was not to be thought of. Another practical argument against committing Reconstruction to a legislature was that, in the unsettled condition of the country, no legislature could be chosen to represent all the counties of the state, except on a general ticket, and such representation was manifestly imperfect, not at all the sort contemplated by the constitution.

The second suggestion was at once weaker and stronger than the first. Its weakness was that it was no more constitutional than Johnson's plan. To this, however, it was replied that none of the three plans was, in reality, constitutional. No legislature was in existence, nor the machinery prescribed by the constitution for electing one. From a Union viewpoint, the revolutionary acts of the secessionists had thrown the constitution out of gear and there was no regular way of putting it again in operation. This was generally admitted by all Union men, but the most conservative pressed for the nearest possible approximation to constitutional forms, while others ridiculed the idea of sacrificing every practical consideration to a pretended legality which was, in truth, no legality at all.

If Reconstruction by means of the legislature should be abandoned on practical grounds, the question remained, should the original convention complete the work or a second one be elected especially for that purpose? The advocates of the latter view took the position that the existing body was in no just sense representative. Few, if any, of the delegates had been chosen in a regular manner, and the wording of the call was positive proof that the people could have had no idea that they were creating a body to formulate constitutional amendments. Here again, however, the objections had more apparent than real weight. If the amendments were not to be proposed in the manner provided for in the constitution, it mattered little in what manner they were proposed. They could not become law until accepted by the sovereign people, and the same people would vote on them in either case. There could be little doubt that an election for a second convention would bring together almost precisely the same individuals as were already deliberating; and, if the people disapproved of the actions of these "self-constituted" leaders, their obvious course was to refuse them their sanction at the polls and thus make a second convention necessary. If, on the other hand, they favored the amendments, time and money would be saved and nothing important lost. In support of this view, there was the impressive precedent of the irregular proceedings resorted to in framing and adopting the federal Constitution of 1789. As Johnson himself clearly pointed out, the convention method deliberately disregarded prescribed forms and depended for its justification upon the inherent sovereignty of the people. What they established received thereby the highest possible sanction. The only necessity, then, was to get the expression of the will of the sovereign; and, whether the first or a second convention submitted proposals, the decisive expression would come from the votes of the same persons at the polls.

The chief advantage of the one-convention plan was in the saving of time. Was there any occasion for haste, aside from the gratification of Johnson's desire for "éclat," which justified the sacrificing of dignity to speed? As has been shown, the call for the convention, issued in November, 1864, contemplated leaving the work of revision to a second body, more formally chosen, and to this arrangement Johnson had offered no objection. But, in the fall and winter, the administration party in Congress had struck rough ground in developing its Reconstruction projects. An especially strong opposition developed to the proposed Thirteenth Amendment. For some time its success seemed doubtful, for all the formidable "Copperhead" strength was arrayed uncompromisingly against it. Under date of January 14, 1865, there is, in the Johnson correspondence, a letter[3] from one W. Bilbo, a prominent Tennessee banker, then in Washington, informing the Governor that the amendment is held up for lack of two more votes in its support. The writer continues: "Can't you come to our assistance with the ten congressional votes of Tennessee? Let the convention at once repeal the secession ordinance, emancipate the slaves, appoint a day within the next fourteen to elect members of Congress, elect them, send them on here so they can help us pass the amendment?" It is at least a plausible surmise that other messages of similar purport came to Johnson. Devoted as he was to the principle of the amendment and now prominently identified with the administration, he would recognize the importance of avoiding a reverse on this cardinal point of its program and of coming promptly to its aid with every available resource. The Congressional vote of Tennessee, he was told, would be decisive of the result. He was about to leave the state, but if, during the few weeks that remained to him as Governor and while his hand still held the helm, Tennessee could be launched on her course and her Congressional candidates placed before the people, his influence was

[3] Johnson Papers, LV, 1878.

powerful enough to direct her in accordance with the views of the administration. Once he was distant in Washington, however, events in his state would be beyond his control, and the dissensions among the Unionists, all too strongly evinced on many previous occasions, made him apprehensive of the outcome. May not this be the explanation of his impatience to accomplish everything possible in the short time available between the defeat of Hood in December and his departure in February?

Another charge against Johnson remains to be treated: that, by the unnecessarily rigid requirements of his "ironclad" oath, he excluded many unquestionably loyal men from participation in Reconstruction, thus destroying their interest in the work, humiliating and aggrieving them, and losing their counsel, influence, and cooperation, besides depriving the new constitution and government of a substantial, impressive indorsement at the polls, for the sole purpose of forcing his own views and his own men upon the state.

It will, no doubt, be generally agreed that the only parties shut out by the oath who had any just claim to be admitted were the pro-slavery loyalists and the "peace Democrats. . . ." Whatever censure they may have deserved for their violent strictures upon the government in a crisis of the nation's fate, they should not have been discriminated against in Tennessee, while their counterparts in the Northern states received toleration. All were equally to be justified or condemned. On this ground, as it seems to me, Johnson's policy may be fairly censured. On the other hand, it must be remembered that the conditions in Tennessee were peculiar. The various loyal factions were of uncertain and shifting strength. The state had been excepted from the Emancipation Proclamation for the express purpose of bringing prestige and impulse to the program of the national administration by herself taking the initiative in freeing her own slaves. With whatever advantages the government expected from this action, the discredit of a defeat would be commensurate. Finally, Lincoln, with his sensitive finger upon the nation's pulse, approved Johnson's course. Usually magnanimous and generous almost to a fault, he gave way, as regards Tennessee, to the latter's representations; and it is safe to say that he did so only after thoroughly diagnosing the situation and satisfying himself that no more lenient policy was feasible. Tennessee seemed always on the point of breaking away from his control, and he could not afford to relax the reins on so intractable a steed. The Union cause required to be in the hands of active, determined men, who, however they might blunder, would not falter. To such Johnson committed it. His three years in office had been one long struggle with timidity and irresolution. It is not to be wondered at that he embraced the brief opportunity offered him to finish the battle himself with few, but dependable and single-hearted fighters at his back.

Biographers of most men who have attained national prominence are able to lighten their narrative with many personal anecdotes, interesting in themselves and helpful in explaining the characters and careers of their subjects. Such advantages must be largely foregone by one who writes of Johnson, at least for the period of the war, when his activities were confined to Tennessee. This is to be explained partly by Johnson's own personality, partly by the impossible circumstances in which he was placed. During these three years, he occupied a position which would have been insupportable by any man less self-sufficient, grim, impervious—one is tempted to say, less fanatical—than he. Never popular with the leaders in his state, his return among his fellow-citizens as the voluntary instrument of the federal government for their repression aroused against him a hatred that expressed itself on every possible occasion and in every possible form of vituperation and insult. And surely no man ever was less qualified than Johnson to overcome prejudice by virtue of his personality. Neither graciousness of address, charm of manner, nor suavity of disposition won or mollified his enemies. He possessed none of the appealing gentleness, broad sympathy, and deep understanding of and love for humanity, none of the saving humor which made up so much of the greatness and power of Lincoln. His mind was narrow, bigoted, uncompromising, suspicious; his nature solitary and reticent; his demeanor coldly repellent or violently combative. Fessenden's remark of him as President, that he had no friends, applied to him equally as Governor. His harsh, domineering intolerance drove from him those who admired his impeccable honesty and patriotism and his brilliant abilities, or, at least, held them only by bonds of esteem rather than devotion. He remained always a solitary man, yielding his full confidence to none.

Of personal letters, to which the biographer looks for the softer tones of a portrait, Johnson received comparatively few and wrote fewer. He was never able to supply the lack of a good elementary education. His pen was not his friend; his spelling and grammar were always faulty. He complains to his wife that the difficulty he experiences in writing often impels him to put the letter aside unfinished.

The studied contempt with which the pro-Southern citizens of Nashville treated him stung his pride, caused him to draw further back within himself, and made him still more resentful. Deputed to extend the protecting aegis of law and orderly government over the state, his utter lack of finesse made him appear to be brandishing a club to frighten the people into subjection, and their animosity centered upon him. The hostility to the federal government and troops, wrote General Nelson to Buell in July, 1862, "seems settled into a fierce hatred to Governor Johnson, to him personally more than officially, for in questioning many people they cannot point to an act that he has not been warranted in doing by their own showing; but still, either in manner of doing it, or that it should be done by him, or from some indefinable cause touching him their resentment is fierce and vindictive, and this country, from being neutral at least, as you left it, is now hostile and in arms."[4]

Johnson returned hatred with all the violent intensity of his nature. As the storm of abuse beat upon him, he became more and more bitter. With him, an affront took on something of the character of the feud, familiar, one may imagine, to his not too remote forebears; the debt must be repaid in full. He developed an almost savage determination to humiliate the "aristocrats," the scorners of free labor, and to make them pay the price of the ruin of the war. More than any other idea, this permeates his public and

[4] *Official Records,* Series 1, XVI, Part I, 816.

private utterances. It was by the constantly reiterated expression, "Treason must be made odious, traitors punished and impoverished," that he became most widely known throughout the country.

The habit of indulging in intoxicants, afterward reputed as Johnson's most conspicuous personal failing as President, had, of course, been formed long before. There is no evidence that it interfered seriously with the performance of his duties, but it occasionally betrayed him into extravagances of action and expression which did him no credit. Charles A. Dana, who, as Assistant Secretary of War, paid him an official visit in Nashville in 1863, reports that the Governor opened their first interview by producing a whisky bottle, and, in his opinion, was addicted to taking "more than most gentlemen would have done."[5]

Carl Schurz gives one of the few interesting personal impressions of Johnson,[6] as he saw him in 1863. "His appearance," he says, "was not prepossessing, at least not to me. His countenance was of a distinctly plebeian cast, somewhat like that of the late Senator Douglas, but it had nothing of Douglas' force and vivacity in it. There was no genial sunlight in it; rather something sullen, something betokening a strong will inspired by bitter feelings. I could well imagine him leading with vindictive energy an uprising of a lower order of society against an aristocracy from whose lordly self-assertion he had suffered, and whose pride he was bent upon humiliating. . . . Judging from his conversation, his mind moved in a narrow circle of ideas as well as of phrases. . . . I could not rid myself of the impression that beneath his staid and sober exterior there were still some wild fires burning which occasionally might burst to the surface. This impression was strengthened by a singular experience. It happened twice or three times that, when I called upon him, I was told by the attendant that the governor was sick and could not see anybody; then, after the lapse of four or five days, he would send for me, and I would find him uncommonly natty in his attire and generally groomed with especial care. He would also wave off any inquiry about his health. When I mentioned this circumstance to one of the most prominent

---

[5] Charles A. Dana, *Recollections of the Civil War* (1902), p. 106.
[6] Carl Schurz, *The Reminiscences of Carl Schurz*, III, 95.

Union men of Nashville, he smiled, and said that the governor had 'his infirmities,' but was 'all right' on the whole.

"My conversation with him always turned upon political subjects. He was a demonstratively fierce Union man—not upon antislavery grounds, but from constitutional reasons, and from hatred of the slaveholding aristocracy, the oppressors and misleaders of the common people, who had resolved to destroy the Republic if they were not permitted to rule it. The constant burden of his speech was that this rebellion against the government of the Union was treason, and that treason was a crime that must be made odious by visiting condign punishment upon the traitors. To hear him expatiate upon this, his favorite theme, one would have thought that if this man ever came into power, the face of the country would soon bristle with gibbets, and foreign lands swarm with fugitives from the avenging sword of the Republic. And such sentiments he uttered not in a tone betraying the slightest excitement, but with the calmness of long-standing and unquestionable conviction."

John M. Palmer, in his *Personal Recollections,* thus estimates Johnson: "He possessed great natural capacity, but his knowledge of the science of government was superficial. He was sincere and earnest in his opinions, but his prejudices were violent and often unjust. His personal dislikes were never concealed. Bailie Peyton said of him that 'he hated a gentleman by instinct.' After listening to him one day, I said: 'Governor, the antislavery men of the North oppose slavery because it is unjust, and hope by abolishing it to make free citizens of those human chattels.' He answered: 'D—n the negroes; I am fighting these traitorous aristocrats, their masters!' "[7]

Almost all the defects of Johnson's character noted by his contemporaries may be explained by the hardships, limitations, and narrowness of his early environment and by the prejudices engendered in a man conscious of natural superiority, but held down by institutions and conventions. The lack of broad, comprehensive interests had, however, a compensating element; it enabled him to concentrate all the strength of his extraordinarily forceful

[7] John M. Palmer, *Personal Recollections,* p. 127.

nature upon the few essentials which he clearly comprehended, and to move to them with overwhelming energy. He had three invaluable assets for the work to which he was called—singleness of mind, tenacity of purpose, indomitable persistency. In the darkest days for the Union, in the spring of 1863, he wrote to his wife: "I feel sometimes like giving all up in dispare; but this will not do we must hold out to the end, this rebelion is wrong and must be put down let cost what it may in the life and treasure. I intend to appropriate the remainder of my life to the redemption of my adopted home East Tennessee and you and Mary[8] must not be weary, it is our fate and we should be willing to bear it cheerfully. Impatience and dissatisfaction will not better it or shorten the time of our suffering."[9] The whole letter reveals a tortured mind and an exhausted body, sustained by an unflagging spirit. With his property confiscated, his family for a time in danger and distress, hated and insulted by his neighbors, maligned by rivals and enemies, often defeated, mortified, and seemingly almost discredited in his labors to reorganize his state, his devotion and patriotism never faltered, but soared higher and surer with every reverse of fortune. When the loyalists of Tennessee were perplexed and almost demoralized, he stood firmly and saw clearly, and by these merits won the confidence of Lincoln and Stanton and was thus able to hold the leadership, overcome all opposition, and command the course of events.

Johnson's weaknesses were those of temperament and training. His claims to honor are based upon loyalty, self-sacrifice, and a steadfast devotion to the cause he believed to be right, which, considering all that he had at stake, can only be described as heroic. The issue joined, he stepped unhesitatingly forward into the front rank for service, regardless of his own comfort and safety, and gave himself unsparingly to saving the state. He worked, says a perhaps too-fulsome panegyrist, "with an industry and energy that never grew weary or asked repose."[10] His reward came in the

[8] Johnson's daughter.
[9] Johnson Papers, XXX, 6689.
[10] Nashville *Times,* January 7, 1865, quoting Atchinson (Kansas) *Champion.*

esteem of those who could best comprehend the value of his services and in elevation to a high post of national distinction. His record as Governor is epitomized in Stanton's letter,[11] accepting his resignation of the office, in March, 1865. The Secretary of War concludes: "Permit me on this occasion to render to you the thanks of this department for your patriotic and able services during the eventful period through which you have exercised the high trusts committed to your charge. In one of the darkest hours of the great struggle for national existence against rebellious foes the government called you from the Senate and from the comparatively safe and easy duties of civil life to place you in the front of the enemy and in a position of personal toil and danger, perhaps more hazardous than was encountered by any other citizen or military officer of the United States. With patriotic promptness you assumed the post, and maintained it under circumstances of unparalleled trials, until recent events have brought safety and deliverance to your state, and to the integrity of that constitutional Union for which you so long and so gallantly periled all that is dear to man on earth. That you may be spared to enjoy the new honors and perform the high duties to which you have been called by the people of the United States is the sincere wish of one who in every official and personal relation has found you worthy of the confidence of the government and the honor and esteem of your fellow-citizens."

[11] *Official Records,* Series 3, IV, 1221; Johnson Papers, LVII, 2426.

ERIC L. McKITRICK

✪

Andrew Johnson, Outsider

The man who succeeded Lincoln, who thought of himself as following in Lincoln's footsteps and carrying out Lincoln's designs, was a lone wolf in almost every sense of the word. He was a man of undoubted ability. Indeed, the order which he brought to the administration of the executive office was in sharp relief to the clutter of Lincoln's time. But the only setting in which Andrew Johnson's powers could become fully engaged was one in which the man would be battling against great odds. The only role whose attributes he fully understood was that of the maverick, operating out on the fringe of things. For the full nourishment and maximum functioning of his mind, matters had to be so arranged that all the organized forces of society could in some sense, real or symbolic, be leagued against him. In such array they could be overborne by the *un*organized forces of whom he always imagined himself the instrument—and assault whose only rhythm was measured out, as it were, by the great heartbeat of the people. These were the terms in which the battle of life had its fullest meaning for Andrew Johnson.

It is often said of Johnson, with much truth, that his plebeian origins bred in him a fierce and independent spirit. One does not, however, think of Lincoln in any such way. One does not say that *his* plebeian origins bred in him "a fierce and independent spirit." Why is this? Had Johnson come of poorer "poor white" stock than

Reprinted from *Andrew Johnson and Reconstruction* by Eric L. McKitrick by permission of the University of Chicago Press. © 1960 by the University of Chicago. All rights reserved.

Lincoln—had his struggle been a harder one? It would certainly seem so; and yet these things are relative and not easy to measure. We know that Johnson eventually became a man of means and a slaveowner; it does not generally occur to us, on the other hand, to describe the Lincolns' circumstances as more than comfortable. We also know that for nearly thirty years prior to the Presidency, Johnson had enjoyed, to all intents and purposes, the highest honors in the public gift—legislator, Governor, Representative, and Senator, whereas Lincoln had only served in the Illinois legislature and gone to Congress for a single term. The key to the contrast between the two men does not seem to be "success" in any objective measure; it lies rather in the way success was conceived. For Johnson, personal fulfillment had long since come to be defined as the fruit of struggle—real, full-bodied, and terrible—against forces specifically organized for thwarting him. Not so for Lincoln. Johnson, all his life, had operated as an outsider; Lincoln, in most of his worldly dealings, and temperamentally as well, was an insider.

The early life of Andrew Johnson was an incredible struggle against grinding destitution that reads like a chapter first of Dickens and then of Horatio Alger, with perhaps a dash of Al Capp. His father, a good-natured porter at Casso's tavern in Raleigh, North Carolina, had lost his life rescuing two drunken gentlemen from an icy stream when Andrew was only three. Andrew's mother, an amiable but rather ineffectual woman known as "Polly the Weaver," apprenticed him to a tailor at fourteen when she could no longer support him. He had no formal education. After a time the young man ran away and hid out while his furious master advertised a reward for his capture. Eventually Andrew, his mother, his ne'er-do-well brother Bill (of "black hair, eyes, and habits"), and his sometime-acquired impecunious stepfather, all headed west over the mountains with their cart. They landed at Greeneville, Tennessee. There Andrew set up a tailor shop, practiced the rudiments of reading, and at nineteen married a wife who taught him to write. Eliza McCardle had a little education but no family connections whatever, being the orphaned daughter of a shoemaker. (Here one thinks, in contrast, of Lincoln's marriage to Mary Todd, the daughter of an aristocratic family with excellent connections.) Through scrimping and hard toil, Johnson bit by bit acquired a home, a new tailor shop, a brick store in Greeneville, and a comfortable farm. He practiced debating with the young men of the town, and in time held several local offices.[1]

In spite of numerous signs that he was really getting on quite decently in the world, the matter of class and social acceptance churned sourly in Andrew Johnson's vitals. His father, the happy menial, had never questioned his meager lot in life; that poor soul had gone to his reward without ever having thought much about the mysteries of "class" at all. Andrew thought of nothing else; his own struggle to rise consumed and obsessed him. Grimly ambitious, he brooded over the wrongs, real and imaginary, which were thoughtlessly foisted upon him by his social betters, and out of his inner world of suspicious fantasy he evolved an extravagant credo of plebeian democracy and honest toil. Once, after a snub from one of the Greeneville gentry, he raged: "Some day I will show the stuck-up aristocrats who is running the country. A cheap purse-proud set they are, not half as good as the man who earns his bread by the sweat of his brow."[2] With a dogged masochism, he never ceased to harp publicly on his own humble origins; he was still doing it on the occasion of his inaugural as Vice-President. Even as Governor of Tennessee, Johnson on one occasion insisted on cutting out a coat for a judge, a former blacksmith who had made a shovel for him; he accompanied the gift with an open letter proclaiming that "the main highway and surest passport to honesty and useful distinction will soon be through the harvest field and the

[1] The material for this portrait is largely drawn from Robert W. Winston's *Andrew Johnson, Plebeian and Patriot* (New York: Henry Holt, 1928). This work, while erratic in its scholarship, has at least the merit of a sympathetic approach to its subject on the level of human biography rather than political doctrine—not the case with George F. Milton's more ambitious biography (*The Age of Hate*), in which Andrew Johnson, the man, is all too seldom seen.

[2] Winston, p. 38. "Andrew Jackson, the pioneer and planter," wrote Thomas P. Abernethy, "was never possessed of class consciousness. Andrew Johnson, the tailor, never escaped it." *From Frontier to Plantation in Tennessee* (Chapel Hill: University of North Carolina Press, 1932), p. 357.

workshop."[3] Throughout it all, Johnson remained inordinately fastidious in matters of dress. One wonders what he must have thought, in later years, of the slovenly habits of the Great Emancipator.

Politically, Johnson's plebeianism served him wonderfully well in the fundamentalist atmosphere of the East Tennessee upcountry. Long hours of cultivating his voice in the solitude of his shop had made him a superb speaker. From the stump he would conjure up the spirit of Old Hickory; he would revive, in order that he might scourge, the ancient and terrible threats of tyranny and Federalism; he could call forth, as Mencken would later say of Bryan in that same country, all the dread "powers and principalities of the air." The simple mountaineers were deeply impressed by his philippics, and they would shiver in appreciation as his words rang through the valley in the gathering twilight.[4] They said of him, as he thundered out his harsh paeans to equality, "Old Andy never went back on his raisin'." But there was no merriment in Johnson's performances. Unlike Lincoln, he had none of that humor which comes from an appreciation of the ever-altering, shimmering complexity of things. "He was dead in earnest," says his biographer, "and he believed with his soul every doctrine he announced."[5]

Johnson's conception of political life was one which had the merit of great simplicity, and in the loosely organized political setting of East Tennessee it was one which could be exploited with

[3] Winston, p. 83.

[4] "As Mr. Johnson grew warm and hurled the terrible thunder of his wrath against the old Federalists," wrote a contemporary, "the shouts sent up by the Democracy could be heard far and wide among the surrounding hills. As he pictured the old Federal party in fearful colors, and pathetically entreated the people to stand firm upon the Constitution, his hearers would huddle closer together, as if for mutual protection, and plant their feet more firmly upon the ground. . . . It was usually nearly night when the crowd dispersed. . . . When night overtook them on their homeward way, in the bewildered condition of their intellects, they recalled dim images of 'blue lights and black cockades,' and in every dark wood they feared to see these monsters, whatever they were, confront them!" Oliver P. Temple, *Notable Men of Tennessee* (New York: Cosmopolitan Press, 1912), pp. 373–374.

[5] Winston, p. 62.

overwhelming personal success in the advancement of a career. Politics for Andrew Johnson was essentially a matter of principles that had to be defended rather than of a party organization that had to win elections. He was a Democrat but never really a party man.

Because of his unwillingness to cooperate with political parties or organizations, Johnson in Congress waged but a guerrilla warfare—a warfare sometimes inside the Democratic party and sometimes outside. Always, however, he stood upon the old platform, equal distribution of government favors, equal treatment of rich and poor, farmer, laborer, mechanic, manufacturer or what not. A strict interpretation of the Constitution and an observance of its letter had now become his guiding principle.[6]

There was such a direct and immediate quality about Johnson's successes on the stump that he could hardly fail to construe reelection as a persuasive test of personal merit owing nothing to "the interests." His constituency sent him back year after year. In such circumstances it was perhaps only natural that he should never feel pressed to put a very high premium on party responsibilities. He was willing, time and again, to break with the organization on any pretext; indeed, much of his career was occupied in fighting it. It is hard to picture Lincoln, on the other hand, with either the taste or the talent for political operations conceived in such terms. Lincoln could not imagine working without his party connections.

It was perfectly in character for Johnson, at the drop of a hat, to "go to the people." Such was the nature of his constituency, combined with the simple values which he represented, that not only was the direct appeal successful time after time, but Johnson's own experience, in the process, could develop and sustain in him an almost religious sense of "the people." If the people did wrong, it was the fault of their conniving leaders. His inaugural as Governor in 1853 saw him transfigured with the democratic faith. On that occasion, he delivered an apocalyptic speech which was received with much amusement by the Whigs and anti-Johnson

[6] *Ibid.*, p. 52.

Democrats but which was greatly approved by the common folk. He dwelt upon the coming "divinity of man," likened the "voice of the people" to the "voice of God," and declared: "It will be readily perceived by all discerning young men, that Democracy is a ladder, corresponding in politics to the one spiritual which Jacob saw in his vision; one up which all, in proportion to their merit, may ascend. While it extends to the humblest of all created beings, here on earth below, it reaches to God on high. . . ."[7]

The texture of Johnson's mind was essentially abstract. Concrete problems never had the power to engage his interest that "principles" had;[8] the principles of equal rights, local self-rule, states' rights as well as Union, and strict constitutionalism had served him through all vicissitudes and had taken on mystic powers with the passage of the years. Faced with a crisis that had no parallels in his past experience, he would have found it next to impossible to imagine that the moral rules which had guided him in his youth should not suffice him then.

Despite Johnson's tendency to boast, he was not a person who had real confidence in his intellectual powers. For a public man, he was obsessed with himself to a degree that exceeded the normal, and most of his speeches, no matter what else they dealt with, may be read as demands for personal vindication and personal approval. Unlike Lincoln, whose "humility" was sustained by the odd arrogance of a superior man's self-knowledge, Johnson lacked assurance. He tended to hesitate in full realization of his own shortcomings. At bottom, general rules were an easy substitute for concrete thinking; confronted with a difficulty, Johnson's mind searched instinctively for such rules in order that it might once more close itself and be at rest. He was not really capable of intellectual courage until after he had made up his mind, and once he had, he would do anything rather than undergo the agony of further doubts. It was a peculiar kind of courage (if such it was):

[7] Oliver Temple observed, "I doubt if Mr. Johnson could ever have gotten many to locate in this empyreal commonwealth" (p. 382).

[8] The major exception (if such it could be called) was Johnson's identification with Homestead legislation, which he promoted for many years with a simple monotony and an evangelical intensity ("free land for free laborers") not unlike that of Bryan for free silver.

"He could bear insult, personal danger, obloquy; but he could not yield his point."[9] In contrast, there is a downright blitheness about Lincoln's last speech, in which he said that bad promises were better broken than kept. Lincoln was never unprepared, should matters of great moment seem to make it necessary, to redefine something as a "bad promise."

The final stage of Johnson's career, culminating in his rise to the ultimate power, was launched with a characteristic act of dissociation. In 1860 and 1861, with superb disdain for his own personal safety, Johnson—then a Senator—defied the secessionists of Tennessee. True to the principles of the sainted Jackson (for whom he had been named),[10] he defended the Constitution and the Union with bitter devotion until no drop of hope for his state was left. He was loyal to the end, and when Tennessee went out, Andrew Johnson stayed on as the loyal Senator from a disloyal state—he "could not yield his point." When the Union armies precariously occupied certain parts of the state in 1862, Lincoln asked Johnson to go to beleaguered Nashville as Military Governor; Johnson hesitated not an instant. For three years, amid unbelievable anxieties and dangers, through nightmares of uncertainty, Johnson stood at his post, playing the role of the outsider under the most heroic circumstances. It was his finest hour; and it was for this that Lincoln in 1864 picked him for his Vice-President.

Johnson had certainly earned his reward. But there was a difficulty which nobody thought much about at the time and the embarrassments of which would not really become apparent until well after Johnson's accession to the Presidency itself. The man had no real connections with the party organization which had placed him there, nor would he ever recognize any. There was little in his past that had given him any preparation for the role of party leader—a role whose essence Abraham Lincoln had understood in his bones.

Might any general predictions have been made as to the future course of the man who took the oath as President on April 15, 1865? What were the prospects for a man whose career had been

[9] Howard K. Beale, *The Critical Year: A Study of Andrew Johnson and Reconstruction* (New York: Harcourt, Brace, 1930), p. 26.
[10] His full name was Andrew Jackson Johnson.

successful on such a basis as Andrew Johnson's? He had never played his chances on the conservative side. He had played them on the margin—but he had always won. The role of the outsider had formed the political personality of this man; it was a role based on essentially nonpolitical behavior, and it had been played through thirty years of politics—thirty years in the thick of things. It was a role to which he was now committed beyond choice, and it was not an asset to a man who had become President of the United States. The social outsider, the political outsider, and now the outsider who had power: such had been the stages of Johnson's rise, and it was not a background that augured well for political sensitivity or for "moderation," institutionally defined. Johnson was temperamentally and sociologically a "radical," whereas the insider, in our politics, has perennially found it very difficult to be that kind of "radical"; he is weighted down by too many connections. To be a good freebooter, one must somehow— like Andrew Johnson—carry as few connections as possible.

Johnson's policy on Reconstruction, despite the hopes of the Republican party, was, after all, fully consistent with all his past habits, and it should not have occasioned (and probably did not occasion) any surprise to men who really knew those habits.

In justice to Johnson, it would be well not to be misled by "evidence" that the President, in the summer and fall of 1865, was somehow edging toward his ancient Democratic associations. He was temperamentally incapable of "selling out" in that sense. It was true that Democrats, emerging from interviews, found his conversation much more to their liking on matters of Reconstruction than did Republicans who discussed similar questions with him. But this satisfaction was based upon the President's principles, which the Democrats soon saw as those most conducive to their own political prospects. And yet for Johnson himself, those doctrines were not really conceived in party terms at all. To all such considerations he seemed oblivious.

Johnson's stand appears to have been settled in his own mind fairly early. Indeed, it was he who, with Representative Crittenden, had produced the resolutions of 1861, which declared that the war objectives should be restricted to defense of the Constitution and the Union and that "as soon as these objects were accomplished the war ought to cease." "I hope," he wrote to Montgomery Blair in 1863, "that the President will not be committed to the proposition of States relapsing into territories and held as such."[11] When John A. Logan called upon Johnson to discuss Reconstruction on May 31, 1865, the President was said to have declared: "General, there's no such thing as reconstruction. These States have not gone out of the Union. Therefore reconstruction is unnecessary."[12]

Flushed with passion, Johnson had exclaimed, in the celebrated audience with Wade and others on April 16, the day after Lincoln died, "Treason must be made infamous and traitors must be impoverished."[13] Then, in view of a pardoning policy which became progressively milder as the months went on, many have supposed that a major shift of intention occurred in the President's mind sometime between his inauguration and the early summer. This softened attitude is attributed variously to the counsels of Secretary Seward, the intrigues of the Blairs, and the blandishments of Southern ladies seeking pardons for their husbands. It is not unlikely that the President derived a certain pleasure from the position in which he found himself vis-à-vis these ladies; to be able to confer his boon upon them could hardly have failed to be a source of some satisfaction. In any case he could be, for all his obstinacy, a forgiving man. We can easily imagine, moreover, his constitutional convictions being fortified in lengthy talks with the Blairs at Silver Spring. But in the long run Johnson made his own decisions, and the really critical aspect of his Reconstruction policy—the constitutional relations of the states to the Union—had probably hardened for him, and thus ceased to vex his mind, early in the war.

The states, then, had never been out of the Union at all, and the constitutional right of the state to regulate its own internal con-

---

[11] Edward McPherson, *The Political History of the United States . . . during the Period of Reconstruction* (Washington: Philp & Solomons, 1871), p. 199.

[12] Chicago *Republican*, quoted in Cincinnati *Enquirer*, July 7, 1865.

[13] George W. Julian, *Political Recollections*, p. 257.

cerns had never ceased to exist in all its vigor. The abstractness of such a dogma, in view of Johnson's willingness to use pressure (however erratically he may have exerted it) in getting the states to ratify the Thirteenth Amendment and repudiate their debt, never seemed to occur to him. He somehow had to convince himself—and apparently did—that these things were being done "voluntarily." Nor could his *laissez-faire* attitude on Negro suffrage fail to strike him as both fair and logical. It was true that, under such a policy, Negro suffrage would in all likelihood be ruled out, but there the inscrutable will of the Fathers (as he saw it) left him no choice. And so with the admission of the Southern Representatives: it was the *constitutional* thing to do, regardless of consequences.

Such were the President's views, doubtless fully articulated by the time he issued his May 29 proclamations. He still held them when Congress met in December, 1865, six months later. He would defend them, against merciless abuse, in his "swing around the circle" the following year. And in December, 1866, those principles would remain doggedly unaltered. In his message to Congress at that time he serenely announced:

Upon this question, so vitally affecting the restoration of the Union and the permanency of our present form of government, my convictions, heretofore expressed, have undergone no change, but, on the contrary, their correctness has been confirmed by reflection and time.[14]

[14] James D. Richardson, *Messages and Papers of the Presidents*, VI, 488.

✪

Johnson and His Policy

Both Andrew Johnson and his Southern policy were important factors in the decision of Reconstruction. Man and policy have alike been distorted by hostile interpretation and need to be re-pictured more accurately. Of the true character of Andrew Johnson we know surprisingly little. Yet for several years he inspired more hatred, stirred more discussion, than any other individual in the land. As man and as executive, his every act swelled this storm of controversy. No political speaker failed to talk of him. But those who really knew him were few.

The animosity of Reconstruction days has printed a very definite picture of our seventeenth President upon tradition; but it is not Andrew Johnson. It is the caricature that his calumniators in Congress and the press fastened upon him, rather a political bogy, a personified policy, than the man who lived in the White House. His enemies worked effectively, for the popular conception of Johnson is that of a vulgar, drunken tailor; a soapbox ranter; an illiterate, ill-mannered, intemperate fellow, stubborn, intolerant, quarrelsome; honest and well-meaning, but a fool, pliant in the hands of traitors, Copperheads, or anybody who would toady to him; a "spiteful, inflated, and unprincipled egotist"; an "insolent, clownish drunkard" whose excesses disgraced the White House, whose family could not be recognized by respectable society,

From *The Critical Year: A Study of Andrew Johnson* by Howard K. Beale, copyright, 1930, by Harcourt, Brace & World, Inc.; renewed, 1958, by Howard K. Beale. Reprinted by permission of the publishers.

whose lack of dignity and incapacity in office made us hang our heads in shame before foreign nations. Time has considerably toned down the picture, but our fathers' generation could never have looked on Andrew Johnson without contempt.

He has always been charged with egotism. He did talk overmuch of himself. But this habit arose rather from an inferiority complex than from egotism. He had entered manhood unable to read; his wife had taught him to write. By his own merit and perseverance, he had risen from the stratum of a poor journeyman tailor to the Presidency. He had lived among a proud slaveholding aristocracy who had snubbed him and scorned him. But his humble origin had proved a political resource which he had learned to exploit. Had others boasted of it, his rise from tailor's bench to White House might have had popular appeal. For the President to do so was bad taste. Besides, there was something effeminate, contemptuous in the tailor's trade. It had not the glamour that rail-splitting had shed over another President from the frontier. And when radicals began to ridicule his trade and social inferiority, they hit upon the most sensitive spot in his armor;[1] they recalled all the indignities and mortifications of a long unhappy career. His boasting was a shield for a naturally sensitive soul. In most matters Johnson lacked assurance, sought advice, hesitated in full realization of his own shortcomings. He truly said of himself: "The elements of my nature, the pursuits of my life, have not made me either in my feelings or in my practice aggressive. My nature, on the contrary, is rather defensive in its character."[2]

In spite of popular belief, there can be no question of Johnson's sobriety. It was a day of hard drinking, but Johnson was not one of the hard drinkers. No evidence exists of his ever drinking to excess during his Senatorship or war Governorship.[3] Then came the fatal day of his inauguration as Vice-President when he was

[1] See, for example, John J. Craven, *Prison Life of Jefferson Davis*, p. 244.

[2] *New York Herald*, August 19, 1866.

[3] Contemporary enemies like Stewart (*Reminiscences*, p. 194), and even historians like Rhodes (*History of the United States from the Compromise of 1850*, V, 618), repeat the charges of inebriety as facts but present no evidence. Clifton R. Hall (*Andrew Johnson, Military Governor of Tennessee*) says, "The habit of indulging in intoxicants, afterward reputed as

unquestionably drunk. The spectacle was distressing to sober men throughout the country. Antiadministration radical papers, Copperhead papers, and scandalmongers published the news with glee. Most conservative journals printed it in shame. Sumner sought to impeach Johnson. But the story was hushed up. Some papers printed the explanation; many did not.

Johnson had just recovered from typhoid fever, and had not wanted to come to Washington, but Lincoln had insisted. On the morning of the inauguration, Johnson still felt weak from his illness. Just before he entered the Senate chamber a friend gave him some whisky to strengthen him for the ceremony. He took too much, or was oversensitive to whisky; at any rate, it went to his head, and he made a sorry, jumbled speech. McCulloch,[4] Doolittle,[5] Hamlin,[6] who accompanied him to the Capitol, and Crook[7] testify to the truth of this explanation. There is no proof that Johnson was ever again intoxicated.

Johnson's most conspicuous personal failing as President, had, of course, been formed long before" (p. 219). Mr. Hall's authorities for this allegation are two: Charles A. Dana, writing thirty years after the event, when he says, Johnson "brought out a jug of whisky . . . and then made it about half and half water. The theoretical, philosophical drinker pours out a little whisky and puts in almost no water at all—drinks it pretty nearly pure—but when a man gets to taking a good deal of water in his whisky, it shows he is in the habit of drinking a good deal. I noticed that the Governor took more whisky than most gentlemen would have done, and I concluded that he took it pretty often" (*Recollections of the Civil War*, p. 106); and Carl Schurz, writing forty-three years afterward, when he says, "It happened twice or three times that, when I called upon him, I was told by the attendant that the Governor was sick and could not see anybody; then, after the lapse of four or five days, he would send for me, and I would find him uncommonly natty in his attire, and generally 'groomed' with especial care. He would also wave off any inquiry about his health. When I mentioned this circumstance to one of the most prominent Union men of Nashville, he smiled, and said that the Governor had 'his infirmities,' but was 'all right' on the whole" (*The Reminiscences of Carl Schurz*, III, 96). Slim evidence, indeed, for so grave an accusation!

[4] H. McCulloch, *Men and Measures*, p. 373.

[5] *Century Magazine*, LXXXV (1912), 198.

[6] Schouler (*History of the United States*) says that Hamlin's statement of the facts was preserved in the Johnson Mss., but it does not seem to be there now (VII, 8). See also Charles E. Hamlin, *Hannibal Hamlin*, p. 497.

[7] Bodyguard to Lincoln, Johnson, Grant, Hayes, Garfield, and Arthur. Colonel William H. Crook, *Through Five Administrations*, p. 82.

But this slip gave a handle to the radicals. They later called up this occasion, and began to speak of him as the "drunken tailor." On February 22, 1866, on April 18, and during his "swing 'round the circle," whenever he made one of his disjointed extemporaneous speeches, they accused him of drunkenness. Papers all over the country printed the accusation, and spoke of his special train as a traveling barroom. Thousands of good people hung their heads in shame at the thought of a "drunken" President.

That Johnson never again drank to excess seems certain from the fact that the radicals did not use it as an impeachment charge. They searched diligently but found no evidence that could be used even in a political trial.[8] But better proof exists. Welles confides in the unprinted portions of his diary that Grant had to leave the Presidential party at Cleveland because he had drunk too heavily;[9] he speaks of the drunkenness of Senators Chandler[10] and Howard[11] of Michigan; and he pictures Robert Johnson as an habitual drunkard, a great trial to his father, and relates how he provided a ship and sent Robert on a long cruise under charge of a dependable captain to relieve the President of anxiety over his escapades.[12] On the occasion of the inauguration as Vice-President, Welles frankly recorded that Johnson was drunk, and hoped there was an explanation.[13] Yet at no other time did Welles even in the privacy of the expurgated sections of his diary mention Johnson's drinking. McCulloch says, "For nearly four years I had

[8] David M. DeWitt, *The Impeachment and Trial of Andrew Johnson*, p. 420; McCulloch, pp. 393–394. McCulloch declares that "there were few public men whose character and conduct would have sustained as severe a scrutiny." The testimony itself Robert W. Winston (*Andrew Johnson, Plebeian and Patriot*) found in the Document Room in Washington.

[9] Welles Ms. Diary, September 17, 1866.

[10] *Ibid.*, December 5, 1866. "Chandler is steeped & steamed in whisky—is coarse, vulgar and reckless."

[11] *Ibid.*, December 5, 1866. "Howard also drinks, but has more culture and is better educated, yet he is an . . . unfit man for Senator."

[12] *Ibid.*, April 24, April 27, and September 19, 1866.

[13] *Ibid.*, March 4, 1865 (II, 252). References to Welles's Diary are always to the manuscript, which varies considerably in places from the printed version. (See H. K. Beale, "Is the Printed Diary of Gideon Welles Reliable?" *American Historical Review*, XXX [1925], 547.) Where there is, as there usually is, a corresponding passage in the published edition, the volume and page are cited in parentheses as here.

daily intercourse with [Johnson], frequently at night, and I never saw him when under the influence of liquor. I have no hesitation in saying that whatever may have been his faults, intemperance was not among them."[14] In a contemporary letter to his friend Talbott, McCulloch declared that "the reports in regard to his habits of personal indulgence are . . . utterly destitute of foundation—slanders of which the authors will themselves be ashamed when the heat of party passion shall have subsided."[15] Doolittle testified, "My relations to him have been such that I have seen him frequently, in the early morning hours, at midday and in the evening. I have had frequent conversations with several of the members of his Cabinet, and with his private secretaries, and I tell you as a fact that ought to be published to the world as an answer to the most infamous charges that have been circulated against him, that there is not one word of truth in the charges that Mr. Johnson is intemperate."[16]

Shortly after the unfortunate inaugural incident, Lincoln testified to a doubting cabinet member, "I have known Andy Johnson for many years; he made a bad slip the other day, but you need not be scared; Andy ain't a drunkard."[17] A Leipzig paper, in describing Johnson's personal habits, told that before dinner he took a glass of whisky as an appetizer, and that "various fine wines [were] then brought in, of which the President [took] but very little, closing the meal uniformly with another ration of coffee."[18] Gobright, who reported the Chicago tour for the Associated Press,[19] Jefferson Davis,[20] Major Truman, who was Johnson's

[14] "There was no liquor in his room. . . . His luncheon, when he had one, was, like mine, a cup of tea and a cracker." McCulloch, p. 374.

[15] *New York Herald,* October 5, 1866.

[16] Speech at the Academy of Music, Philadelphia, May 19, 1866, *Speeches of Hon. Edgar Cowan . . . Jas. R. Doolittle . . . Hugh McCulloch* (National Union Club Documents), p. 12.

[17] McCulloch, p. 373.

[18] Article in a Leipzig (Germany) newspaper, reprinted in the *New York Herald,* August 13, 1866.

[19] Gobright was grilled by the impeachment investigators. "Testimony Taken before the Judiciary Committee . . . in the Investigation of the Charges against Andrew Johnson," *Reports of Committees,* 40th Congress, 1st Session, No. 1314, House Report No. 7, pp. 525–532.

[20] Craven, p. 245.

private secretary,[21] Crook, Johnson's bodyguard,[22] and even Parson Brownlow[23] testified to Johnson's sobriety. Welles, McCulloch, Doolittle, Truman, and Crook were honorable men in a position to know; Lincoln's word cannot be doubted; the German newspaper could have had no possible motive for falsehood. Brownlow and Davis were Johnson's enemies. No trustworthy contradiction exists. Johnson's habitual intoxication existed only in wild rumors, in disproved stories such as Beecher's,[24] in mendacious campaign propaganda, in the radical press, and in the memoirs of old men who could only have known by hearsay or who, like Dana and Schurz, able to know the truth, had personal axes to grind in repeating rumors that would hurt an old enemy. Such testimony is worthless. But Johnson's fourth of March slip set the tone of the radical campaign, and laid him open to indignities.

In his astounding book,[25] published in 1867, General Baker, wartime head of the Secret Service, printed at length the evidence taken at the trial of a Mrs. Cobb. The manifest purpose was, without subjecting the author to libel prosecution, to stigmatize the President by innuendo as a keeper of harlots, to picture the White House under Johnson as a house of prostitution. He described the manipulations of a group of women who acted as pardon brokers, selling for cash the pardons they wrung from Johnson by appeals to his sympathy; he insinuated that their success lay in power they held over the President. Baker does not prove that these women were more than pretty flirts who capitalized their smiles with department clerks, though undoubtedly some had unsavory reputations.[26] But even Baker's account shows, if read carefully, that

---

[21] *Century Magazine*, LXXXV (1913), 438.

[22] Crook "never once saw him under the influence of liquor." As he was with Johnson almost constantly in Washington and on the Chicago trip, his knowledge should be exact. As he disliked Johnson until he knew him well, and admired Grant, Hayes, and Lincoln, his testimony should be impartial.

[23] Winston, p. 104. Winston could not find any charge of drinking in Tennessee newspapers.

[24] Beale, *The Critical Year*, pp. 78–79.

[25] Lafayette C. Baker, *History of the U.S. Secret Service.*

[26] Baker and this troupe of women were entirely discredited before the House investigating committee that would have been only too glad to use their testimony. H. McCulloch, p. 394; R. W. Winston, pp. 415–416.

whatever influence these women did have was with Robert Johnson and not with the President.[27] Andrew Johnson's heart always
melted before the pleadings of a woman, especially a pretty one,
even in the stern days of his war Governorship, but no evidence has
even been adduced to show that he was other than strictly honorable in his connections with them. The picture that Baker seeks to
paint has no other substantiation than wild rumors in opposition
papers. The singularity and sensationalism of his story, and the
fact that it was written in anger at his dismissal, make his charges
quite untrustworthy. On the other hand, abundant reliable evidence, the known regularity of his life, and his devotion to his
large family, all testify to Johnson's high character.

Johnson's reputation suffered from the enmity of newspaper-
men. In whatever he did or said, he was vigorous and picturesque,
a type that reporters idolize or victimize. Never popular with any
group, he was particularly hated by press correspondents, because
like Grant he dealt with them brusquely when they interfered with
the efficient administration of the war. In Tennessee he had no
time for interviews; he was indifferent to their favor. Even when he
meant to be polite, pressure of important affairs often made him
curt. With importunate reporters he dealt summarily. While he was
the popular War Governor, newspapers lauded him; his daring and
vigor made him a favorite in sensational stories. Correspondents
bided their time and bore their grudges. After he became President
they saw their chance and wreaked all the accumulated grievances
of the years upon his head.[28]

[27] Other evidence exists against Robert, who was at this time private
secretary to his father. It was soon after this that Johnson's anxiety over his
son became so great that Welles and Seward contrived to send the son
abroad on a warship. An Illinois lieutenant of Trumbull wrote of Robert:
"There is too much whisky in the White House, and harlots go into the
private secretary's office unannounced in broad daylight. Mrs. C[obb] did
that since the trial while a friend of mine was waiting for an audience . . .
and she came out leaning on the arm of a drunken son of the Prest. There
were a large number . . . waiting . . . and saw it all." N. B. Judd to L.
Trumbull, February 14, 1866 (Trumbull Mss., LXIV). Robert was a notorious debauchee; the profligacy of the son was easily turned by Johnson's
enemies into ill repute for the father.

[28] For example, Dana's story of his drunkenness in Tennessee (p. 106).

To destroy this old picture is easier than to draw a new one, for Johnson defies intimacy. Of only average height, he was nonetheless broad-shouldered and imposing. His complexion was swarthy, his features good. He had sparkling, penetrating eyes. A mass of thick dark hair topped his head. Deep lined into his countenance was a look of mingled determination and distress. A stolidity resulting from patient suffering under accustomed hardship, and a somber serious-mindedness, not often relieved by any sign of joviality, were characteristic. His greatest physical asset was a voice, mellow and pleasing in tone, but of such power that without appearing to raise it, he could make himself heard to the outer edge of vast throngs of people. His manner and the peculiar magnetism of his personality as he spoke to a crowd lent a vigor and dignity to speeches that in print were unimpressive.

Yet it was Johnson's extemporaneous speeches that most seriously injured his reputation. His training had been in upland Tennessee political campaigning. To auditors he carried conviction. Reported in a newspaper, especially an unfriendly one, his speeches became jumbled harangue. His Tennessee habit of parrying words with the crowd gave opposition reporters a coveted opportunity to belittle him. Against skillful heckling he could not maintain his dignity. Taken out of their surroundings, Johnson's extemporaneous speeches are undignified, sometimes illiterate, often in bad taste. But the political gathering of the day was accustomed to his kind of stump oratory from Senators, Governors of states, and ministers. Johnson's outbursts compare favorably with speeches of John A. Logan, Thad Stevens, Senator Chandler, Senator Wade, Governor Oglesby, Governor Brownlow, or Wendell Phillips, who denounced him for lack of dignity.[29] Had his sentiments been radical, his speeches would have won him praise from the men whom they "shocked." But they did supply enemies with an extraordinary stock of ridicule.

His prepared addresses and messages were impressive.[30] John-

[29] The speeches of the scholarly Sumner were exceptional.

[30] Whether he wrote them himself or sought aid, as with his first annual message, from men like Bancroft, matters little. The ideas were his if not the phraseology.

son's very enemies testify to "his clear and forcible powers of expression" and his ability, "when calm and collected," to state his opinions impressively.[31] His messages to Congress remain models of clarity and convincing reason, and in his own day, not even the suspicious Welles guessed that he did not write them himself.

Johnson was methodical, as no President had been since John Quincy Adams. He instituted what the White House had never before boasted—a system of records of all business transacted. His letter books were carefully preserved as were all letters received. He even kept scrapbooks of the times. The vast collection of records and papers thus preserved testifies to Johnson's orderliness and administrative efficiency, as does the expedition with which he handled the quantity of work that Reconstruction and the new pardon system imposed upon his personal staff. He revolutionized the administration of the executive offices.

His industry was amazing. When he came to Washington in the spring of 1865, he was still weak from typhoid fever. All summer he was ill. Welles repeatedly urged him to take a rest, or at least a sail.[32] In the latter part of June he was so weak that strong will power could no longer sustain him, and for ten days he had to drop work.[33] But ill as he was, he stayed on in Washington through the summer heat of 1865 and 1866. He arose early and retired late. All day he received throngs of office-hunters, pardon-seekers, advice-givers, who crowded his anterooms.[34] Numerous delegations of petitioners or well-wishers from North and South paid their respects, and often received a speech in return. Johnson did not know how to turn people away. Our Presidents until recently have been expected to make themselves available to a pestiferous horde of callers. But with Johnson, to the usual crowd were added swarms of Southerners with grievances to air or

[31] *Christian Examiner,* LXXXI (November 1866), 404.

[32] For example, Welles Ms. Diary, July 9, 24, and August 1, 1865 (II, 329, 342, 347).

[33] H. McCulloch to S. M. Forbes, July 3, 1865 (McCulloch Mss., II).

[34] When the Cabinet did not meet and no official visitors were to be received, as was often the case during the summer, Johnson was victimized by the anteroom crowd from early morning until evening. For a description of the crowds of rebels that monopolized his time see Whitelaw Reid, *After the War,* pp. 304–308.

pardons to seek, and useless congratulatory committees. These throngs occupied long hours with trifles, while important matters waited. Many a leader of Northern opinion despaired and went home discouraged because this host of nonentities deprived him of the President's ear, or angry because the President's time was monopolized by ex-rebels. Eventually his friends protested, and the crowd was at last thinned out, but that was not until the fall of 1866.[35]

Aside from these interviews, Johnson was a busy man. He read long reports, heard opinions of advisers, formulated policies, handled the routine of administration, held frequent cabinet meetings, and wrote letters, telegrams, and orders to subordinates all over the country. His days were long and difficult. Doolittle tells how "assiduously and . . . industriously" Johnson worked "from the early morning hours till late at night."[36] He rose at seven in winter and six in summer. Until ten he wrote, read, and studied; he was an omnivorous reader. From ten to eleven he interviewed visitors; at eleven he lunched; from twelve to one he met his Cabinet or received distinguished callers, and then again admitted the throngs of pardon-seekers and place-hunters. If he got time he took a walk at three, but often he received the swarms of callers without relief until dinner at four. At dinner he discussed the news of the day with his nearest friends. Then at five he retired with a cat and a huge coffee pot to his study, where he worked until midnight, reading, writing, and holding conferences with intimates. At eight he emerged long enough to have tea with his family. The endurance of the man who, in ill health, under strain of abuse and oppressively weighty problems, could work from six in the morning until midnight month after month without vacation or recreation is appalling. This calm, taciturn, hard-working human being is hardly recognizable as the bawling, drunken demagogue of the radical newspapers.

Regularity and hard work were not even relieved by normal

[35] On October 3, 1866, the *New York Herald* commented that the "President's edict against office brokers . . . [was] having a salutary effect and [was] greatly lessening the amount of his daily labor."

[36] *Speeches of Hon. Edgar Cowan . . . Jas. R. Doolittle . . . Hugh McCulloch,* p. 12.

recreations. When Johnson became President, he had never attended a theater, and he saw only a few plays in Washington. He remarked once that he had been to a circus and to a minstrel show, and had enjoyed them; but that he never found time for such diversions, because he preferred to read and study. His only relaxation was a drive or an occasional picnic with his grandchildren. This attitude made White House festivities somber observances of duty. There were more dinners and receptions than in the succeeding administrations; they were dignified, sometimes brilliant; but they were solemn, never gay.

Except for Robert, the President's family was respected and accepted without question in Washington society. His daughters, Mrs. Patterson and Mrs. Stover, were women of great charm and tact.[37] His eldest daughter, Senator Patterson's wife, presided over the household and was a gracious hostess. In the background was Mrs. Johnson, an invalid in an upper room, known only to family intimates. Her presence there was not generally known; only twice did she appear in public. But she was a good woman and intelligent; she had been an invaluable aid to Johnson ever since the penniless, obscure days when she taught him to write. To her he was passionately devoted, and she remained his most trusted counselor. Johnson's bodyguard testifies that "her influence was a strong one, and it was exerted in the direction of toleration and gentleness." She was sweet-faced and sweet-spirited; Johnson's response to the slightest movement of her hands, or her "Now, Andrew," evidenced his respect and her influence. She was slowly dying of old-fashioned consumption. The death of her eldest son, the debauchery of her next, and the bitter attacks on her husband made her life unhappy. Indeed, she said she had been "more content when her husband was an industrious young tailor."[38] To understand Johnson one must picture him in this family group, surrounded by his four children, a son-in-law and five grandchildren, with his patient, gentle, invalid wife in their midst.

[37] Even Mrs. John A. Logan, wife of one of Johnson's bitterest enemies who saw Washington society through many decades, testified to this. *Reminiscences of a Soldier's Wife*, pp. 226, 240. See also H. McCulloch, p. 406.

[38] The description of Mrs. Johnson comes from one of the few who ever mentions her. W. H. Crook, p. 87.

Johnson's devotion to duty was tireless. He was doggedly persistent, dauntlessly courageous. Even his enemies admitted his rugged honesty, his "great native force of intellect and exceeding strength of will . . . his love for the Union [and] his genuine patriotism."[39] It was these characteristics that had made him the notable leader of prewar Tennessee, the fearless Senator of 1861 who alone among Southerners remained loyally at his post, and the efficient War Governor under great trial and personal danger in whom Lincoln felt complete confidence. By ridicule the radicals burlesqued these same traits and certain upcountry Tennessee peculiarities into grave faults. Crude, Johnson was, of course, but his was the crudity of the American frontier of which his countrymen were proud. In another time and place he would have been a popular idol.

Just before the election of 1866, the unemotional, noncommittal Secretary of the Treasury wrote, "Men may differ with him in regard to his manner of dealing with the States recently in rebellion, but no fair man could have been with him, as I have been during the trying eighteen months of his administration, without being impressed with his love of country and his devotion to duty, with the unselfishness and uprightness of his character, and the honesty of his purposes."[40]

Weaknesses Johnson had, too. One was inordinate faith in his own power of persuasion. He felt that if only he could present his case in person to the people and appeal to their wisdom and sense of justice, they would unquestionably support him. His trip to Chicago wrought great harm, but he seemed not to realize that it was injuring him.[41] His faith in his ability to win votes on the Southern question led him to neglect really effective issues.

Johnson was never popular. A peculiar magnetism he did have

[39] *Christian Examiner*, LXXXI (November 1866), 404. McCulloch says that in "intellectual force he had few superiors" (p. 406).

[40] H. McCulloch to W. H. Talbott, *New York Herald*, October 5, 1866.

[41] This trip did cure him of extemporaneous speaking. Through the ordeal of impeachment he admirably preserved his dignity and his silence, in strong contrast to most of his Congressional denunciators. But he learned his lesson too late.

that attracted people who talked with him personally. George L. Stearns, a Boston radical, was temporarily won by an interview.[42] Yet he possessed none of the personal charm that gives men popularity. He could sway a crowd; he could impress individuals. But he never succeeded in making men love him. When he led, it was by force of will.

Johnson's reserve deprived him of intimate friends. He was exasperatingly noncommittal. Often this was an advantage. He listened well; in an interview he could let the other man do all the talking, agree without committing himself, and send the man away satisfied without avowing his own view. More often his reserve hurt him. In cabinet meetings he listened patiently to all opinions, but seldom expressed one. Welles frequently recorded in his diary what he had suggested to the President with the remark that he "seemed to agree," and later the comment that he had not acted on the advice. Of all things, Johnson most needed the cooperation of close friends. Welles, McCulloch, Doolittle, Randall, Browning, Cowan, the Blairs, Ewing, Stanton, Seward were with him constantly; they had access to him for private conversation at any hour of the day or night. They advised; they wrote reports; they argued with him. But none of them really knew Johnson. Welles was probably as good a friend as any. Yet from the diary it is evident that Johnson never really confided in him. In a galaxy of extraordinarily lifelike portraits, Johnson, the center of them all, is the one Welles fails to vivify. His was an inscrutable soul. In the midst of exciting times, surrounded by crowds of people, he remained lonely in the White House.

Indecision was another failing. Amid a bewilderment of conflicting advice and professed friendship, Johnson was perplexed. Since he was not directly in touch with Northern sentiment, he had to depend upon advisers who were. But whom was he to trust? The Blairs, Welles, Seward, and Stanton distrusted one another, and warned him each against the other. Radicals, moderate Republicans, moderate Democrats, Copperheads, and Southerners tendered advice and denounced each other. Torn between opposing

[42] He was so much impressed that he asked and got Johnson's permission to publish the conversation. October 8, 1865 (Johnson Mss., LXXVIII).

factions, Johnson hesitated, and did nothing. Early in 1866 a moderate program aggressively sponsored, drastic changes in federal offices and the Cabinet, a break with extreme radicals, would have won his policy a party. But he hesitated for months, reluctant to break the Union party, while the radicals through vigorous leadership won moderate after moderate to their cause.

Johnson's very courage and determination once he had made up his mind were often converted from virtues into faults. He did not know how to compromise. His mind had one compartment for right and one for wrong, but no middle chamber where the two could commingle. When Johnson did finally become convinced of the justice or rectitude of a cause, all the powers of earth could not turn him from it. He could bear insult, personal danger, obloquy; but he could not yield his point. He could not accept the situation as he found it, turn partial support to his ends, or yield on details to attain large advantages. In the restoration of the Southern states, Johnson saw the salvation and future happiness of the country; fundamental principles were at stake: both his duty and his honor were involved. He could gladly face death or political ruin, but he could not be swerved from the path whither every fiber of his passionate soul told him duty led. His admirable, courageous, but ruinous determination was based on the same inflexible sense of honor that underlay Sumner's unreasoning opposition. In other times and other men, Americans have lauded this quality. But it was disastrous at a time when infinite tact, yielding here, forcing there, was necessary. Johnson failed to carry the day—yet he failed but by a little and under great odds, and on Reconstruction and constitutional interpretation the future has vindicated him. Had the balance of events turned slightly the other way—had he succeeded—this very uncompromising sense of duty which brought obloquy upon his name would have been accredited the highest virtue of a great man. Johnson possessed those characteristics that make men blessed or damned, famous or infamous, because chance leads them to success or failure.

Johnson, responsible for enforcing the country's laws, had to face the Southern situation immediately upon his inauguration. First in the field with a constructive policy, he was rebuilding the South while others were still debating. He was convinced that this Southern problem must be settled before other issues were considered.

Fundamentally Johnson's program was based upon conviction that kindness and generosity alone would restore the Union, upon confidence in the Southern people as essentially good, and upon faith in democracy as practicable even in time of crisis. Johnson believed that, aside from a few indispensable guarantees, the details of readjustment should be left to the loyal people of the states in question, whom he considered infinitely better fitted to work out their problems than military officers or Northern politicians. "If a State is to be nursed until it again gets strength, it must be nursed by its friends, not smothered by its enemies," he declared.[43] And again, "The only safety of the nation lies in a generous and expansive plan of conciliation, and the longer this is delayed, the more difficult will it be to bring the North and the South into harmony. . . . The idea of legislating for one-third of the population of the country, and passing constitutional amendments without allowing them any voice in the matter . . . is full of danger to the future peace and welfare of the nation. They cannot be treated as subjugated people or as vassal colonies without a germ of hatred being introduced, which will some day or other, though the time may be distant, develop mischief of the most serious character."[44] He believed that the observance of political equality as a matter of justice would encourage the people of the South to be "more and more constant and persevering in their renewed allegiance," while military force would be "contrary to the genius and spirit of our free institutions, and exhaustive of the national resources."[45]

Johnson had spent a lifetime fighting a Southern aristocracy. He was proud of being a plebeian, and looked upon himself as the great guardian of the rights of the common man. Now he saw in New England a new type of aristocracy, based upon Hamiltonian

---

[43] *Speeches of Andrew Johnson,* edited by F. Moore, pp. 483–484.
[44] Boston *Evening Commercial,* July 21, 1866.
[45] Proclamation, April 2, 1866. James D. Richardson, *Messages and Papers of the Presidents,* VI, 431–432.

principles of government for "the rich and the well born" and upon the new business principles of government for the benefit of industry. This new Northeastern civilization seemed to Johnson as dangerous to Jacksonian principles and the welfare of the common man as had the rule of the old slavocracy. He had opposed, too, the determination of a minority of great slaveholders to impose their ideas upon the rest of the country, and could not now brook a New England civilization which avowed the purpose of remolding the South to fit New England standards. He saw in this new type of Hamiltonian centralism a serious menace to the Jeffersonian principle of states' rights upon which his political beliefs were grounded. While Johnson had disliked the slave system, he was nonetheless a Southerner who understood the Negro problem. Abolitionism had been anathema. And much that New England now demanded seemed to smack of it. Besides, he could not believe New Englanders entirely sincere in their denunciations of the disunionism of Southerners. In February, 1861, he had pointedly enumerated New England's past demands for disunion.[46] Her new determination to keep Southern states out, he regarded as a new form of opposition to the Union for which he had risked life and reputation. For a combination of reasons, then, he felt a strong prejudice against New England, and, as a Southerner, could not sympathize with her 1866 ambitions.

He was a democrat, too. His greatest boast was that he was a common man, the friend of common men. "I am a Democrat now," he had said in 1862; "I have been one all my life; I expect to live and die one . . . they shall never divert me from the polar star by which I have ever been guided from early life—the great principles of Democracy upon which this Government rests."[47] His training had bred in him implicit faith in the people and distrust of politicians. On the eve of civil war he had said, "We have some bad men in the South . . . and we have some bad men in the North, who want to dissolve this Union in order to gratify their unhallowed ambition. . . . If the question could be taken away from politicians; if it could be taken away from the Congress

[46] *Congressional Globe,* 36th Congress, 2nd Session, p. 769.
[47] *Ibid.,* 37th Congress, 2nd Session, p. 586.

of the United States, . . . [the people] would settle it without the slightest difficulty, and bid defiance to secessionists and disunionists."[48] He told a delegation from the Cleveland convention: "We must return to constitutional limits establishing the great fact that ours is a government of limited powers with a written constitution, with boundaries both national and State, and that these limitations and boundaries must be observed and strictly respected if free government is to exist; and, coming out of a rebellion, we ought to demonstrate to mankind that a free government cannot live on hate and distrust."[49] To deny Southerners the rights of self-government because they could not be trusted to govern themselves properly, seemed to Johnson a betrayal of democratic principles.

Though Johnson stood ready to punish the man who was in arms against the government, he was just as willing to welcome him back to full fellowship when he showed himself repentant and once more loyal. In the very definition of repentance and loyalty inhered the fundamental conflict between Johnson and the radicals. Repentance to Johnson meant sorrow for having taken up arms against the government, and, as a proof thereof, repudiation of debts incurred in rebellion; loyalty connoted a present desire to maintain the Union, and live under the Constitution with slavery and the right of secession eliminated. But the radicals saw in Southerners no repentance short of condemning themselves, their soldiers, and their leaders as sinners against God and traitors against the government, no loyalty short of repudiating their own society and adopting Northern political, economic, and social standards. Between these two points of view, there was a gulf that could have been bridged only by tolerance and earnest effort on both sides.

Johnson's program of restoration followed that of Lincoln, yet carried out virtually the policy that he had advocated long before he became Vice-President. The basic terms were laid down in two proclamations of May 29, 1865. One granted amnesty with restoration of property,[50] except slaves, to all but fourteen excepted

[48] *Ibid.*, 36th Congress, 2nd Session, p. 767.
[49] *New York Herald*, September 26, 1866.
[50] Except where legal proceedings under confiscation laws had already been instituted.

classes of former Confederates when they should take a solemn oath of allegiance.[51] But he restored confiscated lands generously and issued pardons freely to those who asked, provided they showed evidence of future loyalty. "I did not expect to keep out all who were excluded from the amnesty, or even a large number of them," he later explained, "but I intended they should sue for pardon, and so realize the enormity of their crime."[52] The second proclamation appointed Holden Provisional Governor of North Carolina with "all the powers necessary and proper to enable such loyal people of the State of North Carolina to restore said State to its constitutional relations to the Federal Government."[53] A convention was to amend the constitution of the state, but no person should be a delegate or vote for a delegate to this convention unless he had subscribed to the amnesty oath, and had been a qualified voter under the state law before the passage of the ordinance of secession. Determination of future qualifications for electors and officeholders was left entirely to the state. This second proclamation ordered the restoration of federal revenue officers, postal service, and courts. Subsequent proclamations soon set in motion the wheels of reorganization in Mississippi, Georgia, Texas, Alabama, South Carolina, and Florida. Similar provisional governments had been established under Lincoln in Tennessee, Louisiana, Virginia, and Arkansas. By July, then, all Secessia was in process of political rehabilitation.

When Johnson announced this policy of leniency, he was denounced by the radicals for inconsistency. As War Governor of Tennessee, he had dealt severely with traitors. While Vice-President and during the assassination furor, he had daily proclaimed that treason should be made odious and traitors should be punished. So summarily, indeed, did he handle the accomplices in Lincoln's assassination that he was criticized for excessive harshness. Now men said he had suddenly reversed his position, and

[51] J. D. Richardson, p. 310.
[52] Conversation with G. L. Stearns, Boston *Daily Advertiser,* October 23, 1865; also Johnson Mss., LXXIX.
[53] J. D. Richardson; p. 312.

they sought to guess the influence that had brought the change. His policy was in reality fundamentally the same in 1866 as it had been in 1863;[54] it was merely at first misunderstood.

When Johnson made his stirring Senatorial speeches against traitors, the Union was in danger; and to the Union Andrew Johnson showed as complete devotion as did Charles Sumner to the Negro. When Johnson was War Governor of Tennessee, that state was the scene of a bitter battle for the very life of the nation. Johnson stopped at nothing in defense of the Union against traitors in arms. When he became President, the victory was won and Lee had surrendered, but the war was by no means over. Johnston's forces were still in the field against Sherman. The problem that had worried Lincoln and Grant and Lee, Johnson still faced—the danger of guerrilla warfare. Grant and Sherman, with Lincoln, bent every effort to sparing the country its prolonged agonies, for they, like Johnson, who had seen it in Tennessee, knew what it meant, as Stanton and Stevens and Sumner could not. Johnson's threats against treason, then, were hurled at desperate leaders who were threatening to scatter the Southern forces in guerrilla bands more dangerous than actual armies.

In April the shock of Lincoln's assassination had made even wise men temporarily lose their heads. In issuing his proclamation of May 2, which accused Davis and other prominent Southerners of complicity in the murder of Lincoln, Johnson had the advice of calm and sage men as well as the opinion of Stanton and Holt who wrote it. Full comprehension of the tension, the distrust, the panic of April and May, 1865, is possible only through feeling the rapidity of the popular pulse as it beat out its rhythm of terror and hatred in the numberless letters that poured in upon such men as Johnson, Sumner, and Joseph Holt, the stern, suspicious Judge Advocate General.[55] Nearly everybody was infected by the spasm

[54] As War Governor he had urged Lincoln to oppose the Wade-Davis proposal and had urged speedy restoration as soon as loyalty was assured. A. Johnson to M. Blair, November 24, 1863 (Edward McPherson, *Political Manual* [1867], p. 73). See also Winston, pp. 252–257, 522–525.

[55] The Holt Mss. present an admirable picture of this phase of the opening days of Johnson's administration.

of fear and wild rumor that overcame the country.[56] Scarcely a Southern leader escaped suspicion. Even benign old Welles was swept off his feet. It is little wonder that in this atmosphere Johnson's ire was aroused against the leading Confederates of whose complicity in Lincoln's murder his Secretary of War, and Attorney General, and Judge Advocate General claimed to have positive proof. Only gradually did passions cool and excitement subside, as slowly the truth of Booth's fanatical intrigue was divulged. By the end of May, however, the war was actually over, the Southern armies were safely demobilized, and guerrilla warfare was no longer an imminent danger but an easily forgettable chimera.

Johnson did long to inflict exemplary punishment upon a few leading traitors. "I shall go to my grave," he wrote in 1868, "with the firm belief that Davis, Cobb, Toombs, and a few others of the arch-conspirators and traitors should have been tried, convicted, and hanged for treason. . . . If it was the last act of my life I'd hang Jeff Davis as an example. I'd show coming generations that, while the rebellion was too popular a revolt to punish many who participated in it, treason should be made odious and arch-traitors should be punished."[57] The criticism aroused by Stanton's conduct of the trial of Booth's co-conspirators, and his own repugnance toward military tribunals, kept him from yielding to the pressure for a military trial of Davis. Johnson desired an example, not revenge. He knew only too well that a military trial would make Davis a martyr. For two years he kept Davis in confinement while he sought legal means to try him. But Chase would not ride the Virginia circuit until the last vestiges of military rule were withdrawn and the habeas corpus restored,[58] and Johnson's legal

---

[56] For example, a lengthy epistle from J. Hamilton of New York gave the details of a Southern plot to assassinate Lincoln, Johnson, Stanton, Grant, and others and put General Sherman in power because of his leniency toward the South. May 29, 1865 (Stanton Mss., XXVII).

[57] A. Johnson to B. C. Truman, August 3, 1868, *Century Magazine,* LXXXV (1913), 438.

[58] S. P. Chase to A. Johnson, October 12, 1865 (Johnson Mss., LXXIX); S. P. Chase to G. W. Brook, District Judge, March 20, 1866 (*ibid.,* XCI); S. P. Chase to J. W. Schuckers, September 24, 1866 (Chase Mss., 2nd Series,

advisers never found the means of surmounting this obstacle. It was, however, only when open warfare with the radicals over-balanced all other considerations, that Johnson gave up his efforts to bring Davis to trial.

While Johnson was threatening leading traitors, he was quietly formulating in cabinet his plan of leniency for the masses. The very North Carolina Proclamation issued on May 29 had been drawn up while Lincoln was yet alive, discussed at his last cabinet meeting, and postponed only to enable Stanton who had drawn it up to furnish the other cabinet members with copies. As soon as Lincoln's funeral was over, the proclamation was again considered, changed somewhat, and made applicable to North Carolina instead of Virginia, whose existent loyal government presented complications. This and the Amnesty Proclamation carefully drawn by Speed were agreed upon while Seward, whom radicals later blamed[59] for Johnson's so-called reversal of policy, was still confined to his house.[60]

Johnson's close advisers favored moderation. The Cabinet agreed upon the policy of the proclamations except that Dennison, Speed, and Stanton would have included Negro suffrage, and Speed and Stanton would have dealt more severely with the leaders. Grant and Sherman urged moderation and speedy restoration; their opinion carried weight. Grant, whose prestige and friend-liness gave him influence over Johnson, attended cabinet meetings and was constantly in consultation with the President. After their subsequent quarrel Johnson wrote, "Grant . . . meant well for the first two years, and much that I did that was denounced was through his advice."[61] Welles and McCulloch, Seward when he was sufficiently recovered, and Senator Doolittle

---

III); J. W. Schuckers, *Life and Public Services of Salmon Portland Chase,* pp. 535–543.

[59] James G. Blaine, *Twenty Years of Congress,* II, 66–70; Sumner's speech, reported in the *New York Herald,* October 3, 1866; O. O. Howard, *Autobiography,* II, 277. Seward gladly accepted credit for molding Johnson's policy, New York speech, *New York Tribune,* September 4, 1866.

[60] Welles Ms. Diary, May 8 and 9, 1865 (II, 301).

[61] A. Johnson to B. C. Truman, August 3, 1868, *Century Magazine,* LXXXV (1913), 439.

were frequently with the President. The Blairs were intimate advisers.[62] In fact, it was to Blair's home at Silver Spring, just out of Washington, that Johnson had retired to avoid the public gaze and recover his dignity after his drunken inauguration as Vice-President. Friends who stood by him then naturally retained influence. Preston King was so close to the President that when Mrs. Lincoln left and Johnson took possession, this New York politician went to the White House to live with him until his family arrived. All summer King remained in Washington to advise.[63] At the very moment when Sumner and Wade were rejoicing at Johnson's radicalism, Doolittle wrote home to his wife, "Johnson is all right . . . God is still with us. O, if we are only true to the country all will yet be safe. . . . Mr. Johnson, King and myself are a trio whose hearts & heads sympathized more closely and more deeply than any other trio in America just now."[64] These close friends of Johnson all favored moderation.[65]

Radicals went to call on Johnson, did most of the talking, and interpreted his taciturnity into approval. The President was a good listener, noncommittal even with close friends. The radicals assumed that a courageous loyalist from the South who had suffered grievously at the hands of rebels would seek revenge. They read *their* meaning into the word "traitor" in his speeches. Blinded by their own enthusiasm, they congratulated themselves that he was their tool. Then when time disillusioned them, they accused Johnson of a political somersault. Some blamed Seward. Others said wheedling of Southern aristocrats who had snubbed him before the war had wrought the change, in a man who would sell his soul for social recognition.[66] Still others accused him of ambition to build

---

[62] Sumner's speech, *New York Herald*, October 3, 1866.

[63] J. G. Blaine, p. 11; Welles Ms. Diary, May 12 and July 24, 1865 (II, 305, 340); G. Welles to Mrs. Welles, August 6 and September 24, 1865 (Welles Mss., LIX).

[64] April 26, 1865, *State Historical Society of Wisconsin Proceedings* (1909), p. 291.

[65] They were not "rebels" or Copperheads, but the same moderate Union men who had advised Lincoln.

[66] J. G. Blaine, pp. 68–70; J. D. Fuller, Pastor of Tremont Temple, Boston, to C. Sumner, December 27, 1865 (Sumner Mss., LXXV).

a party of Southerners and Westerners, "traitors" and "Copper-heads," that would retain him in the Presidency. These men, if sincere, did not know Johnson. The truth was that the development of his policy had been steady and logical from the beginnings under Lincoln and his own experiments in Tennessee to its final form late in 1865.

To the application of his policy Johnson gave personal attention. He appointed Provisional Governors who called conventions chosen on the basis of the amnesty oath and the old qualifications for voting. The conventions amended state constitutions, determined future suffrage qualifications, and then arranged elections of legislatures and governors. These legislatures chose United States Senators and held elections for members of the House of Representatives. Meanwhile the Provisional Governors and troops remained. Only when he was convinced that he could do so safely, did Johnson turn over the state governments to the elected officials.

The whole problem was made infinitely more difficult for Johnson by the foolish acts of Southerners themselves. Southern legislators whom he was trying to help were as uncompromising on the one side as Northern radicals were on the other. In fact, during 1865 Southern extremists caused Johnson more concern than did those of the North. Then when Southerners went to the polls, they elected their old leaders, often unpardoned, sometimes notorious rebels, instead of the less prominent candidates who had a passive war record. To put faith in former leaders was natural, but extremely impolitic. It ruined what chance Johnson's policy had of immediate success. Besides, unreasonable and hot-headed editors and politicians talked wildly. Returned soldiers took in general a rational view of the situation, but many of them could not undo the damage wrought by a few noisy agitators.[67]

In handling this trying situation Johnson displayed unusual patience and wisdom. With one eye on Northern politics, he untiringly counseled the South to be reasonable and tactful. After the

[67] Even Sidney Andrews, a radical journalist who found little good in the South, reported the ex-soldiers "the best citizens" in the South, and warned his radical friends that the Union depended on "the bearing of the men who were privates and minor officers in the armies of Lee and Johnston." *Atlantic Monthly,* XVII (February 1866), 242.

election in 1865 he wired Governor Holden, "The results of the recent elections in North Carolina have greatly damaged the prospects of the State in the restoration of its Governmental relations. Should the action and the spirit of the Legislature be in the same direction, it will greatly increase the mischief already done, and might be fatal. It is hoped the action and spirit manifested by the Legislature will be so directed as rather to repair than to increase the difficulties under which the State has already placed itself."[68] The President advised the Southern members-elect not to present themselves at the organization of Congress. "It will be better policy," he said, "to present their certificates of election after the two Houses [are] organized, which will then be a simple question under the Constitution of the members taking their seats. Each House must judge for itself the election returns and qualifications of its members."[69] When the Mississippi legislature hesitated about ratifying the Thirteenth Amendment, he wired, "Failure to adopt the Amendment will create the belief that the action of the convention abolishing Slavery, will hereafter by the same body be revoked. . . . I trust in God, that the Legislature will adopt the amendment, and thereby make the way clear for the admission of Senators and Representatives to their seats in the present Congress."[70] To South Carolina and Georgia he wired similar counsel.[71]

Lenient as he was, there were limits beyond which Johnson would not yield. As an evidence of loyalty prerequisite to a special pardon, he required an amnesty oath. Southerners attempted to vote on the strength of this oath before they had been pardoned. Johnson promised to try to pardon all who deserved it by the time their votes were needed, but he emphatically forbade their voting until the pardon was granted.[72] When unpardoned rebels were

[68] November 27, 1865 (Johnson Mss., "Telegrams").

[69] A. Johnson to B. F. Perry, November 27, 1865 (*ibid.*, LXXXI, and "Telegrams").

[70] A. Johnson to Governor W. L. Sharkey, November 1, 1865 (*ibid.*, "Telegrams").

[71] A. Johnson to Governor Perry, October 28, 1865; to Governor Johnson, November 26, 1865 (*ibid.*, "Telegrams").

[72] A. Johnson to Governor Johnson, September 29, 1865; to Governor Holden, September 21, 1865 (*ibid.*, "Telegrams").

elected, the President refused to allow them to assume office. Humphreys was not recognized as Governor of Mississippi until Johnson saw fit to pardon him;[73] in New Orleans Monroe was suspended from the mayoralty until he had made application and received a pardon.[74] Later after sufficient time for application had passed, Johnson refused altogether to allow Semmes of Mobile, still unpardoned, to occupy an office for which he had been chosen.[75] Johnson knew how to be firm when he chose.

To the wisdom of Johnson's choice of Provisional Governors even the radicals testified.[76] In cooperation with these Governors Johnson worked out the details of Southern policy. He kept in close touch with each of them, wrote letters, sent telegrams, interviewed prominent Southerners and Northern travelers in Secessia, studied reports, and heard and gave advice. He well realized the delicacy of his task. To move too speedily, he, too, felt would endanger the Union cause. He spoke plainly to a group of Virginians: "In going into the recent rebellion against the Government of the United States the people of the South erred; and in returning . . . I am free to say that all the responsible positions and places *ought to be confined distinctly and clearly to men who are loyal.* If, for instance, there are only five thousand loyal men in a State, or a less number, but sufficient to take charge of the political machinery of the State, *those five thousand men, or the lesser number, are entitled to it, if all the rest should be otherwise inclined.* I look upon it as fundamental that the *exercise of political power should be confined to loyal men.*"[77] But "loyal men" according to Johnson were either those not excepted by the classification of May 29 or those excepted but specially pardoned after having subscribed to the amnesty oath. To swell the ranks of

[73] A. Johnson to Major General Thomas, November 19, 1866 (*ibid.,* "Telegrams").

[74] Edward McPherson, *Political Manual* (1866), p. 28.

[75] *New York Herald,* October 2, 1866.

[76] For example, M. Howard of Hartford to G. Welles, July 27, 1865 (Welles Mss., LIX).

[77] Reply to "Virginia Resolutions" (Johnson Mss., LXXXVI). Italics are Johnson's.

loyalty Johnson favored full restoration of property and civil rights to men sincerely anxious to return to good citizenship.[78] He enlisted the aid of prominent Southerners applying for pardon. For example, when Joseph E. Brown, an 1860 secessionist and War Governor of Georgia, was imprisoned in Washington after the war, Johnson released him, talked with him, and sent him home on parole to serve the Union cause. "I think," the President told Stanton, "that his return home can be turned to good account. He will at once go to work and do all that he can in restoring the State. I have no doubt that he will act in good faith. He can not, under the circumstances, act otherwise."[79] Brown became a strong advocate of the Union and of acceptance of Northern terms of Reconstruction. He became a United States Senator; in 1868 he voted for Grant; he was forced into the Democratic party in 1872 only by Republican excesses. Such another pardoned leader was Alexander H. Stephens, Vice-President of the Confederacy. After release from prison, he labored sedulously under Johnson's surveillance for moderation among Southerners.[80] Yet Johnson urged Stephens not to run for office. "It would be exceedingly impolitic," he wired, "for Mr. A. H. Stephen's [*sic*] name to be used in connection with the Senatorial election. If elected he would not be permitted to take his seat. . . . He stands charged with Treason, and no disposition has been made of his case. His present position will enable him to do far more good than any other."[81] Stephens had emphatically refused to allow his name to stand lest it embarrass the President.[82] But he was elected over this protest. His telegram to Johnson explained even this much-heralded "defiance" of Congress. "I was elected yesterday to the United States Senate," it runs, " . . . under

[78] He issued an order that land should be restored when a pardon was granted to ex-rebels. McPherson (1866), pp. 12–13.

[79] June 3, 1865 (Stanton Mss., XXVII).

[80] See, for example, Alexander H. Stephens, *Recollections,* pp. 544, 546–548.

[81] A. Johnson to Major General Steedman, November 24, 1865 (Johnson Mss., "Telegrams").

[82] J. S. Harris of Milledgeville, Georgia, to A. Johnson, December 29, 1865 (*ibid.,* LXXXIII).

circumstances particularly embarrasing [sic] which will be fully explained by mail. An effort may be made to impress you with the belief that this was the result of a disposition . . . to oppose the policy of the Administration. . . . My full conviction is that it sprung from an earnest belief whether erroneous or not, that it would most effectually aid that policy which it is well known I am faithfully laboring to carry out."[83] Stephens did greatly aid Johnson. He even helped persuade the Georgia legislature to pass laws securing Negroes the very civil rights that the radicals were seeking to impose by Congressional action.[84]

In applying this same policy of giving Southerners an active interest in peace and Union, Johnson encouraged them to organize a militia that radicals denounced as preparation for another civil war. September 1, 1865, he wired Governor Parsons of Alabama, "I would suggest for your consideration the propriety of raising in each county an armed mounted *posse comitatus* organized under your Militia Law and under such provisions as you need to secure their loyalty and obedience to your authority and that of the Military Authorities, to repress crime and arrest criminals. A similar organization by me in Tennessee when Military Governor worked well. Governor Sharkey has begun to raise such a force in Mississippi. It seems to me that in some such way your citizens would be committed to the cause of Law and Order and their loyalty to the Union would become not merely passive but active. In any event while Society is reorganizing, the people would themselves by Vigilance Committees or by like unauthorized, spontaneous, and quasi-illegal manner endeavor to repress lawlessness and punish marauding. And it seems preferable to give this natural impulse a proper legal shape and control than to have it illegal and uncontrolled."[85] When Schurz protested against the Mississippi militia, and encouraged General Slocum in prohibiting it, Johnson wired in rebuke: "I presume General Slocum will issue no order interfering with Governor Sharkey in restoring functions

[83] February 1, 1866 (*ibid.*, "Telegrams").
[84] A. H. Stephens to A. Johnson, March 23, 1866 (*ibid.*, XCI).
[85] *Ibid.*, "Telegrams."

of the State Government without first consulting the Government. . . . It is believed there can be organized in each county a force of citizens or militia to suppress crime, preserve order, and enforce the civil authority . . . which would enable the Federal Government to reduce the Army and withdraw to a great extent the forces from the State. . . . The great object is to induce the people to come forward in defense of the State and Federal Government. . . . The people must be trusted with their Government."[86]

In the relations between military and civil authorities Johnson faced a problem. He knew that military authority was necessary in portions of the South; even when he declared by proclamation that the rebellion had ended, he announced against the advice of many of his friends that "the President's proclamation does not remove martial law, or operate in any way upon the Freedmen's Bureau in the exercise of its legitimate jurisdiction."[87] He wished civil and military officers to cooperate in hastening the return of normal conditions. Military commanders were ordered to "aid and assist the . . . provisional governor" and to "abstain from in any way hindering, impeding, or discouraging the loyal people from the organization of a State government."[88] Where the military and civil authorities did cooperate, good government and order were rapidly restored. Where they did not, Johnson sometimes backed the military, as when he upheld General Thomas' suspension of an order of the legislature of Mississippi to disarm all Negroes;[89] he sometimes supported the civil authorities, as when he upheld in Florida the arrest of General Foster's officers for fast riding in violation of civil ordinances,[90] and when he ordered an imprisoned sheriff in Mississippi to be released, Lieutenant Colonel Gibson who had arrested him to be relieved of his command, and the general in charge to "direct that no military interference be had

---

[86] Schurz, p. 192; also C. Schurz to C. Sumner, C. Schurz, *Speeches, Correspondence, and Political Papers,* I, 269.

[87] McPherson (1866), p. 17.

[88] Richardson, pp. 312–314.

[89] A. Johnson to General Thomas, December 12, 1865 (Johnson Mss., LXXXII).

[90] *New York Herald,* December 20, 1866.

against civil process respecting the matter."[91] Johnson's maxim was never to allow the military force to interfere "in any case where justice [could] be attained through the medium of civil authority."[92]

Three demands Johnson did make of the Southern states: repeal of the ordinances of secession, ratification of the Thirteenth Amendment, and repudiation of the rebel debts, Confederate and state. But even these fundamental and unquestionably just conditions, Johnson was determined to secure by voluntary action. He would not use force beyond withholding pardons or delaying recognition of individual officials, but he advised and persuaded, and used every line of Southern influence to secure their adoption. For example, when he heard through Governor Holden that the North Carolina convention had tabled a law prohibiting the payment of the war debt of the state,[93] Johnson wired, "Every Dollar of the Debt created to aid the rebellion against the United States should be repudiated . . . forever. . . . It . . . cannot be recognized by the people of any state, professing themselves loyal to the Government of the United States, and in the Union. . . . I trust and hope, that the people of North Carolina, will wash their hands of everything that partakes in the slightest degree of the Rebellion."[94] The next day the tabled resolution of repudiation was called forth and passed, 84–12. From Georgia, Governor Johnson wired, "We need some aid to repeal the war debt. Send me word on the subject."[95] Johnson responded, "The people of Georgia should not hesitate one single moment in repudiating every single Dollar of debt created for the purpose of aiding the rebellion against the Government of the United States. . . . It should at once be made known at home and abroad, that no debt contracted for the purpose of dissolving the Union of the States,

---

[91] A. Johnson to Major General P. J. Osterhaus, November 3, 1865 (Johnson Mss., "Telegrams").

[92] E. D. Townsend to D. Tillson, April 17, 1866, McPherson (1866), p. 17.

[93] McPherson (1866), p. 19.

[94] October 18, 1865 (Johnson Mss., "Executive Mansion Letters"); printed in McPherson (1866), p. 19.

[95] October 27, 1865, McPherson (1866), p. 20.

can, or ever will be paid."[96] Ten days later the Georgia convention passed the repudiation ordinance, 133–117.[97] The South
Carolinians quibbled to a degree that must have exasperated
Johnson, and their convention finally adjourned without repudiating the state debt; but it did repeal the ordinance of secession, and
declared slavery abolished "by action of the United States authorities."[98] Johnson displayed infinite tact and patience, but upon his
three demands he stood firm.

He also urged upon the states protection of the civil rights of
Negroes. "There is no concession required on the part of the
people of Mississippi," he told Governor-Elect Humphreys, "or
the Legislature, other than a loyal compliance with the laws and
constitution of the United States, and the adoption of such measures, giving protection to all freedmen or freemen, in person and
property without regard to color, as will entitle them to resume
all their constitutional relations in the Federal Union. . . . There
is no disposition, arbitrarily, on the part of the Government, to
dictate what their action should be, but on the contrary, simply
and kindly advise a policy that is believed will result in restoring
all the relations which should exist between the States comprising
the Federal Union."[99]

Johnson realized that the basis of Southern representation
would have to be changed to prevent Southern power in Congress
from being actually increased by the Thirteenth Amendment which
automatically abolished the old three-fifths rule. Hence he suggested in January, 1866, a compromise amendment which read:
"Representatives shall be apportioned among the several States
. . . according to the number of qualified male voters, as prescribed by each State. Direct taxes shall be apportioned among the
several States . . . according to the value of all property subject
to taxation in each State."[100] But his proposal was ignored. He
had doubted the propriety of making this amendment in January.

[96] October 28, 1865 (Johnson Mss., "Telegrams").
[97] McPherson (1866), p. 20.
[98] *Ibid.*, pp. 22–24.
[99] November 17, 1865 (Johnson Mss., "Telegrams").
[100] The proposal was made to Senator Dixon, and was published in the
National Intelligencer, January 29, 1866. There is a copy in the Johnson
Mss., XCV, in William G. Moore's handwriting.

By July he believed that the question could never be permanently settled until all the states were represented, but that the menace of overrepresentation of the South was a mere bugbear anyway since no change could occur until after the census-taking of 1870, by which date a proper remedy could have been determined.[101]

Johnson even favored limited Negro suffrage. But he believed that this was a matter for the states to decide.[102] Southerners must be allowed to work out the problem for themselves. Johnson knew the mutual hatred of poor white and Negro.[103] He felt that the Negro would fare better in the hands of the old slaveholding class than under Northerners and poor white loyalists. In his first message to Congress, he said, "The freedmen, if they show patience and manly virtues, will sooner obtain a participation in the elective franchise through the States than through the General Government, even if it had power to intervene."[104] As a citizen of Tennessee Johnson would have sought the suffrage for intelligent and property-holding Negroes, and ex-soldiers;[105] as President he could only recommend it to the states. "I hope and trust," he wrote Governor Sharkey of Mississippi, "your convention [will grant this qualified suffrage], and, as a consequence, the Radicals, who are wild upon negro franchise, will be completely foiled in their attempt to keep the southern States from renewing their relations to the Union by not accepting their senators and representatives."[106] Universal suffrage, Johnson, a Southerner who knew the Negro, could not favor.

Through the summer and fall the people watched Johnson's program in operation, and on the whole, approved. In September the

101 Interview with Johnson, Boston *Evening Commercial,* July 21, 1866.

102 On his trip South on the President's behalf, Watterson assured the people that the Chases and Sumners would never drive Johnson from the position that the suffrage question belonged to the states. H. M. Watterson to A. Johnson, June 27, 1865 (Johnson Mss., LXVIII).

103 Conversation of A. Johnson with G. L. Stearns, Boston *Daily Advertiser,* October 23, 1865; also Johnson Mss., LXXIX.

104 J. D. Richardson, p. 360.

105 Conversation with G. L. Stearns cited above.

106 August 15, 1865, McPherson (1866), p. 19.

Wisconsin convention supported Johnson by a huge majority.[107] Senator Dixon repeatedly,[108] and Babcock as late as April,[109] promised the overwhelming approval of Connecticut voters. In February men like Cochrane of New York,[110] Geiger of Ohio,[111] and General Sherman in Missouri,[112] declared that, whatever the politicians did, the people would support Johnson. Grant testified to the popularity of the moderate cause.[113]

The hearty support of nearly all the great Union generals, Grant, Sherman, Thomas, Hancock, Meade, Schofield, Ewing, and War Governors like Morton of Indiana and Andrew of Massachusetts won for Johnson's cause great prestige with the people.[114] Beecher offered thanks that "God has raised you up for such a crisis & endowed you with the ability and disposition, to serve the Nation rather than yourself or any mere party."[115]

Radical leaders realized the strength of popular support of Johnson. Just before the first veto the shrewd Chicago journalist, Charles H. Ray, wrote Trumbull, "I greatly fear that the result of the disposition that many of our friends counsel will be to drive him into the enemy's ranks. Now take my prophecy on one thing: If he will agree to your bill giving the freedmen the civil rights that the whites enjoy, and if he halts at that, and war is made on him because he will not go to the extent of negro suffrage, he will beat all who assail him. The party may be split, the government may go out of Republican hands; but Andy Johnson will be the cock of the walk."[116] After the veto and Johnson's much denounced February speech, Loring wrote from the Massachusetts legislature, "I

[107] The old abolitionist element was completely snowed under. J. R. Doolittle to A. Johnson, September 8, 1865 (Johnson Mss., LXXVI).

[108] For example, September 26, 1865 (*ibid.*, LXXVII).

[109] J. F. Babcock to G. Welles, April 6, 1866 (Welles Mss., LX).

[110] J. Cochrane to A. Johnson, February 12, 1866 (Johnson Mss., LXXXVI).

[111] J. H. Geiger to J. R. Doolittle, February 11, 1866 (*loc. cit.*).

[112] W. T. Sherman to A. Johnson, February 11, 1866 (*loc. cit.*).

[113] U. S. Grant, *Personal Memoirs,* pp. 510–511.

[114] R. W. Winston, pp., 340, 347.

[115] H. W. Beecher to A. Johnson, October 23, 1865 (Johnson Mss., LXXIX).

[116] February 7, 1866 (Trumbull Mss., LXIII).

find a peculiar desire for delay, & a reluctance to move against the President. . . . I am somewhat astonished at the affection manifested for a man, whose course towards the party which elected him, entitles him to anything but affection."[117] In November, 1865, Wade dubbed Johnson "a knave or a fool," but feared he had a majority of the people behind him.[118] Morton, later to become a bitter opponent, wrote Johnson, "Since the publication of your message, I have conversed with a number of the first men in New York, in the financial and commercial departments of business, and have found all to heartily approve it. . . . The great body of the people in the North will endorse your doctrines and policy, and this the members of Congress will find out before they are ninety days older."[119]

Johnson's annual message commending his policy to Congress was masterful. Charles Francis Adams wrote, "The annual message, and the report of the Secretary of the Treasury, raised the character of the nation immensely in Europe; I know of nothing better in the annals even when Washington was chief and Hamilton his financier."[120] Watterson, Bancroft, and General Dix agreed with this verdict.[121] Even Lowell praised it.[122] Sheridan, Commander of the Military Division of the Gulf, after Schurz's condemnatory report was in Johnson's hands, wrote praising the President's position. "We can well afford," he said, "to be lenient

[117] G. B. Loring to C. Sumner, February 26, 1866 (Sumner Mss., LXXVII).

[118] B. F. Wade to C. Sumner, November 1, 1865 (*ibid.*, LXXV).

[119] December 7, 1865 (Johnson Mss., LXXXII). Other leaders who later became radicals testified at this time to the popularity of his policy. General J. T. Pratt of Connecticut to A. Johnson, September 11, 1865 (*ibid.*, LXXVI); A. Badeau, Grant's staff assistant, to E. B. Washburne, October 20, 1865 (Washburne Mss., XVI). Forney of the Philadelphia *Press* believed in December that if the party opposed Johnson, it would "go to pieces." J. W. Forney to C. Sumner, December 26, 1865 (Sumner Mss., LXXV).

[120] C. F. Adams to Sidney Brooks, Hugh McCulloch, *Men and Measures,* pp. 219–220; also Detroit *Advertiser and Tribune,* December 6, 1865.

[121] H. M. Watterson to A. Johnson, December 7, 1865, George Bancroft to A. Johnson, December 6, 1865, J. A. Dix to A. Johnson, December 7, 1865 (Johnson Mss., LXXXII). Bancroft, who had written the message for Johnson, watched with special interest its effect, and wrote, "*All* of all parties applaud the ground you have taken."

[122] *North American Review,* CII (January 1866), 250–260.

to this last annoyance, impotent ill feeling. . . . It is so hard by any species of legislation to correct this feeling, magnanimity is the safest and most manly course. How hard it would be to change the opinions of Mr. Wendell Phillips and make him a Vallandigham democrat by any species of legislation. I have the most abiding faith in the solution of the question of a restored Union, if we can only wait and trust to a little time and the working of natural causes."[123] Had a referendum been taken in December, 1865, Johnson's policy would have been approved overwhelmingly.[124] How popular support was diverted from Johnson to the radicals is the story of the campaign.

[123] P. H. Sheridan to A. Johnson, November 26, 1865 (Johnson Mss., LXXXI).
[124] Rhodes concedes this (V, 549).

✪

Andrew Johnson:
The Last Jacksonian

On April 15, 1865, the day after the assassination of Abraham Lincoln, a small group of Radical Republicans met in Washington to plan their political strategy for the critical times ahead. Among them were Senator Benjamin F. Wade of Ohio, Senator Zachariah Chandler of Michigan, and Representative George W. Julian of Indiana—all members of the powerful Congressional Committee on the Conduct of the War, a committee that had vigorously opposed Lincoln's conservative plan of Reconstruction. The radicals were determined not to lose the fruits of the war through a "soft" peace—one that would enable the Southern rebel leaders to regain the positions of political and economic power they had held before the war. This, the radicals feared, would be the inevitable result of Lincoln's generous terms; and, according to Julian, some of them consequently believed that Lincoln's death was "a godsend to the country." Providence, said Senator Chandler, had kept Lincoln in office as long as he was useful, and then put another and better man in his place.

This new and supposedly better man was Vice-President Andrew Johnson, who the radicals believed sympathized with their views. To be sure, Johnson was a Southerner and in prewar

From *The Era of Reconstruction,* by Kenneth M. Stampp. © Copyright 1965 by Kenneth M. Stampp. Reprinted by permission of Alfred A. Knopf, Inc.

politics had been a Democrat—indeed, *still* claimed to be a Democrat. But his recent deeds and utterances about the rebellion made the initial radical confidence in him quite understandable. Like his old hero, Andrew Jackson of Tennessee, Johnson had been a consistent and unqualified Unionist. When Tennessee seceded from the Union, he repudiated the action of his state and remained in his seat in the United States Senate. He even agreed to serve on the Committee on the Conduct of the War, where he worked harmoniously with Wade and Chandler. In 1862, when federal troops occupied much of Tennessee, Lincoln appointed Johnson Military Governor of the state. Two years later Johnson accepted the Vice-Presidential nomination on what purported to be a wartime coalition ticket. During the political campaign he delighted the radicals when he castigated the bloated aristocrats of the South and called for their destruction. "I say the traitor has ceased to be a citizen," he cried, "and in joining the rebellion has become a public enemy." In demanding that the rebels be brought to justice, he said many times: "Treason must be made odious and traitors must be punished and impoverished."

When Johnson succeeded to the Presidency, the North was in a bitter mood, and his verbal assaults on the Southern rebels continued as violently as ever. He offered rewards for the arrest of Jefferson Davis and other Confederate leaders, as well as for the accomplices of John Wilkes Booth. He seemed determined to bring at least some of the prominent Confederates to trial for treason; he showed an interest in the Confiscation Act of 1862 as a device to break up the large Southern estates; and he made it clear that he was now committed to the complete abolition of slavery. To a delegation of Pennsylvanians he said: "To those who have deceived, to the conscious, influential traitor, who attempted to destroy the life of the nation—I would say, on you be inflicted the severest penalties of your crimes." In short, Johnson gave no sign of misplaced charity as he prepared to make treason odious and to punish traitors. Ten days after Lincoln's death, Senator Chandler reported that Johnson "is a radical as I am and as fully up to the mark. If he has good men around him, there will be no danger in the future."

In the early days of his administration, Johnson had plenty of good radical friends around him, and he was quite willing to consult with them. His former colleagues on the Committee on the Conduct of the War seemed to expect that they would become his unofficial advisers. They had a most satisfactory interview with him, during which Johnson listened with apparent sympathy while they did most of the talking. At the close of the interview, Senator Wade said happily: "Johnson, we have faith in you. By the gods, there will be no trouble now in running the government." And the beaming President replied with a variation on an old theme: "Treason must be made infamous and traitors must be impoverished."

The radicals departed assuming that the governments Lincoln had organized in four Southern states would be repudiated, that the Cabinet would be reorganized, that a few dozen leading rebels would be brought to trial, and that either Congress would be called into special session or political Reconstruction would be delayed until Congress met in regular session the following December. In May, 1865, one of the radicals, Carl Schurz, made a most favorable assessment of Johnson: "The objects he aims at are all the most progressive friends of human liberty can desire." The New York *Independent,* a radical weekly, rejoiced that Providence had "trained a Southern loyalist in the midst of traitors, a Southern democrat in the midst of aristocrats . . . to be lifted at last to the presidency of the United States, that he might be charged with the duty of dealing punishment to these self-same assassins of the Union."

Three years later, the radicals in the House of Representatives impeached Johnson for "high misdemeanors," brought him to trial before the Senate, and came within one vote of convicting him and removing him from office. This dramatic shift in Johnson's fortunes resulted in part from subsequent modifications of his ideas about Reconstruction, in part from his own limitations as a politician, and in part from the utter failure of the radicals to understand him. Even in the early weeks of apparent harmony, the area of agreement between Johnson and the radicals was quite narrow. The vast expanses of ideological conflict remained concealed, sometimes because the President was less than candid in his interviews with the radicals, sometimes because he and his visitors spoke only in the vaguest generalities. Their common grounds were, first, their mutual desire to suppress the Southern rebellion and preserve the Union; second, their mutual support of the Thirteenth Amendment; and, third, their mutual hatred of the Southern planter aristocracy and desire to destroy it—and on the last of these, as we shall see, Johnson soon began to waver. Beyond these matters Johnson and the radicals had nothing in common.

The radicals wanted to make the process of political Reconstruction relatively slow and complicated. They would keep Southerners out of Congress a while longer in order to reduce their political influence. Meanwhile the radicals would consolidate the position and power of the Republican party, which still had to prove its capacity to survive the sectional crisis that had created it. For a variety of reasons, practical and idealistic, the radicals were determined to use federal power to extend civil and political rights to Southern Negroes. In addition, many of them (not all) hoped to preserve the legislation passed during the Civil War for the purpose of encouraging or subsidizing American business enterprise, for example, the national banking act and the protective tariff. None of these goals interested Johnson; indeed, some of them represented evils to be avoided at all costs.

Andrew Johnson, we must remember, was not a Republican, radical or conservative; in spite of his admiration for Lincoln, he was almost as far removed ideologically from the wartime President as he was from the radicals. He did not welcome the vast acceleration of social and economic change for which the Civil War was responsible. In an age of railroads, manufacturing corporations, and commercialized agriculture, Johnson still romanticized the self-sufficient yeoman farmer, still regarded cities as centers of moral decay. In an age of national consolidation, Johnson, in spite of his devotion to the Union, still believed in political decentralization and states' rights. In his static world, Thomas Jefferson and Andrew Jackson were sufficient guides to the principles of public morality and the mysteries of political economy; and the Democratic party, in spite of its misguided Southern leaders, was the safest custodian of the nation's destiny.

In short, Andrew Johnson practiced the politics of nostalgia; and he discovered in his own career, in which he took infinite pride, full vindication of his old-fashioned social philosophy. Johnson was a self-made man, the embodiment of the American success story, though hardly one of its more attractive products. Born in North Carolina, he endured in his childhood the rigors of extreme poverty. At a tender age, without formal schooling, he was thrust into the world to make his own living. In 1826 he moved across the mountains into East Tennessee, a region of small farms and few slaves, where he settled in the village of Greeneville and opened a tailor shop. There he gained his first taste of success and public recognition: his tailor shop gave him a comfortable income; his wife taught him to write; he read some books; and he joined a debating society. Soon he was in politics, from the first a Jacksonian Democrat, a champion of the village artisans and yeoman farmers, and a bitter foe of the proud and affluent Whigs. "Some day I will show the stuck-up aristocrats who is running the country," he vowed early in his career. "A cheap purse-proud set they are, not half as good as the man who earns his bread by the sweat of his brow."[1]

Johnson's political career was a record of almost unbroken success as he advanced from alderman to mayor of Greeneville, to the state legislature, to the federal Congress for five successive terms, to the Governorship of Tennessee for two terms, and then in 1857 to the United States Senate. In Southern politics he was regarded as something of a radical; and though his understanding of social problems was often primitive, his rhetoric sometimes that of the demagogue, there is no reason to doubt his sincere devotion to the welfare of the common white man of the South. "The people need friends," he said. "They have a great deal to bear." In

---

[1] "For Johnson, personal fulfillment had long since come to be defined as the fruit of struggle—real, full-bodied, and terrible—against forces specifically organized for thwarting him. . . . Johnson, all his life, had operated as an outsider." Eric L. McKitrick, *Andrew Johnson and Reconstruction* (Chicago, 1960), p. 86.

Tennessee politics his most notable crusade was for a system of free, tax-supported public schools. In national politics he was one of the earliest advocates of a so-called Homestead Act, a measure designed to give actual settlers a gift of 160 acres of land from the public domain. As he pressed for its passage, he repeatedly paraphrased Jefferson's defense of the agrarian interest and the Jacksonian's alarm at the passage of the American Arcadian Utopia. "I do not look upon the growth of cities and the accumulation of population around the cities as being the most desirable objects in this country," he said. "Let us try to prevent their further accumulation. . . . I want no miserable city rabble on the one hand; I want no pampered, bloated, corrupt aristocracy on the other; I want the middle portion of society to be built up and sustained. . . . Let us go on interesting men in becoming connected with the soil; . . . prevent their accumulation in the streets of your cities; and in doing this you will dispense with the necessity for your pauper system."

But Johnson's prewar radicalism did not make him an opponent of slavery; in fact, he defended the South's peculiar institution and eventually acquired a few slaves of his own. Ever the democrat, his objection to the slave system was that only a privileged few enjoyed its benefits, and not the mass of white men. In one of the most twisted prayers ever uttered for the welfare of the common man, he once said: "I wish to God every head of a family in the United States had one slave to take the drudgery and menial service off his family." Never did Johnson expand his democratic creed to include the American Negro; like the Southern Populists in the late nineteenth century, his was a democracy for white men only. George W. Julian recalled that early in the war Johnson had maintained that emancipation was impossible without immediate colonization. Julian believed that at heart he was "as decided a hater of the negro . . . as the rebels from whom he had separated." But by 1864 Johnson saw that slavery was going to be a casualty of the war, and he accepted this result for two reasons, as he explained: "first, because it is a right in itself, and second, because in the emancipation of the slaves, we break down an odious and dangerous aristocracy."

When Johnson became President and was confronted with the problem of Reconstruction, his principal goal at first seemed to be to undermine the Southern planter class. But this does not mean that he had at last come to terms with the new centers of political and economic power: the burgeoning cities with their ambitious merchants, manufacturers, and financiers. Still the agrarian, still the backward-looking Jacksonian Democrat, he could see no gain for the common man if a Northern moneyed aristocracy replaced a Southern landed aristocracy in the seats of power. Johnson was particularly concerned about the influence of a new class of public-security holders that had emerged during the Civil War. After the war he echoed Jefferson's fear of an aristocracy of liquid wealth: "The aristocracy based on $3,000,000,000 of property in slaves . . . has disappeared; but an aristocracy, based on over $2,500,-000,000 of national securities, has arisen in the Northern states, to assume that political control which the consolidation of great financial and political interest formerly gave to the slave oligarchy of the late rebel states. . . . We have all read history, and is it not certain, that of all aristocracies mere wealth is the most odious, rapacious, and tyrannical? It goes for the last dollar the poor and helpless have got; and with such a vast machine as this government under its control, that dollar will be fetched. It is an aristocracy that can see in the people only a prey for extortion."

Eventually, Johnson suggested a way to reduce the power of this aristocracy, too. In his last annual message he told Congress that during the war investors had used depreciated paper money to purchase government securities paying high interest rates; thus the government had received in gold only a fraction of the face value of the securities it had issued. Therefore, said Johnson, "it may be assumed that the holders of our securities have already received upon their bonds a larger amount than their original investment." This being the case, he proposed as an equitable settlement the continued payment of the interest on the government debt for sixteen more years, after which the government's obligation should be considered paid in full. "Our national credit should be sacredly observed," Johnson concluded, "but in making provision for our creditors we should not forget what is due to the masses of the people."

Meanwhile, Johnson also made it clear that he regarded the protective tariff as an unjust burden upon consumers; the national banking system as a dangerous monopoly; and the sale of timber and mineral lands from the public domain to private corporations as a betrayal of the Homestead policy adopted in 1862. "The public domain," he said, "is a national trust, set apart and held for the general welfare upon principles of equal justice, and not to be bestowed as a special privilege upon a favored class." In pure Jacksonian rhetoric, he denounced those who sought to obtain special favors from government. "Monopolies, perpetuities, and class legislation," he insisted, "are contrary to the genius of free government. . . . Wherever monopoly attains a foothold, it is sure to be a source of danger, discord, and trouble. . . . The government is subordinate to the people; but, as the agent and representative of the people, it must be held superior to monopolies, which in themselves ought never to be granted."

Johnson aimed his blows at the Southern lords of the manor, then, not to give aid and comfort to the new masters of capital, but to strengthen the position of the American yeomanry. To him, as to Jefferson, they were "the chosen people of God." Time after time they had been betrayed by powerful combinations of vested interests who sought to control the government for their own selfish ends: first by Hamilton and the Federalist commercial aristocracy, until Jefferson restored the government to the tillers of the soil; then by Nicholas Biddle and the national banking interest, until Jackson destroyed them with a crushing veto; then by John C. Calhoun and the planter aristocracy, whom Johnson had been fighting during his long political career.

But Johnson was now in a position to make this time of political Reconstruction a time of triumph for the yeoman class. This was the class that he hoped to bring to power in the New South—the class whose interests he would make decisive in the formulation of public policy. For this end, a reorganized and strengthened Democratic party, cleansed of its disloyal prewar leadership, would be a reliable instrument; and with an agrarian-oriented Democracy in control, the country would return to first principles and paradise would be regained.[2]

Unfortunately for Johnson, the Radical Republicans, especially those from the states of the Northeast, had a somewhat different vision of paradise. As the radicals gradually realized what Johnson's goals actually were, they reluctantly decided that their opposition to executive leadership would have to be renewed.

The irreconcilable differences between their respective programs made conflict inevitable, but this alone does not explain the level of extreme violence it ultimately reached. Johnson's background and personality—his shortcomings as a politician—were also responsible for the numerous unseemly incidents of his administration. This is not to suggest that the radicals were guiltless, for the language they used in their attacks upon the President was often inexcusable. But Johnson, if he hoped to exercise executive leadership, could ill afford the luxury of answering in kind. Unfortunately, this was a luxury he could not resist, even at the cost of compromising the dignity of his office. Unlike Lincoln, he was not a master of men—not even master of himself.

Johnson's origins, as we have seen, were as humble as Lincoln's, his rise to fame just as spectacular. But Lincoln made his log-cabin, rail-splitting background, his embodiment of the American success story, a political asset; Johnson made it a liability, for he was heavy-handed in exploiting it. His humble origin and the scorn and contempt the planter class had heaped upon him in earlier years made him bitter, pugnacious, and self-assertive. He had no ease, no grace, no self-confidence. Many times he permitted radicals, with whose views he disagreed, to depart from an interview convinced that there was no disagreement at all. "He listened so attentively," Carl Schurz once reported, "that I was almost sure he would heed my advice." Moreover, his lack of self-confidence

---

[2] For a while, in 1866, Johnson considered forming a new national conservative party. Secretary of State William H. Seward had been urging a "reorganization of parties that would attract the support of Southerners and of Northern Democrats by a speedy and generous restoration of the secession states." LaWanda and John H. Cox, *Politics, Principle, and Prejudice, 1865–1866* (New York, 1963), p. 222. But this was after Johnson's program had clearly failed; and, in any case, nothing came of the idea.

made him indecisive at crucial times. Gideon Welles, Johnson's Secretary of the Navy, noted that "it has been the misfortune, the weakness, the great error of the President to delay—hesitate before acting." Yet Welles knew of no man who was more firm once he had taken a stand. Johnson's firmness, however, took the form of inflexibility, for there was in him a streak of stiff stubbornness that served him ill. Having made up his mind, he would not compromise; he would not yield a minor point to gain a major objective; he was utterly devoid of tact.

Early in his career Johnson had won a reputation as an orator, but his was a brand of oratory fashioned in the rough school of East Tennessee politics, where the graceful rhetoric, rounded periods, and classical allusions of a Jefferson Davis had little appeal. Johnson had waged his political campaigns in basic English; and after he became President he reverted to these tactics easily, almost instinctively, in the heat of debate. His enemies did not find it difficult to provoke him to verbal indiscretions.

Radical disillusionment with Johnson began as soon as he ceased gnashing his teeth and shaking his fist at rebels and started actually to formulate Reconstruction policies. The war was over now; the South was defeated; and the political realities called for something more than bold posturing and terrible threats. Southerners, stunned in defeat, waited to hear the terms with which they would have to comply. How smoothly Reconstruction would proceed depended in part on how decisively federal authorities acted immediately after the surrender. Early in May, Schurz wrote Sumner: "If we only make a vigorous start in the right direction the problem will be easily solved. But if too much latitude is given to the mischievous elements in the South for the next few weeks, it will be exceedingly difficult to set matters right again."

Johnson responded with a series of public statements and executive proclamations that left the radicals momentarily stunned, because they seemed so utterly contrary to his former position. The new President, it now appeared, was as convinced as Lincoln had been that Reconstruction was the responsibility of the executive department and not of Congress. He did not propose to call Congress into special session, or to delay Reconstruction until

December when Congress would meet in regular session. Rather, he would start and finish it in the seven months before Congress assembled and then present Congress with a *fait accompli*. Nor did he propose to reorganize Lincoln's conservative Cabinet, or to accept the radicals as his unofficial advisers. Instead, he proposed, like Lincoln, to go it alone; and if Lincoln's position was vulnerable for ignoring Congress, Johnson's position was well-nigh indefensible. The circumstances that brought him to the head of the executive department gave him no popular mandate and enabled indignant and disrespectful radicals to refer to him as "His Accidency the President."

Nevertheless, Johnson announced that he would continue to apply Lincoln's plan of Reconstruction, though, in fact, he modified its terms and significantly changed its purpose. On May 9, 1865, he officially recognized the Pierpont government as the legal government of Virginia. Three weeks later, on May 29, he formalized his program in two proclamations. In the first of these he prescribed an oath of allegiance that the mass of Southern people would be permitted to take; those who took it would receive amnesty and pardon and the restoration of all rights of property, except slaves, unless confiscation proceedings had already been instituted. In other words, taking the oath brought with it the recovery of civil and political rights, immunity from prosecution for treason or conspiracy, and exemption from the provisions of the Confiscation Act.

Johnson, however, listed fourteen classes of persons who were not entitled to the benefits of his amnesty, and these exceptions were more numerous than Lincoln's. While the war was still in progress, he had said: "Many humble men, the peasantry and yeomanry of the South, who have been decoyed, or perhaps driven into rebellion, may look forward with reasonable hope for an amnesty. But the intelligent and influential leaders must suffer." The exceptions, as one would expect, included Confederate civil and military officers; but the thirteenth classification was by far the most interesting and significant. For here Johnson acted as the class-conscious plebeian—the radical agrarian who was setting out to remake the social and political life of the South. All those who had supported the Confederacy and whose taxable property was valued at $20,000 or more were barred from taking the Johnson oath and obtaining amnesty. "You know perfectly well," Johnson told a delegation of Virginians, "it was the wealthy men of the South who dragooned the people into secession." These men were to have no part in political Reconstruction. If power were to be transferred to the yeomanry, this would be a practical step in that direction; for without pardons the large property holders would be politically disenfranchised and still liable to confiscation proceedings. But all was not lost for them, for Johnson did provide that members of the excepted classes could apply for special pardons; he promised that each of them would receive a fair hearing.

The second proclamation of May 29 outlined the steps for the formation of loyal state governments.[3] In each of the Southern states the President would appoint a Provisional Governor whose duty it would be to call a state convention and supervise the election of delegates to it. Only those who could qualify under the state laws in effect in 1860 and who had taken the amnesty oath would be entitled to vote or stand for election. The convention could then prescribe permanent voting and office-holding requirements, after which an election would be held for a regular Governor, state legislature, and members of Congress. Less formally, Johnson demanded that the Southern states proclaim the illegality of their ordinances of secession, repudiate all Confederate debts, and ratify the Thirteenth Amendment. The process of political Reconstruction would then be completed, and the President would revoke martial law and withdraw the federal troops.

This is the program that Johnson launched in the Southern states during the summer of 1865, while the Congressional radicals looked on helplessly. Within a few months the conventions had finished their business, the state elections had been held, and Presidential proclamations had retired the Provisional Governors and turned political power over to the newly elected Governors

[3] The proclamation of May 29 applied only to North Carolina. Within the next few weeks similar proclamations put the same program into effect in the other Southern states where Reconstruction had not yet begun. As in Virginia, Johnson accepted the Lincoln governments in Arkansas, Louisiana, and Tennessee.

and legislatures. In December, when Congress assembled, Johnson announced that the process of Reconstruction was completed. The Southern people, he said, had returned to their allegiance in good faith; the Southern states had been restored to their proper position in the Union; federal courts, customs houses, and post offices were open; and it was the duty of Congress now to seat Southern Senators and Representatives.[4] In the South, he concluded, "the aspect of affairs is more promising than, in view of all the circumstances, could well have been expected." In short, Johnson congratulated himself on a job well done.

Or at least that was his public posture. Whether inwardly he was as pleased with the outcome of his Reconstruction program as outwardly he pretended to be may well be doubted. Eventually Congress rejected the Johnson governments in the South, formulated its own policies, and at last, in 1867, put in motion a new plan of Reconstruction—thereby wounding the President as painfully as he had previously wounded Congress. The historical tradition, therefore, is that the radical repudiation of Presidential Reconstruction represented Andrew Johnson's ultimate defeat and humiliation. But this is dubious history, because the President had already suffered a devastating defeat even before Congress assembled. Actually, the radical attack upon him saved him from having to face up to his own personal failure. For Johnson, in implementing his Reconstruction program, had somehow either lost sight of his original goals or lacked the firmness and political skill he would have needed to attain them.

At the outset he had taken a bold stand. The prewar leaders of the South, he had said, "must be conquered and a new set of men brought forward who are to vitalize and develop the Union feeling in the South." Moreover, the great plantations "must be seized and divided into small portions and sold to honest, industrious men." But by December, 1865, Johnson's dream of an agrarian Utopia had been lost; he was almost the prisoner of the men he had set

---

[4] In Texas Johnson's program of Reconstruction was not completed until the following spring. On August 20, 1866, Johnson formally proclaimed "that the insurrection . . . is at an end, and is henceforth to be so regarded."

out to destroy; and he was committed to a swift termination of political Reconstruction in the name of states' rights. His resort to narrow constitutionalism to defend what was now an aimless policy was for all practical purposes a declaration of political bankruptcy.[5]

Why, then, did Johnson fail? He failed primarily because of an erroneous assumption about the attitude of the Southern white masses toward the planter class. From the beginning of his political career, Johnson had believed that the Southern yeomanry were the helpless victims of a ruling aristocracy, waiting hopefully for new leaders who would champion their cause. Secession, he repeatedly claimed, had been engineered by a small clique of planter politicians against the will of the majority. But after the war, with the planter aristocracy defeated and discredited, with Johnson in a position to give the yeomanry their chance, he expected them to find leadership that would enable them to control the Southern conventions and state governments organized under his plan of Reconstruction.

Unfortunately, Johnson had become the captive of his own Jacksonian rhetoric and vastly oversimplified the problem he faced. To be sure, there had been tensions in the relations between farmers and planters in the ante-bellum South; among the masses there had always been an undercurrent of envy and resentment. But much of the time these unsophisticated rural folk had also exhibited toward the planters a certain measure of respect and admiration, and a willingness to accept their political leadership. Though some undemocratic political practices still survived in the South, the great majority of white nonslaveholders nevertheless had the franchise, and the aristocracy had to exert its influence within an essentially democratic political framework. It was the wealth, education, and self-confidence of the slaveholders—their

---

[5] Johnson's own plan of Reconstruction—he preferred the term *restoration*—was not based on a strict states'-rights constitutional position. For he required the Southern states to do certain things, such as repudiating Confederate debts and abolishing slavery, before they could participate in the government. He used the states'-rights argument only when Congress laid down additional terms. Thaddeus Stevens, on several occasions, accurately pointed to Johnson's inconsistency.

mastery of the techniques that bring political success in a democracy—that enabled them to exert great influence on their humble neighbors. They had not dragged a reluctant people out of the Union in 1861, for the vast majority of the white yeomen in the Confederate states had favored secession. And the vast majority still seemed to be satisfied with the old leadership when the war ended and the Confederacy collapsed.

Nothing, then, had really changed in the South when Johnson prepared to establish new state governments; there was no significant grass-roots movement for a change in political leadership. According to John W. De Forest, a Union officer, Southern politics still reflected "the somewhat feudal, somewhat patriarchal, social position of the large planter. . . . Every community has its great man . . . around whom his fellow-citizens gather when they want information, and to whose monologues they listen with a respect akin to humility. . . . [Everywhere] that I went . . . I found the chivalrous Southron still under the domination of his ancient leaders." And the Southern elections of 1865 bore him out. In Mississippi the new legislature did reflect an increase in the power of the small landholders; and in Tennessee the Unionists won complete control. But in general the planters and Confederate leaders captured the Johnson governments. Many of the new Governors and legislators had been active rebels and boasted of their wartime activities in their political campaigns. Scores of them belonged to one or another of the categories that Johnson had excluded from his general amnesty. The new Governor of South Carolina, James L. Orr, had served in the Confederate Senate; the new Governor of Mississippi, Benjamin G. Humphreys, had been a Confederate brigadier general. The great majority of those elected to Congress had been Confederate military officers, cabinet officers, or Congressmen; among them was Alexander H. Stephens of Georgia, Confederate Vice-President, elected to the United States Senate.

Johnson poured out his bitter disappointment to William W. Holden, his Provisional Governor in North Carolina. In that state six of the seven men elected to Congress were not entitled to take the amnesty oath, and many members of the legislature had not yet received Presidential pardons. "The results of the recent elections in North Carolina," Johnson told Holden, "have greatly damaged the prospects of the State in the restoration of its governmental relations. Should the action and spirit of the legislature be in the same direction it will greatly increase the mischief already done and might be fatal."

Johnson was then forced to make a crucial decision. Somehow he had to deal with Southerners in the excepted classes who had been denied the benefits of his amnesty proclamation but had nevertheless been elected to public office. Since they symbolized the defeat of his Southern program, he might have refused to permit them to take office and called for new elections. He might even have concluded that his attempt at political Reconstruction was premature and that federal control would have to continue for a while longer. Clearly there had not been time enough for the recruitment of new Southern leadership and for the organizational work that was needed if Johnson's goals were to be achieved. But Johnson did none of these things. Instead he issued special pardons in wholesale lots—to delegates to the state conventions, to Governors, to members of the legislatures, to Congressmen-Elect, and to mayors and other local officials. Planters, prewar politicians, Confederate military leaders often had merely to call on the President—sometimes only to write to him—to get the desired pardons. Altogether Johnson had granted some 13,500 special pardons when, on September 7, 1867, he issued a second amnesty proclamation which left only a few hundred former Confederates unpardoned.[6] "Had it not been for the special pardons," an angry Georgia Unionist complained to Thaddeus Stevens, "the genuine Union men could of carried the state and sent original Union men to Congress." In Virginia, a Union officer told a Congressional committee, pardoned rebels "seem to have assumed . . . political control, and to exercise an influence upon society that they did not before they received those pardons. . . . The Union people were

[6] In a third proclamation, on July 4, 1868, Johnson granted pardons to all but a handful of ex-rebels, and the following Christmas Day he pardoned these last few as well.

in the minority after these secessionists got their pardons, and had to take back seats."

Moreover, Johnson soon lost interest in land reform through confiscation. By the end of 1865 he had dropped all but a few flagrant cases, and early the next year he abandoned confiscation entirely. His Attorney General ruled that the Confiscation Act of 1862 was valid only in wartime and could not be enforced after the restoration of peace.

In short, Johnson had given up. There would be no social or political revolution in the South after all. Southern Unionists and others who had hoped to bar the prewar politicians from positions of power in the New South now turned against the President; his former enemies, who had despised him in earlier years, now came to his defense. A South Carolina planter, Henry W. Ravenel, described this remarkable change: "How hard it is to know really the character of public men," he wrote. "I had always heard of [President Johnson] as a demagogue and pot house politician in Tennessee of the lowest order. . . . I freely acknowledge that my first impressions of him [were] erroneous. . . . [He] has placed himself in opposition to the radicals . . . and by his acts and influence has shielded the South from [their] vindictive policy."

Why Johnson abandoned his goals so precipitately, why he first disenfranchised the Southern aristocracy by denying them amnesty and then gave them individual pardons with such unseemly haste, has always been something of a mystery. Perhaps Johnson, being a confirmed democrat, saw no alternative once they had been duly elected to office. Perhaps his growing fear of Northern capitalists eventually caused him to see the value of the planter class as a countervailing political force. Perhaps he simply lacked the iron will, the quality of ruthlessness, he would have needed to achieve his goals. Perhaps he was, after all, at heart a conservative who shrank from the prospect of political turmoil and economic upheaval once he had experienced the sobering responsibility of power. Perhaps he was influenced by his adroit Secretary of State, William H. Seward, who urged a generous Reconstruction policy to facilitate the creation of a great national conservative party.

Perhaps his ambition for a Presidential nomination in 1868 diverted him from his original course.

All these may have been important reasons for Johnson's behavior, but there is still another that needs to be considered. It is that Johnson, in 1865, betrayed a weakness that is common among men of his background and experience, though far from universal. The memory of his early poverty, the scars he bore from his political battles, the snubs he had received from the haughty planter aristocracy, all had left him with a raw ego and a craving for recognition and respect.[7] Like the Southern common people for whom he spoke, Johnson's resentment of the planter class was, after all, combined with a certain grudging admiration. If his vanity demanded that he gain recognition and respect, then nothing could satisfy him more than forcing this class to seek mercy from his hands. By denying amnesty to all Confederate leaders and large property holders and requiring them to apply to him for special pardons, this is precisely what he obliged them to do. Those who scorned him were now flattering him, appealing to his generosity, begging for the franchise and the protection of their property—but influencing his policy as well.

As early as June 5, 1865, Schurz warned Sumner that Southern delegations were "crowding into Washington" and that the President was permitting "his judgment to be controlled by their representations." A few weeks later, Henry D. Cooke wrote Representative John Sherman of Ohio that Washington was "full of Southern people, and the President is occupied half his time in receiving delegations from Dixie. The effect of this is an increasingly evident leaning towards a more conservative policy." On September 11, representatives of nine Southern states visited Johnson for the purpose, as one of them explained, "of manifesting the sincere respect and regard they entertain for you . . . and to say . . . that they have great confidence in your wisdom to heal the wounds that have been made, and in your disposition to exercise all the leniency which can be commended by a sound and judicious policy." With an air of self-righteousness Johnson re-

[7] These characteristics were evident in nearly all of his speeches, before and after he became President.

minded his visitors of the "taunts, the jeers, the scowls, with which I was treated." He had warned the misguided Southern leaders, and now he had "lived to see the realization of my predictions and the fatal error of those whom I vainly essayed to save from the results I could not but foresee."

For Johnson this was obviously an intoxicating experience, and he became a little giddy as delegation after delegation of contrite Southerners assured him that the fate of the South was in his hands. Before long he began to sound less and less like an angry plebeian, more and more like a mellow patrician in his defense of Southern rights. No longer did he speak of punishing traitors and making treason odious; rather, he said: "I did not expect to keep out all who were excluded from the amnesty, or even a large number of them, but I intended they should sue for pardon, and so realize the enormity of their crime." The pardons flowed from the President's office to men who realized nothing of the sort, to men who accepted him now, humbled themselves before him, showered him with praise—and captured his governments in the South. Why, then, did Johnson fail? The answer, in part, is that the planter politicians proved to be more skillful than he; finding his weakness, they exploited his vanity and thus defeated him with remarkable ease.

More than that: after reducing the Johnson plan of Reconstruction to a shambles, the planter politicians maneuvered the President into so compromising a position that he was obliged to side with them against the Radical Republicans. To have done otherwise would have been to admit failure and, in consequence, to invite Congress to take command. This was a humiliation that Johnson could not bear, and to avoid it he boldly assured Congress that his program had been a complete success. He defended the men who controlled the governments he had created. He claimed that they were now thoroughly loyal and repentant; that they had accepted the results of the war and were acting in good faith; that their feelings toward Northerners were nothing but friendly; and that they were dealing fairly with their former slaves. Had all this been true, Johnson's position still would have been strong, and he would doubtless have been able to force Congress eventually to recognize his governments in the South. But all this was far from true, for the Southern politicians whom Johnson defended were discrediting him by their irresponsible behavior. As a result, they were to blame not only for defeating his Reconstruction plans but also for strengthening the radicals and making certain their ultimate victory over the President.

In December, 1865, after listening to Johnson's message to Congress, the radicals claimed that he had grossly misrepresented conditions in the South. The radicals insisted that the men who had won control of his Southern state governments were still rebels at heart; that they had not been reconciled to defeat and would seize the first opportunity to launch another rebellion; that they were persecuting Northern settlers; and that they were reducing the Negroes to slavery once more.

Johnson and the radicals both searched for evidence to prove their cases, and both found numerous eyewitnesses to support them. General Grant, Harvey M. Watterson, and Benjamin C. Truman, a pro-Johnson newspaper correspondent, toured the South and submitted reports highly pleasing to Johnson. Grant concluded "that the mass of thinking men of the South accept the present situation of affairs in good faith." Writing in April, 1866, Truman reported that "the great, substantial, and prevailing element" in the South "is more loyal now than it was at the end of the war." Johnson also sent Carl Schurz on a tour of the South, but Schurz's preliminary reports, in the form of letters to the President and to the Boston *Advertiser,* indicated that his observations would be far more pleasing to the radicals. Johnson did not ask Schurz for a report, but Schurz wrote one anyway; and the radicals, after forcing Johnson to submit it to Congress, used it to good advantage. Early in 1866, scores of witnesses testified before the Joint Committee on Reconstruction, which Congress had created the previous December, and most of them gave aid and comfort to the radicals. In addition, many Southern Unionists wrote private letters to the President and to Republican members of Congress complaining bitterly about conditions in the South under the Johnson governments. None of these reports was free from bias of one kind or another, but in many ways Schurz's report was the best of them. Though partial to the radicals, it was systematically organized, relatively restrained, remarkably perceptive, and reasonably candid.

From the conflicting testimony a few generalizations about conditions in the South and the attitudes of Southerners would seem to be valid. Southerners did understand that they had been defeated, and they were cooperating in the establishment of new state governments under Johnson's formula. Rumors that they were plotting another rebellion were pure nonsense. Most of those who were eligible to take Johnson's oath of allegiance hastened to do so; most of those who were not eligible petitioned for special pardons. As Schurz reported, whatever differences may exist among Southerners, "on one point they are agreed: further resistance to the power of the national government is useless, and submission to its authority a matter of necessity."

However, a large number of Southerners were bitter in defeat; few of them would have agreed that what they had done in 1861 was morally wrong, or that the right had triumphed. Benjamin C. Truman noted that "boisterous demagogues" and "reckless editors" were still pouring forth "obnoxious utterances." Schurz found among the Southern people "an utter absence of national feeling." Loyalty consisted of "submission to necessity," and submission was advocated as "the only means by which they could rid themselves of the federal soldiers and obtain once more control of their own affairs." Certainly Southerners were not conceding any more than they had to. Many of them were exhibiting a strong hostility toward Northerners who had settled in the South during or after the war, and, if anything, an even stronger hostility toward Southerners who had been Unionists.

Moreover, it would be far from the truth to say that white Southerners generally were reconciled to the Negro's new status as a freedman. Many former slaveholders shared the regret of Louis Manigault, a Georgia planter, that the "former mutual and pleasing feeling of Master towards Slave and vice versa is now as a dream of the past." The whites intensely resented the presence of Negro troops in the South; the more brutal whites committed countless acts of violence against the freedmen; and men of all classes considered any deviation on the part of Negroes from the subservience of slavery days as "insolence." Carl Schurz met planters who were trying to deal fairly with the freedmen, but he also presented overwhelming evidence that the Negroes needed federal protection. In North Carolina, reported General G. F. Granger, "the poor negro hears on all sides . . . that he is after all notwithstanding his freedom, now and forever more, 'nothing but a damned nigger.'" R. W. Flournoy of Mississippi, a large slaveholder before the war, now genuinely concerned about the freedman's welfare, told Thaddeus Stevens: "To leave the negro to be dealt with by those whose prejudices are of the most bitter character against him, will be barbarous."

Given the prevailing attitudes—all of them human enough and quite understandable—Southern political leaders made many tactless blunders, as even the none-too-tactful President himself privately recognized. In the fall of 1865, Gideon Welles, a firm supporter of Johnson's Reconstruction program, recorded in his diary quite a different picture of conditions in the South than the one to which the administration was officially committed: "The tone of sentiment and action of [the] people of the South," he wrote, "is injudicious and indiscreet in many respects. . . . The entire South seem to be stupid and vindictive, know not their friends, and are pursuing just the course which their opponents, the Radicals, desire. I fear a terrible ordeal awaits them in the future."

Most of these blunders, which shocked the Northern people and strengthened the radicals, reflected the pride of the Southern people and expressed their belief in the justness of their cause. The North, wrote Confederate General Wade Hampton of South Carolina, had no right to expect that the South would "at once profess unbounded love to that Union from which for four years she tried to escape." It was, therefore, perhaps too much to expect Southerners to welcome Northerners and admit them to their homes, or to reward Southern Unionists for opposing the Confederacy by electing them to public office. Appointments in the Johnson governments also went to ex-Confederates. A Louisiana Unionist complained to Schurz that the offices "are now being distributed to men who held commissions in the rebel army, who signed the ordinance of secession . . . [and] who took a leading part in the rebel movement; you can see them now as judges, sheriffs, and important officers of the new state." In January, 1866, *Harper's Weekly* reported indignantly that General Hampton "was received with all the honors by the Legislature of Alabama, and responded to their acclamations by eulogizing the noble and heroic effort of the people of that State to destroy the United States Government."

Several Southern conventions still would not agree that secession had been illegal; therefore, they merely repealed, rather than repudiated, the ordinances of secession and thus yielded nothing in principle. The Johnson legislature in Arkansas voted pensions for Confederate veterans; Mississippi refused to ratify the Thirteenth Amendment; South Carolina refused to repudiate the Confederate debt. Under the aegis of Johnsonian Reconstruction was born a popular type of postwar Southern politician who played the role of professional ex-Confederate and Yankee-baiter.

Most damaging were the policies pursued by the Johnson governments toward the Negroes. Though Johnson, like Lincoln, first hoped to eliminate the race issue by colonizing the Negroes outside the United States, by 1865 he seemed to have realized that the Negroes were going to be a permanent part of the Southern population. Yet his Reconstruction terms did not require the Southern states to deal fairly with the Negroes; his only demand was that they accept the abolition of slavery. Beyond this, he thought, the federal government had no jurisdiction; questions of education, social relationships, and civil and political rights must be settled by the individual states. On one occasion Johnson suggested to Provisional Governor William L. Sharkey of Mississippi that the vote be given to Negroes who could meet literacy and property requirements. This, he explained, would "disarm" the radicals, who were "wild upon negro franchise." But he did not make this a condition of recognition. "My position as President," he once said, "is different from what it would be if I were in Tennessee. There I should try to introduce negro suffrage gradually. . . . It would not do to let the negroes have universal suffrage now; it would breed a war of races." Actually, Johnson was never enthusiastic about Negro suffrage, because he feared that the votes of these economically helpless people would be controlled by the large landholders. And since Johnson showed virtually no interest in the Negroes—no desire to give them federal protection—he helped to push them into the arms of the radicals.

So did the Johnson governments in the South, for all of them restricted the suffrage to the whites. Governor Humphreys of Mississippi affirmed in his Inaugural Address "that ours is and it shall ever be, a government of white men." In Louisiana a state Democratic convention resolved that "we hold this to be a Government of White People, made and to be perpetuated for the exclusive political benefit of the White Race, and . . . that the people of African descent cannot be considered as citizens of the United States." In short, one vital prop of Negro freedom—political rights—was withheld.

A second prop—education—was also denied the Negroes. Schurz observed that "the popular prejudice is almost as bitterly set against the negro's having the advantage of education as it was when the negro was a slave. . . . Hundreds of times I heard the old assertion repeated, that 'learning will spoil the nigger for work,' and that 'negro education will be the ruin of the South.' Another most singular notion still holds a potent sway over the minds of the masses—it is, that the elevation of the blacks will be the degradation of the whites." As a result of these attitudes, none of the Johnson governments made any effective provision for Negro education. Moreover, white public opinion was generally hostile to the efforts of private benevolent societies to establish Negro schools.

The Johnsonians also made quite clear what they thought the Negro's economic role in the New South should be. The future envisioned for him was that of an illiterate, unskilled, propertyless, agricultural worker. A delegate to the Texas constitutional convention said: "I concede them nothing but the station of 'hewers of wood and drawers of water.'" This design, of course, was meant to assure the whites of a perpetual supply of cheap labor, but it also reflected their belief that the Negro had the capacity for nothing better. John B. Baldwin of Virginia told the Joint Committee on Reconstruction: "I do not believe that, as a race, they will ever have the persistence of purpose, or the energy, or the intellectual vigor to rise to anything like intellectual equality with the white race. I think that they will get along very well in the ordinary domestic relations, as servants and inferiors." An Alabama patriarch, seeking a remedy for what he called the evils of abolition, urged Southerners to "secure the services of the negroes, teach them their places, and how to keep them, and convince them at last that we are indeed their best friends." The Negro, he said, "is proud to call you master yet. In the name of humanity, let him do so."

The leaders of the Johnson governments combined these attitudes with a general conviction that the Negro would not work without compulsion of some kind. The Negro's innate indolence, said a Virginia planter, could only be dealt with by "prudent legislation." This conviction produced the best-remembered enactments of the Johnson legislatures: the so-called Black Codes framed to control the Negroes and severely restrict their civil rights. The crucial point about these codes was their ultimate purpose. They were not designed to help the Negro through the admittedly difficult transition from the status of slave to that of a responsible freeman. They were not intended to prepare him for a constructive role in the social, political, and economic life of the South. Few believed that such a role was possible. Rather, the purpose of the Black Codes was to keep the Negro, as long as possible, exactly what he was: a propertyless rural laborer under strict controls, without political rights, and with inferior legal rights. As Schurz quite accurately explained them, they were "a striking embodiment of the idea that although the former owner has lost his individual right of property in the former slave, 'the blacks at large belong to the whites at large.'" To put it bluntly, the Black Codes placed the Negro in a kind of twilight zone between slavery and freedom.

Among their numerous provisions, the codes legalized Negro marriages, permitted Negroes to hold and dispose of property, to sue and be sued. They also took steps toward the establishment of racial segregation in public places. They prohibited interracial marriages, prohibited Negroes from serving on juries or testifying against white men, and re-enacted many of the criminal provisions of the prewar slave codes. In the economic sphere, South Carolina prohibited Negroes from entering any employment except agricultural labor without a special license; Mississippi would not permit them to buy or rent farm land; these states and others provided that Negroes found without lawful employment were to be arrested as vagrants and auctioned off or hired to landholders who would pay their fines. Louisiana required all Negro agricultural laborers to make contracts with landholders during the first ten days of January; once made, the contracts were binding for the year. Thereafter the Negroes were not permitted to leave their places of employment without permission. A Negro who refused to labor for his employer was to be arrested and put to forced labor on public works without compensation until he agreed to go back to his job.

This return to a modified form of involuntary servitude caused Negroes, at numerous meetings, to call on Congress for protection. The *Chicago Tribune* warned Mississippi that the North would convert her "into a frog pond" before permitting slavery to be re-established. A minority of cautious Southerners had advised against the Black Codes—a Mississippian was "amazed at such stupidity." Eventually military officers suspended much of the Mississippi code and threw out the entire South Carolina code.

But President Johnson had acquiesced in the Black Codes without a murmur. On December 18, 1865, in a special message to the Senate, he made an oblique reference to them as "measures . . . to confer upon freedmen the privileges which are essential to their comfort, protection, and security." Problems, he added, "are naturally to be expected from the great and sudden change in the relations between the two races; but systems are gradually developing themselves under which the freedman will receive the protection to which he is justly entitled, and, by means of his labor, make himself a useful and independent member of the community in which he has a home."

As Congress began to take a hand, Johnson's control over the process of Reconstruction came to an end. For him one can scarcely imagine an end more disastrous. A program that began with the dream of a new day for the Southern yeomanry terminated with the landlords fashioning a new kind of bondage for their black laborers, and with Johnson their witting or unwitting ally. Such a settlement the Radical Republicans refused to accept; and before Congress had finished, it had armed the federal government with power to make Negro emancipation more than nominal. If this could have been accomplished in any other way, the alternative never appeared during the era of Reconstruction.

And yet, a persistent historical tradition holds that the Radical Republicans were responsible for the tragic form that Southern race relations took in the late nineteenth and early twentieth centuries. According to this tradition, everything was working smoothly—the two races were making a harmonious adjustment—under Johnson's wise program, until the radicals intervened. The truth is that, before the radical program began, the Johnson governments themselves had introduced the whole pattern of disenfranchisement, discrimination, and segregation into the postwar South. And there, quite possibly, matters might still stand, had Andrew Johnson had his way.

✪

Johnson and the Negro

No uncertainty about the President caused more concern among Republicans, particularly those of the Eastern states, than his attitude toward the freedmen. As a people, Americans have always been alert to motives and intent behind matters judged of moral consequence; and both Johnson's contemporaries and historians have passed judgment upon his attitude toward the Negro. This raises a question which admits of no easy answer.

The December [1865] message . . . was generally received as reassuring. Sharp and bitter dissent, however, came from Wendell Phillips' *National Anti-Slavery Standard;* it found the tone of the President toward the freedmen "utterly repulsive."[1] The *Liberator,* William Lloyd Garrison's venerable weekly, also challenged Johnson's sincerity. Fair words, according to the *Liberator,* must be interpreted by acts; and it saw the President as working to place the governments of the Southern states in the hands of those already re-enacting Black Codes.[2] A more moderate and friendly challenge to the President, but one that, for this very reason, must have been the more disconcerting to its readers, was voiced by the Brooklyn *Daily Union.*[3]

[1] *National Anti-Slavery Standard,* December 9, 1865, clippings on Annual Message (Scrapbook, Johnson Mss.).
[2] *Liberator,* December 15, 1865 (*ibid.*).
[3] Brooklyn *Daily Union,* December 8, 1865 (*ibid.*).

Reprinted with permission from *Politics, Principle, and Prejudice, 1865–1866* by LaWanda Cox and John H. Cox (New York: Free Press of Glencoe, 1963), pp. 151–171.

If the nation is bound to defend the rights of the blacks, why has not the President incorporated such a defence in the conditions of re-admission? If justice only is the thing which can save us from suffer-ing in the solution of the negro problem, why has the President quietly ignored justice just at the point where it becomes most abso-lutely essential that it should be observed? Just when the President proposes to establish each State securely and impregnably behind the banners of resumed Statehood, why does he leave the negro helpless?

President Johnson himself told a delegation of Negroes in February, 1866, that the "feelings of my own heart" had been "for the colored man"; that he had opposed slavery, first, because it had been a great monopoly that enabled an aristocracy to derive great profits and rule with an iron hand and, secondly, because of the abstract principle of slavery. But as a political leader in prewar Tennessee, Andrew Johnson, though an antagonist of the slave-holding aristocracy, had not been known as an opponent of slavery. A kindly master to the slaves of his household, he had on occasion spoken harsh words in respect to the Negro. It is clear that he regarded the whites as a race superior to the blacks, and that he harbored a deep antagonism to Northern abolitionism.[4] Shortly after Johnson took office as President, the antislavery *New York Tribune* pointed out that the new chief executive would not be open to charges of "nigger-worship" since he had "always till now voted and acted as though Blacks had no rights which Whites are bound to respect."[5] Although the tone of the *Tribune's* com-ment was friendly, its characterization may not have been alto-gether fair. During his wartime Governorship of Tennessee, John-son pledged to the Negro populace that he would be their "Moses"; he recognized that the war would kill slavery, welcomed its passing as the end of a disturbing element in the body politic, and loyally strove to implement Lincoln's desire that Tennessee

[4] Lloyd P. Stryker, *Andrew Johnson: A Study in Courage* (New York, 1936), Chap. 5; Robert W. Winston, *Andrew Johnson, Plebeian and Patriot* (New York, 1928), pp. 134, 142, 145, 266. See also Leroy P. Graf, "Andrew Johnson and the Coming of the War," *Tennessee Historical Quarterly,* XIX (September 1960), 215.

[5] *New York Tribune,* April 22, 1865.

should officially bury the institution.[6] He did not, however, attempt to prevent the exclusion of Negroes "not only from the ballot box, but also from the witness-box," a fact that the Democratic press later delighted in citing.[7]

In October, 1865, President Johnson went far toward repudiating the view associated with the Blairs and the Democracy, and one most obnoxious to Republican friends of the Negro, namely that "this is a white man's country." "This is your country as well as anybody else's country," he told a regiment of Negro soldiers who had gathered to pay him tribute. "This country is founded upon the principle of equality. . . . He that is meritorious and virtuous, intellectual and well informed, must stand highest, without regard to color."[8] Private letters to the President, however, strongly suggest that Johnson's views were close to those of the Democracy. A Tennessee friend remembered well "your remark, and that was, Gorham, I am for a *White* Man's Government in America."[9] Harvey Watterson, Johnson's trusted representative in the South, commended a general for command in North Carolina. "Like yourself, too, he is for a white man's government, and in favor of free white citizens controlling this country."[10] There is grave doubt that Johnson's private views were ever completely emancipated from his heritage of Southern racial attitudes. His private secretary, in 1868, noted in his shorthand diary that "the President has at times exhibited a morbid distress and feeling against the negroes." He made note of the President's querulous demand, on seeing a half dozen Negroes at work about the White House grounds, whether "all the white men had been discharged." The secretary consoled the President with the comment that "the

[6] Nashville speech, June 9, 1864, McPherson, *Political Manual for 1866*, p. 46 n.; *Collected Works of Abraham Lincoln*, VIII, pp. 216–217; Milton Lomask, *Andrew Johnson: President on Trial* (New York, 1960), pp. 16–17, 24–26; George F. Milton, *The Age of Hate: Andrew Johnson and the Radicals* (New York, 1930), pp. 136–137.

[7] *New York World*, September 18, 1865.

[8] McPherson, pp. 50–51.

[9] "Gorham" to Johnson, June 3, 1865 (Johnson Mss.).

[10] Watterson to Johnson, June 20, 1865 (*ibid.*).

evident discrimination made here on behalf of the negroes, was sufficient to excite the disgust of all reflecting men."[11]

Johnson's public statements, even that to the Negro soldiers quoted above, seemed to carry an implication that colonization or separate Negro communities might well prove the ultimate solution of the Negro problem. The great question, Johnson told the colored regiment, is whether "this race can be incorporated and mixed with the people of the United States—to make a harmonious and permanent ingredient in the population. . . . Let us make the experiment, and make it in good faith. . . . If we have to become a separate and distinct people (although I trust that the system can be made to work harmoniously) . . . Providence . . . will point out the way, and the mode, and the manner by which these people are to be separated."[12] The December message also spoke of an "experiment in good faith" and cautioned against hasty assumptions that the two races could not live side by side. Some weeks later the President spoke with great emphasis to a Negro delegation of the mutual enmity between "the colored man and the non-slaveholders" and urged the Negro leaders, who had come with a plea for suffrage, to tell their people that they could "live and advance in civilization to better advantage elsewhere than crowded right down there in the South."[13] Although the Thirty-eighth Congress had attempted to put an end to colonization schemes, James Mitchell, who had been appointed Commissioner of Emigration by Lincoln in 1862, clung to his office. In the fall of 1865, Mitchell was actively canvassing political centers from New York to Wisconsin for support of colonization. He reported to President Johnson that he had found many men "anxious to go with us on the question of the separation of the White and Black races."[14] Men close to the President desired

[11] Entry of April 9, 1868, transcript of Moore's diary (*ibid.*).

[12] McPherson, p. 51; see also report of Johnson's interview with colored clergymen, *New York Herald,* May 12, 1865.

[13] McPherson, p. 55.

[14] Mitchell to Johnson, November 21, 1865 (Johnson Mss.); see also Mitchell to Seward, September 14, 1865, and his printed pamphlet *Brief on Emigration and Colonization and Report in Answer to a Resolution of the Senate* (Washington, 1865), both in Seward Mss.

separation as the solution of the Negro problem, and Johnson himself may have viewed it with greater favor than his public comment indicated.[15]

Even on the question of Negro suffrage, where Johnson's position seems clearer than on most questions relating to the freedmen, there was room for uncertainty and contradiction. Before his proclamation of May 29, 1865, establishing a provisional government for North Carolina, he considered the possibility of imposing Negro suffrage upon the rebellious states with enough sympathy to kindle the hopes of men committed to this end. Once this first step toward restoration was followed in mid-June by a similar government for Mississippi without extending the vote to any portion of the Negro people, Johnson's policy was generally recognized as based upon the position that the question of suffrage pertained exclusively to the states. There was a lively difference of opinion, however, as to whether or not the President approved and desired extension of the suffrage to Negroes by state action. In a June interview with a white delegation from South Carolina, Johnson indicated that he feared the late slaveholders would control the Negro vote, if suffrage were granted, and use it against the poorer white men of the South.[16] A few days later Secretary Welles, while defending the administration's hands-off policy in respect to state suffrage, reassured Charles Sumner that there was not "on the part of the President or his advisers any opposition to most liberal extensions of the elective franchises."[17]

In the battle over Negro suffrage waged in Connecticut during the fall of 1865, the Democracy—as we have seen—identified their opposition with the President's cause. Johnson's Connecticut Secretary of Navy, Gideon Welles, was reported in the local press as having expressed without hesitation "his opinion as decidedly opposed to negro suffrage," and this was used as evidence that "President Johnson is opposed to negro suffrage, as he is opposed to forcing negro voting upon the South." Connecticut Republicans,

[15] Compare Howard K. Beale, *The Critical Year: A Study of Andrew Johnson and Reconstruction* (New York, 1930), pp. 180–181.

[16] Report of interview, *New York Herald*, June 25, 1865.

[17] Welles to Sumner, June 30, 1865, (Welles Mss. Library of Congress).

who were fighting hard for the liberalizing amendment to their state constitution, were alarmed at this damaging blow to the cause and appealed to Welles for a public contradiction. Welles declined to make a statement for publication but authorized a denial that he had "expressed any opinion on the subject of the constitutional amendment now pending."[18]

Just as the voters of Connecticut were deciding the issue with the Democrats and against the Republicans, a dedicated but conciliatory antislavery man from neighboring Massachusetts, George L. Stearns, sought from the President a direct answer to this now politically freighted question. In an interview which he later obtained permission to make public, Stearns heard from the President that were he in Tennessee "I should try to introduce negro suffrage gradually; first those who had served in the army; those who could read and write; and perhaps a property qualification for the others, say $200 or $250. It would not do to let the negro have universal suffrage now; it would breed a war of races."[19] This statement greatly pleased Eastern Republicans. Greeley's *Tribune,* for example, commented that judicious men would "rejoice that Mr. Johnson is willing to use even his indirect and unofficial influence that justice may be done to the blacks of the South." The *World* was not unduly disturbed. If the *Tribune* or anyone else can find satisfaction in Johnson's "private views which he steadily refuses to embody in official action we do not object. Give us his official acts, and you are welcome to his private sentiments."[20]

Much of Johnson's popularity among Southerners rested upon the conviction that the President alone stood between them and the dire fate of Negro suffrage. They relied not only upon his official policy in restricting elections under the provisional governments to

[18] C. D. Warner to Welles, September 20, 1865, including clipping from Hartford *Times* of September 19, 1865; W. A. Croffut to Welles, September 20, 1865; Welles to Warner, September 22, 1865; Welles to Croffut, September 22, 1865 (Welles Mss. Library of Congress).

[19] Interview of October 3, 1865, McPherson, pp. 48–49. This appeared in the press of October 23, 1865.

[20] *New York Tribune,* October 23, 1865; *New York World,* October 24, 1865.

whites but also upon unofficial assurances. Watterson during his stay in North Carolina had let it be known "in the right quarter" that the President would never be driven by "the Chases and Sumners" from the position "that the suffrage question belongs to the States alone."[21] Letters that reached the President made unmistakably clear the Southern aversion to an extension of the suffrage and the gratitude for his stand.[22] Like the *World,* Southerners could pass over Johnson's remarks to Stearns, approving a limited state grant of voting privileges to Negroes, so long as he left the question in their hands. The prediction of an Alabama Unionist proved erroneous; the statement in favor of qualified Negro suffrage, he wrote the President, "is enough for these southern people not only to condemn you while lieving [*sic*]—but will try to blacken your future name and history."[23] The Alabaman was not in error, however, in assuming an overwhelming opposition to Negro voting in the South. In view of this attitude, which was undoubtedly clear to Johnson, the following sentence in his December message appears evasive and misleading:[24]

In my judgment, the freedmen, if they show patience and manly virtues, will sooner obtain a participation in the elective franchise through the States than through the General Government, even if it had power to intervene.

President Johnson's often cited recommendation to the Provisional Governor of Mississippi that the state grant limited suffrage to the Negro requires examination in a larger perspective than it has generally received. The Mississippi convention which met in Jackson on August 14, 1865, was the first such convention to assemble under Johnson's plan of restoration. On August 15, the

[21] Watterson to Johnson, June 27, 1865 (Johnson Mss.).

[22] Letters to Johnson from C. D. McLean, June 29, 1865; Watterson, July 8, 1865; J. E. Brown, July 24, 1865; J. B. Steedman, August 15, 1865; W. Conner, September 13, 1865; also A. G. Mackey to C. Schurz, July 23, 1865; M. C. Johnson to M. Blair, August 21, 1865 (*ibid.*).

[23] J. C. Bradley to Johnson, November 15, 1865 (*ibid.*).

[24] McPherson, p. 6. Note that Mississippi's rejection of the President's recommendation of limited Negro suffrage, discussed below, preceded the December message.

President sent to Governor W. L. Sharkey a telegram urging abolition of slavery in the state constitution and the ratification of the pending Thirteenth Amendment. The telegram continued:[25]

If you could extend the elective franchise to all persons of color who can read the constitution of the United States in English and write their names, and to all persons of color who own real estate valued at not less than two hundred and fifty dollars and pay taxes thereon, you would completely disarm the adversary and set an example the other states will follow.

This you can do with perfect safety. . . . I hope and trust your convention will do this, and as a consequence the Radicals, who are wild upon negro franchise, will be completely foiled in their attempts to keep the Southern States from renewing their relations to the Union by not accepting their Senators and Representatives.

On August 20, Sharkey wired back that the convention would amend the state constitution to abolish slavery, but that the right to testify in court and the right of suffrage would probably be left to the legislature.[26] The President replied that he was "much gratified to hear of your proceedings being so favorable," and that "your convention can adopt the Amendment to the Constitution of the United States or recommend its adoption by the Legislature." He pointed out "the importance of being prompt and circumspect in all that is being done," since the Mississippi proceeding would "set an example that will be followed by all the other States." But not one word in the reply made reference to his previous recommendation for qualified Negro suffrage.[27] Four days later the President sent another telegram of commendation, promising an early removal of federal troops and expressing his belief that if the other Southern states followed Mississippi's example the day of restoration was not distant. Again he omitted any mention of the suffrage issue. Governor Sharkey read this telegram to the legislature, which heard it with satisfaction.[28]

[25] Johnson to Sharkey, August 15, 1865 (Johnson Mss.).

[26] Sharkey to Johnson, August 20, 1865 (ibid.).

[27] Johnson to Sharkey, August 21, 1865 (ibid.).

[28] Johnson to Sharkey, August 25, 1865 (ibid.); New York Herald, August 26, 1865.

The convention soon adjourned, and Sharkey sent the President a report of its actions including its charge to the legislature to enact laws to protect the Negro in his rights of person and property. He continued, "How it will do this I cannot say, possibly it may allow the negro to testify. . . . The right of suffrage I do not think will be extended to them; indeed there is an inclination to limit the right of suffrage with the white man. In regard to the amendment of the Constitution of the United States prohibiting slavery I do not think the State ever will adopt the second article or provision of the amendment." He continued with complaints against the military and the Freedmen's Bureau and concluded by asserting that both he and the people of Mississippi thought they were entitled now to be relieved of martial law and "to be treated as though the rebellion had ended."[29]

In the face of this recalcitrant reaction to his recommendations and the almost peremptory request for complete self-rule, Johnson permitted his congratulatory message to remain without qualification, public or private. He did not, however, completely remand Mississippi to the inclinations of its people. Two weeks after the assembling of the Mississippi legislature Johnson renewed his pressure for ratification of the antislavery amendment in a telegram to Governor Sharkey of November 1, 1865, holding out the inducement that its adoption would "make the way clear for the admission of Senators and Representatives to their seats in the present Congress." Once again he abandoned the recommendation for an extension of the vote to qualified Negroes.[30] On the sixteenth, while a joint committee was considering the amendment, the elected Governor, Benjamin Humphreys, sought additional reassurances. He reported that the legislators appeared willing to permit freedmen to testify in courts if assured the federal troops would be withdrawn, but they feared "that one concession will only lead to others. What assurances can I give on the subject?"[31] In his reply the next day, the President stated:[32]

[29] Sharkey to Johnson, August 28, 1865 (Johnson Mss.).
[30] Johnson to Sharkey, November 1, 1865 (*ibid.*).
[31] Humphreys to Johnson, November 16, 1865 (*ibid.*).
[32] Johnson to Humphreys, November 17, 1865 (*ibid.*).

There can be no other or greater assurance given than has heretofore been on the part of the President. There is no concession required on the part of the people of Mississippi or the Legislature, other than a loyal compliance with the laws and constitution of the United States, and the adoption of such measures giving protection to all freedmen, or freemen, in person and property without regard to color, as will entitle them to resume all their constitutional relations in the Federal Union. . . .

There must be confidence between the Government and the States— while the Government confides in the people—the people must have faith in the Government. This must be mutual and reciprocal, or all that has been done will be thrown away.

While refusing to make a definite commitment in respect to withdrawal of troops and while placing legislation to protect the freedmen under the designation of "concession required," in this same telegram Johnson gave the assurance, quoted earlier, that he was not dictating action but only offering kindly advice. Within ten days, the Mississippi legislature adopted a civil rights act for freedmen so inequitable that the administration had to set aside certain of its provisions. The legislature also accepted the recommendation of its joint committee *not* to ratify the antislavery amendment.[33]

Thus, in the face of Southern hostility and defiance, Johnson completely discarded his Negro suffrage recommendation.[34] He had urged an extension of voting privileges, not as a matter of equity or of personal conviction, but as an expedient to outmaneuver the radicals. Perhaps he felt confident of an early restoration without this concession. He did not repeat the advice of August 15, either to Mississippi or to any other of the Southern states. Greeley's "judicious men" might rejoice at the Stearns's interview

[33] McPherson, pp. 20, 31.

[34] In early September, Johnson had been quoted as recommending Negro suffrage on the basis of literacy to a Louisianan with the argument that "there were not five hundred negroes in Louisiana that can stand this test, but it will be doing justice and will stop northern clamor." A month later, he was reported as telling an Alabaman that "political rights, such as suffrage, sitting on juries, &c are not expected to be conferred on them at this time." Springfield *Republican,* September 9, 1865, October 9, 1865; see also October 17, 1865.

of October 3 and hope that the President would use his "indirect and unofficial influence" for qualified Negro suffrage; but he had already tried and abandoned the effort. In his December message Johnson argued at length the case for state control of suffrage on the basis of history and the Constitution. He did not include the suggestion forwarded by his friend and political adviser, Lewis Campbell, that he recommend an end to suffrage restrictions which deprived of the vote men of any class—"white, black, or mixed"—who possessed virtue, intelligence and patriotism.[35] Most Republican advocates of Negro suffrage accepted Johnson's argument as sincere but took issue with his logic. It is not difficult to understand their view that Johnson had as much right under the Constitution to obtain an extension of suffrage from the rebel states as he had to establish provisional governments, insist that they abolish slavery, ratify the Thirteenth Amendment, and repudiate their acts of secession and war debt. Even the *Herald* had stated that the President undoubtedly had the power in closing up the rebellion to insist upon Negro suffrage but deemed it wiser to leave the matter to the states.[36] The correspondence between Johnson and the Mississippi Governors illustrates the inconsistency and embarrassment in his "advice-not-dictation" posture, as well as the ineffectual character of his endorsement of limited suffrage for the freedmen.

Two other incidents throw some additional light upon Johnson's attitude toward Negro suffrage. On January 18, 1866, the House of Representatives passed by a large majority, though no Democrat voted yea, a bill striking the word "white" from the qualifications for voters in the District of Columbia. A preceding motion would have recommitted the bill with instructions to amend by extending the suffrage only to those who could read the Constitution or had served in the Union forces. These changes would have brought the measure in line with Johnson's position. The Union Republicans split on this motion, but the Democrats to a man

---

[35] Campbell to Johnson, November 16, 1865 (Johnson Mss.).
[36] W. B. Phillips to Johnson, November 24, 1865, with clipping from *Herald* enclosed (*ibid.*).

voted against it, thereby defeating a qualified extension of the suffrage.[37] *The New York Times* accused the Democrats of two aims: to stir up trouble between the Union party and the President, and to facilitate passage of a measure that could be used to agitate the Negro question in their constituencies.[38]

Johnson received word that there were enough votes in the Senate to defeat the bill and was requested to send for the Senators who were "sound," tell them his views and unite with them for action.[39] His response is not a matter of record, but on January 28 he had an interview with his loyal Republican supporter, Senator Dixon of Connecticut, which was at once made public. Here he "expressed the opinion that the agitation of the negro franchise question in the District of Columbia at this time was the mere entering-wedge to the agitation of the question throughout the States, and was ill-timed, uncalled for, and calculated to do great harm." The interview dealt principally with his position in respect to amending the Constitution, a matter then engaging the urgent attention of the Joint Committee on Reconstruction and of Congress. Johnson held that any amendment at the time was of dubious propriety, would tend to diminish respect for the Constitution, and was quite unnecessary. However, if any were to be made, he knew of none better than the simple proposition that direct taxation be based upon the value of property and representation be based upon the number of voters. Such an amendment, he thought, "would remove from Congress all issues in reference to the political equality of the races" and leave to the states the absolute determination of "qualifications of their own voters with regard to color."[40] Johnson's reluctant approval for an amendment that would give to the South a choice between lessened representation and an extension of suffrage to Negroes represented the farthest limit of his support for a measure of Negro suffrage. In respect to the substance of the District of Columbia bill he avoided approval or disapproval, or any suggestion for its modification.

[37] McPherson, pp. 114–115.
[38] *The New York Times,* January 22, 1866.
[39] G. C. Smith to Johnson, January 20, 1866 (Johnson Mss.).
[40] McPherson, pp. 51–52.

An amendment of the nature Johnson haltingly endorsed at the end of January, 1866, by then had no chance of obtaining Congressional approval. The proposal that representation be based upon voters had been made by Robert Schenck, Representative from Ohio, at the opening of Congress; it had been approved by Thaddeus Stevens and the Joint Committee on Reconstruction, but it had run into opposition from New Englanders. Their objection was that this formula would result in an inequitable decrease of representation for their section. Due to westward emigration New England's population, the current basis of apportionment, had a disproportionate number of women and children to men; also, the number of voters in the New England states was relatively less than in other states because of educational requirements for voting. New England objections had led to a revision of the proposed amendment retaining population as the basis of representation but providing a reduction wherever the franchise was denied on the basis of race.[41] The President's endorsement of the original proposal could have no practical effect except to embarrass the New England radicals. A Johnson political strategist was urging in March that a vote be pressed on the representation-based-on-voters amendment. New England would reject it, and thereby "show the country that New England selfishness is not willing to accept any basis of representation that diminishes her political power"—this would "shut their mouths."[42]

Ten days after the interview with Senator Dixon, the President received a delegation of Negroes that included Frederick Douglass, who came to express the hope that their people would be fully enfranchised. In reply, Johnson spoke with emotion of the scorn which he insisted the slave had held for the poor white man and was the basis for a continuing enmity between Negro and nonslaveholder. The colored man had gained much as the result of the rebellion, he said, the poor white had lost a great deal; on what principle of justice could they be "placed in a condition different

---

[41] Kendrick, *Journal of the Joint Committee on Reconstruction,* pp. 41, 51, 199; Joseph B. James, *The Framing of the Fourteenth Amendment* (Urbana, 1956), pp. 37, 46, 60.

[42] R. P. L. Baber to Johnson, March 29, 1866 (Johnson Mss.).

from what they were before?" It would commence a war of races; to force universal suffrage without the consent of the community would deny the "first great principle of the right of the people to govern themselves." Without recognizing any inconsistency in his devotion to the principle of government by consent of the governed, Johnson claimed for white Southerners the right to determine whether or not the Negro should vote. He made no allusion to the desirability of a beginning through a qualified franchise.[43]

The interview buried the hopes of those who still looked to the President for unofficial support in breaching the race barrier against Negro suffrage. It delighted many a believer in white supremacy. "I cannot forbear to express to you the great pleasure I felt on reading your remarks to the colored man," wrote an old friend. He continued:[44]

The principles you enunciated are the same expressed to me in a conversation I had with you last Autumn, and in which I fully agreed with you. You said to me then that every one would, and *must* admit that the white race was superior to the black, and that while we ought to do our best to bring them [the blacks] up to our present level, that in doing so we should, at the same time raise our own intellectual status so that the relative position of the two races would be the same. . . .

I am astonished, and more than astonished, at the persistency with which the radical idea of placing negroes on an equality with whites, *in every particular,* is pressed in Congress. . . . Until the tide of fanaticism, which is now in full flood, shall turn, as it must, unless sanity has departed from the people, we must place our trust in you to keep us safe "from the pestilence that walketh in darkness, and the destruction that wasteth at noon-day."

Men of like views might have looked with even greater confidence to the President as the bulwark against Negro "equality" had they been privy to Johnson's private reactions to the delegation headed by Douglass. According to one of the President's private secretaries who was present at the occasion, on the departure of the "darky delegation" the President "uttered the following terse Saxon: 'Those d——d sons of b——s thought they had me in a

---

[43] McPherson, pp. 52–55.
[44] R. R. French to Johnson, February 8, 1866 (Johnson Mss.).

trap! I know that d——d Douglass; he's just like any nigger, and he would sooner cut a white man's throat than not.' "[45]

Republican opinion was far from united in respect to Negro suffrage, but it was substantially agreed that the freedmen should enjoy all other rights and privileges pertaining to free men and citizens. On the matter of these civil rights, Johnson's pre-veto record seemed to indicate that here he stood squarely with Northern liberal opinion. There were grave apprehensions, however, that Presidential authority might prove inadequate to obtain from the South that measure of justice which was considered the freedman's due, or at least, obtain it in time to effect speedy restoration. During the meeting of the Mississippi convention in August, 1865, *The New York Times,* which enjoyed an unofficial status as spokesman for the administration, gave warning in an editorial entitled "The Real Question as to the Future Political Status of the Negro." The "real question" was not whether the freedman should vote but whether he should be protected against injustice and oppression. The North would be watching to see that the convention did not proceed "upon the principle that the colored race are to be kept in a state of subordination, and made the subject of peculiar restraints and exactions." This would be "the great index" to whether or not restoration would soon be effected. "The government, anxious as it is to hasten this end, can make no concession here."[46] The *Times* was not happy with the work of the convention though it acknowledged that Northern doubts might be settled if the Mississippi legislature faithfully fulfilled the duties assigned it by the convention. But why, it asked, was so important a matter left to the faithfulness or unfaithfulness of legislators?[47]

Ever loyal to the President, and adhering to his position as they saw it, the editorial staff of the *Times* succinctly posed the difference that divided the President and the Republican radicals. "President Johnson founds all his practical policy upon the pre-

[45] P. Ripley to Marble, February 8, 1866 (Marble Mss.).
[46] *The New York Times,* August 19, 1865; see also August 18, 1865, August 26, 1865.
[47] *Ibid.,* August 29, 1865.

sumption that the South is fit to be trusted. His radical opponents found theirs upon the presumption that the South is unfit to be trusted." Though the *Times* agreed with the President, there was yet a doubt and a threat in its comment. "When the contrary is shown, then and not until then, will the time come for a different policy."[48] The *Times* hoped for speedy reinstatement of the Southern states, but recognized that in Congress various questions would first be considered, particularly whether more complete securities should not be required for the protection of the rights of the freedmen.[49] As political activity accelerated under Johnson's plan of conventions, elections, and legislative action, the *Times* hoped for a "clean sweep of the old black codes, and giving to the blacks substantially the same equality with the white men before the law, that prevails in the Northern states." No solid ground was left for opposition to admission of the formerly rebellious states, it asserted, save assurance that once reinstated in all their old municipal powers these would not be used to harm the freedmen; on this the government must find some kind of security in advance of readmission. The Southern people would not be put in unlimited control of the freedmen until they had given proof that they would befriend and not injure him. As of mid-October, "no such proof has yet been given."[50]

The news from Mississippi in October and November was not reassuring. Where the question of Negro testimony had entered the local canvass for the legislature, the nonadmission candidates had won the elections. The defeat by a decided majority of a Negro testimony bill after the legislature convened was hailed by a local paper as a "Glorious Result," an honor to the legislators who had withstood "home threats" and "outside influences." "They have been importuned, threatened, reasoned with and implored to admit the negro to equality in our judicial tribunals, but the *representatives of the people* have frowned upon the proposition, and will never permit the slave of yesterday to confront his former master

[48] *Ibid.*, September 14, 1865.
[49] *Ibid.*, September 21, 1865.
[50] *Ibid.*, October 3, 13, 15, 1865.

in the witness-box."[51] Henry J. Raymond, the *Times* editor, was telling cheering Republicans in mid-October that the President's plan included such provision in Southern constitutions and laws "as shall put all their citizens upon an equality before the law."[52] Editorially, the *Times* reinforced the point by stating that President Johnson had given "the power and influence of his position without reserve" to securing for the freedmen "all the great civil safeguards of person and property. . . . They have made themselves felt in no small measure through his Provisional Governors and through the Freedmen's Bureau; and the effects will be made palpable to all in the favorable enactments for the freedmen, in the legislatures of the late rebel states, soon to assemble."[53] To underscore the differences between the Democracy and the President, the *Times* pointed out that the former held that for restoration the Southern states had only to reorganize "in accordance with their own will" while the President insisted that full rights were not restored until certain conditions had been met including "effective laws . . . for the protection of the natural rights of the freedmen."[54] In a rejoinder to the Louisville *Journal,* which had criticized Northerners for meddling with the status of the freedmen, the *Times* warned that the South could disarm the "fanatics" by taking measures to secure the Negroes in their civil rights, to educate them, and to prepare them for responsible duties. *"If the South will not do this, the nation* MUST. *It cannot be left undone."* The influential Louisville *Journal* would do better to stimulate the

[51] Jackson *Daily News,* November 14, 1865, clipping enclosed in R. S. Donaldson to J. W. Weber, November 17, 1865 (Johnson Mss.); *The New York Times,* October 5, 8, 11, 1865. After the President's telegrams of November 17, 1865, one to elected Governor Humphreys and the other to Provisional Governor Sharkey, expressly mentioning Negro testimony, the Mississippi legislature did yield a circumscribed right of testimony but only as part of a general act that included harsh and discriminating provisions against the Negro in respect to the ownership and leasing of lands and the enforcement of labor contracts. For the act, see McPherson, p. 31.

[52] Speech of Raymond reported in *The New York Times,* October 15, 1865.

[53] *The New York Times,* October 23, 1865.

[54] *Ibid.,* November 6, 1865.

Southern people to their duty rather than waste its energies in denouncing Northerners.[55]

The New York Democratic convention, while embracing the President and his policy, denounced any attempt by prolonging military rule or denying representation to coerce the Southern states "to adopt negro equality or negro suffrage" as tending to subvert the principles of government and the liberties of the people.[56] However, the Democracy's chief organ, the *World*, recognized as an integral part of Johnson's program "entire equality before the law" for the emancipated slaves. It even urged upon the South that it give Negroes the right to testify in court, and pointed with pleasure to favorable reaction to its suggestion in Southern and Northern Democratic newspapers. "In this fact is a conclusive refutation of the charge falsely made against the Democratic party that they are willing to exclude negro freedmen from that justice and *equality before the law* which is their right. . . . We believe that we express the views of President Johnson, as we know that we do the views of the great mass of the Democratic party of the North, in saying that this *equality before the law* ought not to be, and cannot prudently be, denied to negro freedmen."[57] The *Herald* reinforced this view of the President's position. "It is the simple policy of recognizing the emancipated blacks as *citizens,* entitled without delay to all the rights and protection of other citizens in the civil courts." An editorial subtitled "What the Southern States Have to Do" listed civil rights for Negroes along with the requirements of abolishing slavery, ratifying the Thirteenth Amendment, repudiating ordinances of secession, and recognizing an obligation to share the national debt. The grant of limited suffrage was placed in a separate category, not a "must," but a "wise" concession.[58]

Thus there was substantial evidence of Johnson's intentions: the agreement of the *Times,* the *World,* and the *Herald;* the President's

[55] *Ibid.,* November 7, 1865, November 8, 1865.
[56] *New York Herald,* September 8, 1865.
[57] Italics added. *New York World,* September 21, 1865, October 21, 1865.
[58] Italics added. *New York Herald,* October 12, 15, 31, 1865.

public telegram to Governor Humphreys, quoted earlier, asserting that the Mississippi legislature must adopt measures to protect freedmen without regard to color; the enforcement of equal rights by the Freedmen's Bureau under the authority of the President. Republicans generally could, and did, credit him with the best intentions in respect to the freedman's civil status. Yet the situation in the South generally, not just in Mississippi, was disturbing. The Southern states, under great pressure, were meeting the President's conditions reluctantly and partially. The President was quoted as saying that the "foolish Georgians were hindering him in the carrying out of his plans a good deal more than the worst of the northern radicals." The cruel part, continued the reporter, is that this occurs just when the President and his friends have been inculcating the idea of nonintervention in the South.[59] Johnson's orders to Provisional Governors to retain their positions even after elected Governors were ready to take over authority were interpreted as a stern Presidential answer to Southern obstinacy.[60] Contrary to the President's known wishes, Southern voters were choosing men to represent them at home and in Congress who had held leadership in the rebellion. Reports abounded that with the liberal grant of pardons and the apparently official standing of the theory that the states were entitled to full rights within the Union, the earlier submissive mood of Southerners was turning to one of thinly disguised defiance. Private letters to the President, Secretary Seward, and Secretary Welles spoke with concern of this changing temper of "obstinancy and bitterness" in the South.[61] The Provi-

---

[59] Springfield *Republican,* November 3, 1865; see also B. C. Truman to W. C. Browning (of the President's staff), November 9, 1865 (Johnson Mss.).

[60] Springfield *Republican,* November 15, 1865, November 18, 1865.

[61] W. W. Boyce to F. P. Blair, October 17, 1865, letters to Johnson from J. C. Bradley, October 13, 1865, November 15, 1865, A. H. Wilson, October 25, 1865, H. Kennedy, November 23, 1865, R. J. Powell, November 26, 1865, F. G. Clark, December 4, 1865, and A. S. Wallace to W. H. Seward, December 25, 1865 (Johnson Mss.); letters to Seward from M. G. Dobbins, November 11, 1865, B. J. Sanford, November 23, 1865, P. Moller, n.d., received November 29, 1865, I. J. Stiles, December 9, 1865, T. Cottman,

sional Governors for North Carolina and Georgia had in despera-
tion appealed to the President for support in obtaining repudiation
of the war debts and general acquiescence in the administration's
program. Johnson had replied with strong telegrams that were used
with effect upon lawmakers.[62] Florida had ratified the amendment
only after a pointed dispatch sent by Secretary Seward on behalf of
the President.[63] Even with open Presidential pressure, South
Carolina had refused to repudiate the debt and Mississippi to ratify
the amendment. Florida and Georgia had balked at declaring the
ordinances of secession "null and void," either "repealing" or
"annulling" them instead.

Resistance to giving the freedmen equal treatment under state
laws was even greater. Some states reluctantly allowed Negroes to
testify in civil courts in order to be free of the jurisdiction of
Freedmen's Bureau courts; but even where this was done under
administrative agreement, lawmakers hesitated to act because of
an overwhelmingly hostile public sentiment against receiving Negro testimony.[64] In the face of this reaction, and despite the sharp
pressure in the case of Mississippi and more discreet pressures
upon other states, certain of Johnson's reactions to the issue of
civil rights, though not publicized at the time, were ominous. In
Alabama both Provisional Governor Lewis E. Parsons and the
Freedmen's Bureau administrator, Wager Swayne, were laboring
to obtain from the convention an organic law to permit Negro

December 11, 1865, A. Dockery to R. I. Powell [?], November 13, 1865,
Seward to Dobbins, November 21, 1865, Seward to Cottman, December 11,
1865 (Seward Mss.); M. Howard to Welles, November 13, 1865, December
2, 1865, December 16, 1865 (Welles Mss. Library of Congress).

[62] W. W. Holden to Johnson, October 17, 1865, Johnson to Holden,
October 18, 1865, R. J. Powell to Johnson, November 26, 1865, Johnson to
Holden, November 27, 1865 (North Carolina); James Johnson to Johnson,
October 27, 1865, Johnson to James Johnson, October 28, 1865 (Georgia);
O. P. Morton to Johnson, October 31, 1865, Johnson to W. L. Sharkey,
November 1, 1865 (Mississippi); Johnson to B. J. Perry, October 28, 1865,
October 31, 1865 (South Carolina); draft telegram with eleven signatures,
to L. E. Parsons and B. Fitzpatrick, September 19, 1865 (Alabama);
Johnson Mss.

[63] Seward to W. Marvin, November 20, 1865 (Seward Mss.).

[64] George R. Bentley, *History of the Freedmen's Bureau* (Philadelphia,
1955), pp. 66–67.

testimony.[65] Governor Parsons reported difficulty to the President in mid-September and asked to be informed "by telegraph immediately, if you regard it indispensible [*sic*] to the interests of the people of Alabama that such a clause should be inserted."[66] No word came from the President. The convention merely enjoined the legislature to pass laws to protect the freedmen. Governor Parsons appealed again to the President. The important question "was and is whether it is necessary to declare in the Constitution that 'no distinction should be made on account of color, as to the competency of witnesses in this state.' There could be no room for cavil if that had been done. . . . But the individual members of Convention, some of them, were afraid of consequences to themselves if they put it in the Constitution. If it had been done the fight [for restoration] would then have to be made on the precise line where I understand you to have placed it—viz—the right of the people of these states to declare who shall vote. . . . I beg to assure you that Alabama approves and will in good faith do all things necessary to sustain your policy with regard to her."[67] The Alabama convention remained in session for another week, but no answer to Governor Parsons' appeal arrived from the President. After the convention's adjournment, Johnson sent a brief telegram commending its proceedings as having "met the highest expectations of all who desire the restoration of the Union. All seems now to be working well, and will result as I believe in a decided success."[68]

From Tennessee also came requests, both unofficially in October and officially in November, that the President send a statement of his views on the subject of Negroes testifying in the courts.

[65] Swayne to O. O. Howard, September 28, 1865, October 2, 1865; Howard to Swayne, October 19, 1865 (Records of the Bureau of Refugees, Freedmen, and Abandoned Lands, War Records Office, National Archives).

[66] Parsons to Johnson, September 13, 1865 (Johnson Mss.).

[67] Parsons to Johnson, September 23, 1865; see also Parsons to Johnson, September 28, 1865 (*ibid.*). From Watterson, who was on hand lobbying with convention leaders, there came word that they were ready to do anything believed to be indispensable for restoration; Watterson made no mention of freedmen's rights. Watterson to Johnson, September 26, 1865 (*ibid.*).

[68] Johnson to Parsons, October 3, 1865 (*ibid.*).

It *"would save infinite trouble,"* so great is "the enthusiasm you have kindled among the people."[69] Johnson finally replied on December 9. He would have answered sooner, he said, but thought his message which "would indicate my views, upon the subject of negro testimony, in all cases where they are parties, would be conclusive. It is to be regretted that our Legislature failed to make some advance at its present session upon this question."[70] Two points in connection with this reply are of special interest: first, the December message made no specific mention of Negro testimony; secondly, Johnson's formula as to the right of Negroes to testify where "they are parties" was much less comprehensive than Governor Parsons' version that "no distinction shall be made on account of color."

Johnson had made specific reference to Negro testimony in an interview granted to a distinguished white delegation from South Carolina October 13, 1865. The statement was reported as follows:[71]

The President thought many of the evils would disappear if they inaugurated the right system. Pass laws protecting the colored man in his person and property and he can collect his debts. He knew how it was in the South. The question when first presented of putting a colored man in the witness stand made them shrug their shoulders. But the colored man's testimony was to be taken for what it was worth by those who examined him and the jury who hear it. Those coming out of slavery cannot do without work. . . . They ought to understand that liberty means simply the right to work and enjoy the products of labor, and that the laws protect them. That being done, and when we come to the period to feel that men must work or starve the country will be prepared to receive a system applicable to both white and black. . . . But get the public mind right and you can treat both alike. Let us get the general principles and the details and collaterals will follow.

Johnson's advice is quoted above at some length, for this statement, like the December message, invited favorable reaction from

[69] J. [?] P. Pryor to Johnson, October 10, 1865, A. J. Fletcher to Johnson, November 20, 1865 (*ibid.*).

[70] Johnson to A. J. Fletcher, December 9, 1865 (*ibid.*).

[71] Reported in *New York Herald*, October 14, 1865.

men of fundamentally differing convictions. Republicans could seize with satisfaction upon the idea of "treating both alike"; Southerners could read into the reference to taking testimony "for what it was worth" an invitation to concede the form without the substance of equality before the law. After bitter battles, Southern legislators, during the period of Johnson's control over the Reconstruction process, conceded to the Negro the right to testify. They limited this, however, to cases in which he was a party and denied to the freedmen—Tennessee made the denial a specific proviso of its testimony bill—the right to sit as jurors.[72] Efforts made in the summer and fall of 1865 by Freedmen's Bureau officers to implement the President's desire to remand jurisdiction over Negroes to civil courts resulted, in a number of instances, in local courts permitting Negro testimony.[73] The results of local justice, however, did not provide substantive protection for the freedmen.[74]

Even more ominous for the future of the freedmen, and for future relations between Johnson and the Republican majority as well, was the concession made by Secretary Seward in the President's name in respect to the Thirteenth Amendment. Southern states were willing to recognize that slavery was dead, but they were not willing to ratify a constitutional provision that gave to Congress the power of enforcement. The fear was that under this authority Congress would pass legislation affecting the status of freedmen in the Southern states. Considerable opinion in and out of Congress held that the amendment gave just such power to

[72] Copy of law of January 25, 1866, with endorsement, C. B. Fisk to O. O. Howard; see also Fisk to Howard, December 19, 1865 (Freedmen's Bureau Records).

[73] Howard to W. W. Holden (O.O. Howard Mss. Bowdoin College Library); Howard to Assistant Commissioners, September 6, 1865; Howard to C. B. Fisk, September 9, 1865; Howard to B. J. Perry, October 21, 1865; W. Swayne to L. E. Parsons, July 29, 1865; Swayne to Howard, August 4, 7, 14, 28, 1865, September 29, 1865; W. L. Sharkey to S. Thomas, September 18, 1865; Thomas to Howard, September 21, 22, 23, 29, 1865, November 13, 1865; Thomas to T. J. Wood, November 23, 1865; F. H. Peirpoint to O. Brown, October 7, 1865 (Freedmen's Bureau Records).

[74] W. Swayne to Howard, November 28, 1865; B. K. Johnston to E. Bamberger, with endorsement of R. S. Donaldson, November 16, 1865; S. Thomas to Howard, November 21, 1865, December 13, 1865; F. D. Sewall report of inspection, April 5, 1866 (*ibid.*); Bentley, pp. 67–68.

protect the rights of Negroes as free men. Even the *Herald* had stated editorially that the amendment "in giving to Congress the 'necessary legislation' to carry the abolition of slavery into effect, gives to Congress some discretionary power touching the late slave codes of the State concerned."[75] Yet in a message to Provisional Governor B. J. Perry of South Carolina, November 6, 1865, Secretary Seward stated: "The objection you mention to the last clause of the constitutional amendment is regarded as querulous and unreasonable, because that clause is really restraining in its effect, instead of enlarging the powers of Congress."[76] South Carolina then ratified the amendment with the following qualification:[77]

That any attempt by Congress toward legislating upon the political status of former slaves, *or their civil relations,* would be contrary to the Constitution of the United States as it now is, or as it would be altered by the proposed amendment, in conflict with the policy of the President, declared in his amnesty proclamation, and with the restoration of that harmony upon which depend the vital interests of the American Union.

Alabama and Florida subsequently accepted the amendment with the proviso that it did not confer upon Congress power "to legislate upon the political status of the freedmen in this State." Mississippi's consent was finally granted contingent upon qualifications even more extended than those of South Carolina. They included the explicit statement that the second section "shall not be construed as a grant of power to Congress to legislate in regard to the freedmen of this state."[78]

Clearly the Southern states were determined to obtain full

[75] *New York Herald,* October 15, 1866. See also Governor O. O. Morton's message, in W. H. Schlater (of the President's staff) to Johnson, November 12, 1865 (Johnson Mss.) and Lyman Trumbull as reported in *The New York Times,* December 20, 1865.

[76] McPherson, p. 23; for newspaper controversy over Seward's interpretation see *New York Tribune,* November 17, 1865, *New York World,* November 18, 1865.

[77] Italics added. McPherson, p. 23.

[78] *Ibid.,* pp. 21, 25; *The New York Times,* December 17, 1865. Cf. Howard D. Hamilton, *Legislative and Judicial History of the Thirteenth Amendment* (Ph.D. Dissertation, University of Illinois, University Microfilms, Ann Arbor, Michigan, 1950), pp. 55–57.

control over the freedmen. In some instances there was open avowal of the intent, once restoration was complete, to repeal civil rights that had been granted under pressure and return the Negro to "his place."[79] Various provisions of the legislation in respect to Negroes under consideration or recently enacted in Mississippi, South Carolina, and other Southern states appeared to be flagrant attempts legally to remand the freedmen to an inferior status. Troubled Republicans found consolation in the President's reported characterization of his policy as an "experiment"; Democrats deprecated or denied the remark and insisted that the President would not be moved from his present policy.[80] The administration gave assurances that it would stand by the freedmen, but it also had been thought to promise early withdrawal of military forces and Freedmen's Bureau jurisdiction in the South.[81] To the confusion and concern that marked the fall and early winter of 1865 was added Seward's curious and limiting interpretation of the enforcement clause of the Thirteenth Amendment.

As Congress began its labors there was much evidence to arouse fears that Southerners were not yet ready to meet the freedman in his new status with justice and without discrimination. The Congressional majority approached the problem with confidence in the President's good intentions. But there were portents, not yet generally recognized, that Johnson's version of "the security of the freedmen in their liberty and in their property" might hold concessions to Southern prejudice that could not be reconciled with the Republican view that Negroes were citizens entitled to equality before the law.

[79] S. Thomas to O. O. Howard, December 13, 1865, M. S. Hopkins to J. Johnson, February 28, 1866 (Freedmen's Bureau Records).

[80] *New York World,* August 28, 1865; *New York Herald,* August 20, 1865.

[81] Cf. Washington correspondent, Springfield *Republican,* November 18, 1865, and C. B. Fisk's report of Presidential interview in *ibid.,* November 23, 1865, with *New York World,* September 13, 1865, *New York Herald,* September 14, 1865, September 21, 1865, November 19, 1865, report of President's letter to W. L. Sharkey in Springfield *Republican,* October 18, 1865, and B. F. Perry to D. E. Sickles, December 7, 1865 (Freedmen's Bureau Records).

ERIC L. McKITRICK

✪

Afterthought: Why Impeachment?

The policy of the United States government toward the South had been settled, despite the opposition of the executive branch, by the decision to undertake military Reconstruction. After that time President Johnson apparently had no measurable influence over such policy, and for almost any practical purpose, the Presidency as an effective and positive force in the nation's affairs ceased to exist.

But the story cannot be closed entirely without a parting question. Why did the Republican majority then turn upon the President and proceed to impeach him? Why did the Republicans, after binding Johnson hand and foot, try to throw him out of office less than a year before his term was to end anyway, and at a time when his successor's nomination had become all but certain? We may well ask why they bothered. It is hard to find anything in the proceeding that was really necessary; indeed, there was much in it that would seem politically quite risky.

The problem is largely one of interpretation. Most the details are well known, this having been one of the best-ventilated episodes in American history. Probably few real secrets of fact remain undisclosed, and the excellent narrative account published in 1903 by David DeWitt is not likely to need redoing for some

Reprinted from *Andrew Johnson and Reconstruction* by Eric L. McKitrick by permission of The University of Chicago Press. © 1960 by the University of Chicago. All rights reserved.

time to come, if indeed ever.[1] Nor is there now much point in trying to "justify" the act of impeachment, if in calm reflection there ever was. The case against its justification has been so well made, and made so often, that we need not anticipate any serious effort to reverse it. Men who actually voted for impeachment at the time confessed, in after years, to stirrings of remorse.[2] But the feelings of normally reasonable men still have a claim on our curiosity, even if those of unreasonable ones are no longer interesting, and the question of why so many were willing to support such a proceeding in the first place is still worth asking.

More than one conjecture, each based on the same essential body of evidence, is possible. There is still, for instance, the thesis of the radical plot, in this case well substantiated, to remove the last obstacle from full Republican domination of the South. This

[1] David M. DeWitt's *The Impeachment and Trial of Andrew Johnson* (New York: Macmillan, 1903) is complete, comprehensive, and elegantly written; it constitutes something of a classic. A short account, whose interest derives chiefly from its author's personal role in the trial, is Edmund G. Ross, *History of the Impeachment of Andrew Johnson* (Santa Fe: New Mexican Printing Co., 1896). The chapters in Milton's *Age of Hate* which relate to this phase of Johnson's administration are especially useful. The bulk of the documentary evidence bearing on the affair may be found in two government publications. *Trial of Andrew Johnson . . . ,* 3 vols. (Washington: Government Printing Office, 1868) contains the record of the trial itself. *Impeachment Investigation Testimony . . .* (Washington: Government Printing Office, 1867), bound together with *House Reports,* 40th Congress, 1st Session, No. 7, "Impeachment of the President," is a massive collection of miscellaneous testimony given before the House Judiciary Committee in 1867 while that body was still trying unsuccessfully to make up a case against the President.

[2] For example, James G. Blaine: "The sober reflection of after years has persuaded many who favored Impeachment that it was not justifiable on the charges made, and that its success would have resulted in greater injury to free institutions than Andrew Johnson in his utmost endeavor was able to inflict." George W. Julian wrote: "The attempt to impeach the President was undoubtedly inspired, mainly, by patriotic motives; but the spirit of intolerance among Republicans . . . set all moderation and common sense at defiance." After describing his own part in the scenes, Shelby Cullom concluded: "And thus ended for the first time, and I hope the last time, the trial of a President of the United States before the Senate, sitting as a Court of Impeachment for high crimes and misdemeanors." Blaine, *Twenty Years,* II, 376; Julian, *Political Recollections,* pp. 317–318; Cullom, *Fifty Years,* p. 158.

was the line taken by DeWitt, and it forms the interpretive basis for his monograph. It is a straightforward and obvious approach, and the most likely point in the entire Johnson administration at which to apply it would be precisely here. Impeachment efforts may not have reached their climax before the late winter months of 1868, but they had been set in motion as early as 1866 in the wake of the fall elections. There was Ashley's resolution in December of that year; efforts were periodically renewed throughout more than a year thereafter; and the most fantastic and unsavory work was done by Ashley, Boutwell, and Butler in trying to connect Johnson with the assassination of Abraham Lincoln. Johnson's "violation" of the Tenure of Office Act was merely the final pretext. The final decision to impeach, in short, was the successful culmination of a long period of labor and planning.

Another line of approach, a variation upon this theme, is a more direct recognition that the removal of Johnson himself would make little objective difference at this stage, but that more general designs of a long-range institutional nature were involved. Here was an opportunity, seldom so aptly presented, for Congress as the legislative branch of the government to seize an added increment of power and to strengthen itself in relation to an executive weakened by the threat of easy removal. The real meaning of the impeachment, therefore, was the opening it gave to profit from the feeling against Andrew Johnson, to readjust the balance of governmental powers, and thus to establish a significant political and constitutional precedent that would favor ministerial responsibility.[3]

Such interpretations, considered theoretically, are certainly not without merit. But here is one point at which the "institutional" approach may actually be less enlightening than it was at earlier

---

[3] "They [many analysts] have concluded that had impeachment proved successful as a weapon to remove a politically unacceptable President, the precedent would have been established for the removal of any President refusing persistently to co-operate with Congress, an eventuality implying the establishment of a parliamentary form of government with legislative ascendancy." Alfred H. Kelly and Winfred A. Harbison, *The American Constitution: Its Origins and Development* (New York: W. W. Norton, 1948), p. 477.

stages of the Reconstruction struggle, when the entire party could imagine itself threatened with division and defeat. To see the Republican majority acting either as a party or in its character as the legislative branch, fulfilling institutional requirements and reaching out for more institutional power, is to see it in the impeachment episode doing precisely all the wrong things. To think of these men acting in rational pursuance of group interests and objects is to derive a number of somewhat misleading conclusions.

The impeachment of the President, from even the crassest of party motives, was an undertaking fraught with political peril. Indeed, the action of the Republican members on the occasions when they did act as a national party and remained collectively, as it were, in their right mind, demonstrated again and again their clear recognition of this liability. It was only too true, of course, that the establishment of carpetbag governments—currently giving the Republicans much anxiety—represented the great opportunity for extending the party's power throughout the South with a Presidential election pending, and for giving it a solid base in the country at large. But the true keys to party security still lay, after all, in the North. All ambitions of a national character, while full of meaning and importance, could have meaning for individuals only to the extent that the security of their own district organizations was not in question. And this could not be taken for granted for a single moment.

Every Northern state had a Republican majority. Yet the margins of 1866 could not guarantee similar margins for another year on other issues, and several states would, in fact, go Democratic in 1867. If public opinion were to rally, not necessarily behind Andrew Johnson himself but in support of the executive office and its stability, the Republicans could conceivably lose control of the North. Their Southern foothold would thereupon be rendered worse than useless. For such a foothold to make any real political difference, the party required a visible and fully legitimate working margin in the North. And it goes without saying that even victory in a national election is small comfort, any time, to a Republican Senator or Representative who happens to have lost his office in a local Democratic sweep. Such is the ultimate liability in a popularly based political system, even in "revolutionary" times, and it has more than a little bearing on, though it assuredly does not clarify, the impeachment of Andrew Johnson.

There is hardly anything new in saying that considerations of morality and reason, or dilemmas created by their absence, have always given at least some measure for assessing men's behavior in our political life. Those considerations have certainly been applied in one way or another to this particular episode, and they may as well be applied again. Perhaps if the impeachment of Johnson were simply thought of as a towering act of abandoned wrath, wholly detached from "reason," it would be surprising to discover how little else was required in the way of explanation. Rather than follow down the trail of the stealthy impeachers, we could, instead, restrict our notice to those occurrences which may have produced such a state of unwholesome madness in the first place.

The final setting was one in which the people had been rendered wholly out of touch with the Presidency. It was one in which, for the other branches, the executive was "coordinate" only by a kind of inverted mockery. The moral air of the nation's politics, like the air of Hamlet's Denmark, had become heavily poisoned. Knavery and Ben Butlerism seemed to have free play in every committee room; buffoonery had erupted in the War Department; distinguished generals were fleeing from the President's efforts to promote them against their will and make them lay siege to a barricaded Secretary of War. The normally conservative Congressman was not simply encouraged in his growing sullenness by the attitude of his radical colleagues; he was, at the final break, egged on by a howling constituency. But why?

Two important considerations bearing on the impeachment could make another look at it very worthwhile. In the first place, much depends on whether the President's role during this period is regarded as an active or a passive one. Johnson had been rendered all but powerless to exercise any functions of real leadership, and we are thereby tempted to think of him as an inert quantity from here on, waiting to be victimized. But that would be a gross misjudgment of Andrew Johnson. For this particular problem

Johnson must be seen as a very active force indeed; otherwise the impeachment could not have occurred. A critical aspect of the picture is that of Johnson *taking the initiative*. His actions from June, 1867, to February, 1868, constituted a long series of provocations, including much premeditated spite over his curtailed prerogatives, which served to drive the Republican North into a state of frenzy and loathing. They made such men as the cautious Bingham, momentarily heedless of consequences, yearn for Johnson's head on a pike simply for the immense relief of having his voice silenced. There was a deep psychological need to eliminate Johnson from American political life forever, and it was principally Johnson himself who had created it. During the trial the oratory and editorial rhetoric teemed with intensely surgical metaphors. The Presidential incumbent no longer functioned in the body politic except to infect it. Out with the infection! Cut it away![4]

The other requirement for bringing the impeachment into being, besides the President's own initiative, was a widespread faith after February 21, 1868, that Johnson's conviction would be simple and swift. A large Republican majority had been brought to a state of mind in which it could easily persuade itself that the President had on that day broken the law. His celebrated but miserably clumsy attempt to oust Secretary Stanton had been specifically anticipated with the framing of the Tenure of Office Act a year before, and now that he had done just what Congress had tried by legislation to prevent him from doing, Congressmen saw no further reason to refrain from doing what they themselves so fervently longed to do. It is now forgotten that the gaping absurdities of that law were hardly so obvious then as they came to seem later; the questionable part of the proceeding could only emerge by demonstration.

Indeed, there was a good deal in the affair that could only emerge by demonstration. The overtones left in history have been those of unworthiness, which is just as well; but while those overtones were certainly there from the first, they were not at the

---

[4] Or, as Joseph Medill put it to John Logan: "Like an aching tooth, every one [*sic*] is impatient to have the old villain out." Quoted in Milton, p. 518.

time the ones that predominated. It is right that history's account should be made up more from the aftermath and afterthoughts than from the causes; but it is also well to observe that this is primarily because the impeachment failed. Had it succeeded, we may be very sure that the echoes of the affair would have been, if still not exactly sweet, at least very different. And we may also be sure that if the prosecutors had not imagined that they had a simple and safe case, they would never have undertaken it. That they, too, would come to have their afterthoughts is still not part of the story's beginning.

Impeachment, again, was a grave and risky step; only under the greatest stress could the majority members bring themselves to take it. Four times a minority tried to bring impeachment forward; three times it was voted down. Up to the final break, there had been no charges that contained legal substance—a point which was remarked upon by most of the party's leaders and editorial spokesmen. Yet four times a rage for impeachment at any price was reawakened by the President's grim refusal to call off his one-man war against everyone who seemed to be of any importance, while even Johnson's own advisers vainly told him that he was best off keeping quiet and doing nothing.

I. FIRST IMPEACHMENT EFFORT: JANUARY–JUNE, 1867

Representative James M. Ashley of Ohio had at some point become obsessed with the feeling that the country was not safe without the President's removal. Ashley's resolution of December 17, 1866, to appoint a committee of inquiry on this subject, however, was smothered when the House refused to vote on it. But as soon as Johnson resumed his vetoing habits (this time with the District of Columbia Negro suffrage bill), Ashley on January 7, 1867, could jump up and say that since none of the older members would offer an impeachment resolution, he would have to do it himself. The resolution passed, though it is not likely that the House took it with very great seriousness. By its terms the Judiciary Committee was to inquire into Johnson's official conduct and determine whether he had done anything impeachable. The assumption seems to have been that the mere existence of such an investigation would serve as a warning and deterrent to Johnson and would be reassuring to all who might doubt the vigilance of Congress.[5]

This investigation, conducted in secret but described daily to the President by Allan Pinkerton, was a grotesque and clownish business not unlike that of Joseph McCarthy and his fifty-seven Communists. The searchers professed to know of evidence that Johnson had bribed public officers, swung around the circle full of whisky, plotted to betray Tennessee in wartime, and conspired with Booth to murder Lincoln. On this final item, Ashley, who was not even a member of the committee, volunteered his services and expended much effort. Ashley was an occult mixture of superstition and lunacy. He seems to have had a theory that the deaths of American Presidents in office were by nature due to Vice-Presidenttial foul play. He was encouraged and assisted in his work by George S. Boutwell of Massachusetts, and the arrival of Benjamin F. Butler in March, 1867, completed as baleful a trio of buzzards as ever perched in the House. Butler made broad hints that pages had been removed from Booth's diary to protect Johnson ("Who spoliated that book?"); and when Jefferson Davis, who was supposed to have shared in the plot, was released on May 13, the already languishing investigation was given some fresh impetus. Supposedly Johnson, involved in both assassination and treason, did not want to try Davis and have all his own secrets revealed.[6]

[5] *Congressional Globe,* 39th Congress, 2nd Session, pp. 154, 320–321. "According to Mr. Sumner," observed *The Nation,* "the whole North is eager for impeachment; but if we may judge from the press, very few people are eager for it. The Washington correspondent of the Springfield *Republican,* who is generally both sensible and accurate, estimates the chance of impeachment as one in a hundred, and the chance of conviction as one in a thousand, which we think is probably a fair estimate of the extent of Mr. Johnson's risk" (IV [January 24, 1867], 61). *Harper's* said: "They [the people] will hear with attention and interest what Mr. Ashley has to say. But if it be a mere repetition of General Butler's speech it will not persuade them that the President ought to be impeached" (XI [January 26, 1867], 50).

[6] Ashley, later called before this same committee to testify, was given a *mauvais quart d'heure* by the Democratic members, who pressed him merci-

It soon became apparent that the only high official who had wanted Davis prosecuted was Johnson himself, the government's case having been spoiled by perjurers. It was also discovered that no pages had been torn from Booth's diary, that the President had not been drunk on the "swing around the circle," and that none of Johnson's canceled checks had been made out to corruptible public employees. Johnson had clearly done nothing impeachable. A majority of the Judiciary Committee, including Chairman James Wilson, had no further stomach for its mission and voted on June 3, 1867, that no evidence of high crimes and misdemeanors existed.[7]

Impeachment at that point was dead, and would have remained so had the President not in effect taken steps to give it new life.

There is now a general impression that Johnson, though opposed to the Reconstruction Acts, proceeded faithfully to carry them out once they had become law. This is true only in the most strained and nominal sense. In less than three months after their passage, he began interfering with the efforts of the federal commanders to put the acts into practice, particularly with regard to registering voters and dealing with civilian officials. One difficulty encountered by the commanders involved the numerous cases in which the registrants were known by the registrars to be swearing false oaths

---

lessly regarding just how much he could substantiate these wild imaginings. "I have had a theory about it," he replied. "I have always believed that President Harrison and President Taylor and President Buchanan were poisoned, and poisoned for the express purpose of putting the Vice Presidents in the presidential office. In the first two instances it was successful. It was attempted with Mr. Buchanan, and failed. It succeeded with Mr. Taylor and Mr. Harrison. Then Mr. Lincoln was assassinated, and from my stand-point I could come to a conclusion. . . . It would not amount to legal evidence." *Impeachment Investigation Testimony*, p. 1199. Butler tried to stir up the members in a speech made on March 26 in which he broadly hinted that Bingham, as one of the government prosecutors in the Davis case, had tampered with Booth's diary in order to protect some highly placed con-spirator who "could profit by assassination." *Congressional Globe,* 40th Congress, 1st Session, pp. 362–364. That Pinkerton was keeping Johnson informed about Ashley's cloak-and-dagger work was discovered by George F. Milton (see p. 411).

[7] *House Reports,* No. 7, "Impeachment of the President," pp. 59–105.

in order to qualify for voting. To meet this and other problems General Pope issued a set of regulations for his district which included provisions for challenging such oaths. Another difficulty was over the course to be followed with civilian officials who failed to cooperate in administering the law. Pope's orders in this case were that when necessary such persons were removable by military authority, Congress having declared that there were no legal governments in these places and that those existing were to be deemed "provisional only." In such measures Pope and the other commanders had the consistent support of General Grant.[8]

But Johnson on June 20, 1867, issued a set of his own orders, and at no point did these orders bear much resemblance to the way the Army was construing the Reconstruction Acts. In a directive embracing a number of questions, he declared that boards of registry had no power to challenge a man's oath, which legally entitled him to vote once he had taken it, and that the only recourse in cases of suspected perjury was to bring suit in the Southern state courts. Participation in rebellion was defined in such a way as to allow the great bulk of white Southerners to qualify in the forthcoming elections. The commanders were said to be without power to remove civilian officials, or to appoint substitutes, or to promulgate decrees having the force of law. The effect of this order would have been to give the existing state governments the most extensive control over the pending elections and to guarantee the largest possible white vote.[9]

Feeling against the President once more flared very high. Inspired by protests from the military that proper control was impossible under such an interpretation of the law, Congress met in July and passed another Reconstruction Act. This act defined the "true intent and meaning" of the first two Reconstruction Acts,

[8] *Senate Executive Documents,* 40th Congress, 1st Session, No. 14, "Correspondence Relative to Reconstruction"; *House Executive Documents,* 40th Congress, 1st Session, No. 20, "Reconstruction"; *Report of the Secretary of War,* 40th Congress, 2nd Session, I, 240–395; Fleming, *Civil War and Reconstruction in Alabama,* pp. 475–480, 488–491.

[9] *House Executive Documents,* 40th Congress, 1st Session, No. 34, "Interpretation of the Reconstruction Acts"; Richardson, *Messages and Papers,* VI, 527–531, 552–556.

and in so doing systematically reversed every point in Johnson's June 20 order. Johnson promptly vetoed this bill and in his message denounced the actions of Congress, declared that he would never willingly surrender his constitutional powers, and exhorted the people to remove by ballot the rod of military despotism.[10]

II. SECOND IMPEACHMENT EFFORT: JULY–DECEMBER, 1867

Despite the Judiciary Committee's previous arid efforts, it now seemed to become plausible all over again that Johnson might really have been guilty of all those treasonable acts—including the assassination of his predecessor—for which a month before no evidence had existed. On July 11 the committee was instructed to proceed afresh with its labors and be ready to report at the next meeting of Congress. Meanwhile Ben Butler, who had quickly emerged as the stoutest demagogue in the House, was placed at the head of a special committee to plumb the depths of Lincoln's murder. This group became known as the "Assassination Committee." Its members schemed and skulked for the remainder of the summer.[11]

Against the earnest advice of General Grant, Johnson in August began removing various officers who were especially obnoxious to him and who were especially zealous in their efforts to carry out the Reconstruction Acts. He started with the Secretary of War himself on August 5, and before he was through he had removed

[10] *Congressional Globe,* 40th Congress, 1st Session, pp. 517–546, 549–558, 569–586, 594–598, 610–615, 617–620, 622, 625–628, 631, 637–638, 640, 729–732, 741–747, Appendix, pp. 43–44; Richardson, pp. 536–545. House and Senate passed bills on this subject on July 9 and 11, respectively; a mutually satisfactory version was completed July 13; the bill was vetoed July 19 and repassed in both Houses on the same day.

[11] The "instructing" really occurred in a negative sense; the House simply failed to act on the question of discharging the committee. The new "Assassination Committee," composed of Representatives Butler, Shellabarger, Julian, Ward, and Randall, was appointed on July 8. It never made a report. *Congressional Globe,* 40th Congress, 1st Session, 522, 592–593, 656–657, 697–698, 720, 725, 761–763, 765–766; Ross, pp. 49–50.

all but one of the district commanders in the South. He ousted Sheridan from command of the Louisiana-Texas district and Sickles from his command in South Carolina. He added Pope and Ord to his list of removals in December. General Swayne, who was head of the Freedmen's Bureau in Alabama and had great influence with the leading men of that state, was removed along with Pope.[12]

Johnson's effort to get rid of the ambiguous Stanton was to drag out for more than six months, during which time the President would manage to shed a certain amount of undeserved luster on an able but very unattractive, unheroic, and devious man. As a result of several changes made during 1866, Johnson now had a cabinet whose members—with the exception of Stanton—he could more or less count on to support his politics. On the other hand, the loyalty of Stanton, who had close ties with the radical group in Congress, had been known for some time to be defective. Stanton had been the only cabinet member to oppose Johnson's order of June 20 or his veto of the July 19 Reconstruction Act, and he had persistently ignored Johnson's well-known desire that he resign.[13]

By August 1 Johnson had finally decided—having meanwhile discovered that Stanton had actually helped write the Act of July 19—that the man must go. On August 5 he asked for the Secretary's resignation, which Stanton refused to give, whereupon Johnson decided to remove him. He had been trying all during this time to persuade Grant to accept the office. Grant was most reluctant to do it, expressing his understanding (one which was quite generally shared) that Stanton was protected by the Tenure of Office Act, a measure which had been passed on the same day as the first Reconstruction Act.[14]

[12] *House Executive Documents,* 40th Congress, 2nd Session, No. 57, "Removal of Hon. E. M. Stanton and Others"; McPherson, *Reconstruction,* pp. 345–346; Fleming, pp. 492–493.

[13] Richardson, p. 584. Gideon Welles's *Diary* is virtually a week-by-week chronicle of the curious relationship between Johnson and Stanton, a relationship in which, behind an elaborate mask of mutual politeness, each was perfectly aware of the other's distrust of himself. This went all the way back to 1865.

[14] "Removal of Hon. E. M. Stanton and Others," pp. 1–2; Milton, p. 447; Richardson, p. 584.

The fashioning of this law had occurred under very complex circumstances, and that section of it which applied to the Stanton case was not a product of the original impetus that had brought the measure into being. The act had grown directly out of the wholesale removals from rank-and-file federal offices made by Johnson both during and after the election campaign of 1866. It was designed primarily to protect Republican officeholders from executive retaliation, which had created a problem of some seriousness, and consequently it had the overwhelming support of Republicans in both Houses. The radicals, however, had taken advantage of rising tension over Reconstruction in January and February, 1867, to add a section protecting cabinet members as well. They had Stanton specifically in mind. This passed the House but ran into strong opposition from Senate moderates, John Sherman in particular.[15]

In the final stages of debate a House-Senate compromise was agreed upon which covered cabinet officers during the term of the President who had appointed them, the question of exactly what constituted "appointment" being left somewhat vague. The Senate accepted the bill in that shape. On the one hand, the House members of the conference committee took this as a full victory for their version of protection for cabinet officers, while, on the other, Sherman assumed, or at least so argued in the Senate, that this part of the bill raised no real issues, since a test at the cabinet level was not likely to arise. He would later come to regret these words. But Sherman himself was far more interested in the ordinary officeholders—his mail was full of appeals from his own

[15] The bill was debated continuously in the Senate from January 10 until January 18, 1867, on which date it was passed. *Congressional Globe,* 39th Congress, 2nd Session, pp. 382–390, 404–412, 433–442, 460–471, 487–497, 517–528, 541–550. The House took it up on February 1, added its own amendment, and passed it the next day. *Ibid.,* pp. 935–944, 969–970. Lyman Trumbull was very much in favor of accepting the House amendment when it arrived back in the Senate but was opposed by Sherman and other moderates. This repeated the pattern of sentiment on appointments which had emerged during the previous session in 1866 in connection with the Post Office Appropriation Bill. The Senate on February 6 refused concurrence in the amended House version. *Ibid.,* pp. 966–969, 978, 1039–1047. For a summary of these debates, with commentary, see DeWitt, pp. 183–199.

appointees for protection—and he was willing to include the disputed section rather than hold up the measure any further.[16]

But whatever may have been the reservations of Senate moderates, there was no question in the general view over what that section was intended to do. A substantial number of Republicans, realizing that Stanton was their only remaining access to the executive department, wanted very much to keep him there and assumed that this was now guaranteed. A touch of irony lay in the fact that Stanton himself did not at the time approve of the measure, and he probably helped Seward write Johnson's veto message. But Stanton nevertheless allowed himself to be convinced that the country's salvation demanded his remaining at the War Department.[17]

[16] For example, "I am glad to see in the movements of the body of Congress so much temperance and steadiness. I hope we shall have as strong a law as Congress can pass regulating appointments and removals from office and restraining abuse of power in that respect." Warner Bateman to John Sherman, December 7, 1866 (Sherman Mss. Library of Congress). Sherman during this time was besieged by protests over Johnson's removals: J. M. Brown to Sherman, November 7, 1866; E. Forsman to Sherman, November 17, 1866; J. F. Dewey to Sherman, December 4 and 14, 1866; citizens' petitions from eighth and ninth Ohio districts, December 8, 1866; M. Walker to Sherman, December 19, 1866; William Stedman to Sherman, January 3, 1867; petition from members of Ohio legislature, January 26, 1867; petition from citizens of Lima, Ohio, n.d. (No. 25934) (Sherman Mss.). The joint conference committee, appointed on February 14, 1867, was composed of Schenck, T. Williams, and J. F. Wilson for the House, and G. Williams, Sherman, and Buckalew for the Senate. The committee's substitute was reported back to the Senate on February 18, to the House on the nineteenth, and was agreed to in both places. The bill was vetoed by the President on March 2 and repassed in both Houses on the same day. *Congressional Globe,* 39th Congress, 2nd Session, pp. 1340, 1514–1518, 1737–1739, 1964–1966; Richardson, pp. 492–498.

[17] Richardson, p. 587; Welles, III, 50–51, 54. The act's basic provisions were: (1) That any civil officer requiring Senate confirmation should, when confirmed, hold office until a successor had been appointed and confirmed in the same manner; (2) that cabinet officers were to be considered in the same category, except that they were to hold office during the term of the President who had appointed them, and one month thereafter, subject to removal by and with Senate consent; (3) that in cases of misconduct during a Senate recess, the President might suspend the offender, appoint a temporary successor, and report the reasons therefor to the Senate within twenty days after its next meeting; should the Senate refuse concurrence, the offender was to be reinstated; (4) that only in cases of death or resignation

After the events of June and July, therefore, Grant's advice to Johnson—that removing Stanton would be contrary to the way the law was understood by the people—was actually quite sound. Johnson hesitated a few days; then on August 5 two items appeared in the President's mail which settled his mind and drove him to action. One was the information, recently brought out in the trial of John Surratt, that Judge Advocate Holt had never properly shown him the petition for clemency which had been forwarded with the papers of Mrs. Surratt back in 1865. Johnson was convinced that Stanton had been back of this. The other was a letter from Sanford Conover, a very shady person whom the government had at one time employed as a spy in the Jefferson Davis case but who was now in jail awaiting sentence for perjury. Conover described elaborate efforts by Ashley and Butler to get him to cook up "evidence" of Johnson's having been in on the assassination plot. The *quid pro quo* was to have been a pardon for Conover—which Holt had already tried to obtain—but having lost hopes of it from that quarter, Conover was now, in effect, double-crossing the "Assassination Committee" with a direct appeal to the President. Regardless of whether the Secretary of War had himself been involved in any of this, Stanton was Holt's superior and was thus officially responsible for his doings. The President accordingly demanded the Secretary's resignation, and when Stanton refused to give it, Johnson began laying plans to remove him.[18]

---

might an officer be replaced during a recess of the Senate, and in such cases the successor's commission would expire at the end of the next session; and (5) that violations of the act would be deemed "high misdemeanors," and would be punishable by fine and/or imprisonment. *Congressional Globe,* 39th Congress, 2nd Session, Appendix, pp. 198–199.

[18] St. George L. Sioussat, "Notes of Colonel W. G. Moore, Private Secretary to President Johnson, 1866–1868," *American Historical Review,* XIX (October 1913), 98–132. The Conover material, the original of which is in the Johnson papers, was released for publication and appeared in the Washington and New York newspapers on August 10, 1867. The President had actually known for some time, from other sources, about these goings-on. See Milton, pp. 413–414. The exchange of notes regarding Johnson's desire for Stanton's resignation and the Secretary's refusal to give it is in Richardson, p. 584, and McPherson, p. 261.

After another week Grant finally agreed to take office on an *ad interim* basis, and on August 12 Stanton was not removed but "suspended," pending a report to the Senate. Thus Johnson, yielding to the reluctance of Grant, remained to the latter's satisfaction within the Tenure of Office Act. Meanwhile Stanton, bowing, as he said, to "superior force," vacated the office to Grant, who thereupon assumed its duties. Johnson hoped and assumed that Grant would ultimately do one of two things: either hold office long enough to let the case be tried in the courts if the Senate refused to concur in the suspension, or else resign in time for Johnson to have someone else in the post by the time the Senate, with its nonconcurrence, should force the case to a test. This assumption would later become the subject of a bitter public debate. But for the time being it could remain (like Stanton) in a state of suspension, since Congress was not then in session. Such was the way things stood when Congress met again late in November, 1867.[19]

Between the time of Stanton's suspension and the meeting of Congress, Johnson managed to enrage the Republicans on certain other counts. His removal of Sheridan was made over the vigorous objections of his new Secretary of War *ad interim,* who predicted that it would "only be regarded as an effort to defeat the laws of Congress." In this Grant was right; the removal, not only of Sheridan but of Sickles as well, set off a great public outcry and added measurably to the growing conviction that Johnson was trying to subvert the Reconstruction Acts. In the autumn, moreover, the Democrats made substantial gains in a number of state elections. Johnson seized the occasion to make a "victory speech" to a crowd of serenaders on November 13 in which he announced that his policy had been vindicated by the people. Thomas Ewing had made agitated but vain efforts beforehand to dissuade the President from making any such speech.[20]

[19] "Removal of Hon. E. M. Stanton and Others," pp. 1–3.
[20] Grant urged against Sheridan's removal both in conversation and in two letters (August 1 and 17, 1867) which he wrote to the President on that subject. Johnson, it appears, had sought advice everywhere; virtually everyone he consulted advised very strongly against the removal, but he proceeded to go ahead and make it anyway. Even the Chief Justice was sent

It was against this background that the House Judiciary Committee (despite the embarrassments of the Conover fiasco, which had been made public on August 10) decided by a narrow 5–4 vote on November 20 to recommend impeachment. On December 2, 1867, three reports were laid before the House. A majority report recommended that the President be impeached on general grounds of "usurpation of power." The second, a Republican minority report written by Chairman Wilson, attacked the majority report on all counts but recommended that Johnson be "censured" for betraying the confidence of those who had placed him in power. The third was a Democratic minority report which supported Johnson throughout.[21]

The regular second session of the Fortieth Congress convened on the same day, December 2. On the following day Johnson sent in his Third Annual Message. In it, he defiantly declared that "cases may occur in which the Executive would be compelled to stand on his rights, and maintain them, regardless of consequences." The House sweated and heaved, but in a record vote taken on December 7 impeachment was defeated. For all their chagrin and ire, the Republicans had again been forced to recognize that they still did not have a case.[22] Had Johnson stopped there, the momentum could not possibly have been revived: the issue would have been closed. But once again he resumed the initiative.

---

for. The latter "begged him for his own sake and for that of the country" not to take such a step. ("He does not realize at all the feeling against him in the country," Chase wrote to Garfield.) No one in the Cabinet, except the irascible Welles, approved of the removal; in fact, "Mr. Browning's face actually seemed to grow thin at the suggestion." "Removal of Hon. E. M. Stanton and Others," pp. 2–4, 7–8; S. P. Chase to Garfield, August 7, 1867 (Garfield Mss. Library of Congress); Welles, pp. 149–157; Sioussat, p. 114. According to the *New York Tribune* on August 27, ". . . the country needs adjustment, security, tranquility, repose, and he persists in keeping it unsettled, distracted, angry, and apprehensive." Johnson's "victory speech" is in *Impeachment Investigation Testimony,* p. 1175.

[21] *House Reports,* No. 7, "Impeachment of the President."

[22] Richardson, pp. 558–581; *Congressional Globe,* 40th Congress, 2nd Session, pp. 67–68, Appendix, pp. 54–65.

III. THIRD IMPEACHMENT EFFORT: JANUARY–FEBRUARY, 1868

Johnson gave the members of Congress two more things to reflect upon over the Christmas holidays. On December 12 he sent to the Senate his reasons for suspending Stanton. On December 18 he sent Congress a message on another subject, the motive for which can hardly be diagnosed as other than simple cussedness. Sheridan's replacement, Winfield S. Hancock, a Democratic general who did not approve of the Reconstruction Acts, had recently issued a military order asserting the supremacy of civil over military government. This was in virtually direct contradiction to the Act of July 19, which Hancock was supposed to be administering in the Texas-Louisiana district. Back in July the House of Representatives had voted special resolutions of thanks to Sheridan, Pope, and Sickles for "able and faithful performance" of duty in their respective districts; Johnson now asked in his message that a similar vote of thanks be tendered to Hancock. The effect of this sally may well be imagined. After the members had gone home, moreover, Johnson proceeded to remove Pope, having already removed the other two.[23]

For the third straight year, Congressmen visited with their constituents during the holiday season and came back to Washington in a frame of mind markedly more radical than when they had

[23] Richardson, pp. 583–594, 595–596; *Congressional Globe,* 40th Congress, 1st Session, pp. 500, 504 (July 5, 1867); *House Executive Documents,* 40th Congress, 2nd Session, No. 58, "General W. S. Hancock." "Mr. Covode. I am anxious to know whether that is genuine or whether it is a hoax. [Laughter.] The Speaker. It is a message from the President." *Congressional Globe,* 40th Congress, 2nd Session, p. 264. Eldridge of Wisconsin, a Democrat, thereupon tried unsuccessfully to get the floor in order to offer the requested resolution. This was on December 18. When he finally did offer it on January 6, 1868, Washburne of Illinois promptly moved a substitute: "That we utterly condemn the conduct of Andrew Johnson, acting President of the United States, for his action in removing that gallant soldier Major General P. H. Sheridan. . . ." *Ibid.,* p. 332. Johnson's order of December 28 removing Pope called also for the removals of Ord and Swayne. McPherson, pp. 345–346.

left. This was no wonder, since in addition to everything else they were now beginning to be flooded with letters from anguished carpetbaggers and Southern Unionists wanting to know what Congress was going to do for them in their efforts—currently meeting numerous obstructions—to set up the new state governments.[24] In a little over three weeks after the recess, the President would be involved in a fresh quarrel, this time with General Grant.

On January 10, 1868, the Senate Committee on Military Affairs issued a report vindicating the suspended Stanton, and on the thirteenth the Senate voted to refuse concurrence in the suspension. On the day after the committee made its report (but before the Senate had acted on it), Grant, by now very uncomfortable, told Johnson that he did not want to stay in office any longer and serve as a test case while violating the Tenure of Office Act. Johnson tried to argue Grant out of his misgivings and managed to exact a half-hearted promise that the General would wait until they

[24] "For some reason," according to DeWitt, ". . . the majority reassembled in a sullen mood. The distinction between conservative and radical seemed to have been obliterated" (p. 316). There is much material in the correspondence of Sherman, Washburne, and Sumner during this period from workers in the various Southern Republican outposts. These testaments of frustration are vibrant with anger over the disruptive effects of Johnson's removals. "The removal of Genls. Pope and Swayne," C. W. Buckley wrote to Washburne on January 9, 1868, from Montgomery, Alabama, "has taken from the work of reconstruction two able and experienced leaders. Their loss to the union men of this state is irreparable, and their removal is followed by such an outburst of rebel hostility . . . that we are on the very eve of violence and bloodshed" (Elihu Washburne Mss. Library of Congress). "Had he [Swayne] remained in command here our work would have been comparatively easy, and success certain. Unfriendly military management has killed us. . . . What next are we to do? . . . We can only look to Congress to come to the rescue." George Ely to Washburne, February 9, 1868. See also W. M. Dunn to John Sherman, November 18, 1867, A. L. Harris to Sherman, November 29, 1867, Foster Blodgett to Sherman, December 30, 1867 (Sherman Mss. Library of Congress); W. H. Gibbs to Washburne, November 26 and 29, 1867, January 29, February 3 and 21, 1868, John C. Underwood to Washburne, December 9 and 16, 1867 (Washburne Mss.); James L. Dunning to Sumner, December 29, 1867, R. R. Williams to Sumner, January 1, 1868, John H. Anxhurst to Sumner, January 1, 1868, Thomas W. Conway to Sumner, January 6, 1868, J. Sumner Powell to Sumner, January 20, 1868, Oscar M. Waring to Sumner, February 11, 1868, G. Norton to Sumner, February 13, 1868, W. Dockray to Sumner, February 22, 1868 (Sumner Mss. Harvard College Library).

had had another talk before taking any action. But Grant, whose peace of mind required that he be shielded from the complicated side of anything, bolted on the following Tuesday after having heard about the Senate's vote the night before. He vacated his office, went back to army headquarters, and washed his hands of all further responsibility for the War Department. Stanton, lurking about the premises, was thereupon free to reoccupy his old office, which he promptly did. Grant then sent a note to the President, again calling attention to the Tenure of Office Act and inclosing a report of the Senate's action, saying that he could no longer serve as Secretary of War *ad interim*.[25]

That same day, Tuesday, January 14, Johnson summoned Grant in before a full cabinet meeting to explain himself, continuing, despite Grant's embarrassed protests, to address him as "Mr. Secretary." He pointed out that Grant had broken their agreement. The General said rather lamely that he had not expected the Senate to act so soon and offered to go personally to Stanton and persuade him to resign. (This he later did, without success.) What followed precipitated another call for impeachment.[26]

Johnson at this point had two alternatives. Although he had caught Grant in a questionable act, he might still retain the cooperation of Grant as General of the Army by simply issuing his executive orders through him and ignoring Stanton. This he was strongly advised to do by Thomas Ewing, and Grant himself was not unwilling to proceed on such a basis. But in order to preserve this rapport Johnson would have had to let the matter of their disagreement drop; there was nothing now to gain and much to lose by continuing to harp on it. In any case the magnitude of Grant's duplicity had to be measured by the size of Johnson's moral claim on him in the first place—and this in turn had to be defined from the standpoint of Johnson's own designs for testing

[25] McPherson, p. 262; Adam Badeau, *Grant in Peace* (Hartford: S. S. Scranton, 1887), pp. 110–112; Sioussat, p. 115; Browning, *Diary*, II, 173–174; Welles, p. 259.

[26] Welles, pp. 259–262; Browning, pp. 173–175; Sioussat, pp. 115–116; McPherson, pp. 283–291.

the Tenure of Office Act, to which Grant had been determined all along not to be a party.

Or, Johnson could do what he in fact did: try to show up the General publicly and demonstrate his own rightness. He released his version of the cabinet interview for publication, which angered Grant and set him to brooding, and thereby inaugurated an exchange of letters all of which found their way into print. Grant, egged on by his friends, wrote the President giving his version of the agreement, which he said did not include his assisting Johnson to get rid of Stanton if it meant breaking the law. The exchange terminated on February 10 with a scathing letter from Johnson, accompanied by statements which the President had obtained from each of the cabinet members saying that he was right and that Grant was in effect lying. Johnson certainly had the better of the exchange, for whatever it might be worth, but he had humiliated and alienated Grant forever.[27]

The fact was that a bargain between Johnson and Grant had never been possible on any but the narrowest of ground—their mutual distaste for Stanton—and to strike any sort of agreement each had had to keep a whole set of reservations strictly in the background. Their views on the two acts of Congress which had caused most of the trouble—the Tenure of Office and Reconstruction Acts—had been miles apart from the first. One of the precipitating reasons for Johnson's desire to replace Stanton was the latter's opposition to his June 20 order and his veto of the July 19 Reconstruction Act. Grant, on the other hand, appears to have thought that if he himself did not accept office Johnson might appoint someone else who would embarrass the Army in carrying out the law. Grant would not have been likely to make this plain when he accepted; when he later did say it, Johnson was quite naturally enraged. Johnson, for his part, wanted to use Grant and his immense prestige to get rid of Stanton and to demonstrate, if

[27] William T. Sherman, *Personal Memoirs of Gen. W. T. Sherman* (3d ed., rev. and corrected; New York: Charles L. Webster, 1890), II, 423; Badeau, pp. 113–115; Welles, pp. 269–276; Sioussat, pp. 117–118; Browning, pp. 178–180. The entire Johnson-Grant exchange is in McPherson, pp. 283–291.

possible, that the Tenure of Office Act was a legal nullity. Had he insisted on the full implications of this at the time, Grant would not have accepted at all. The General would only take the appointment within the bounds allowable by the same Act, which he said he intended to obey. Johnson would later deny that *his* agreement to these terms—suspension and *ad interim* replacement, rather than direct removal and reappointment—had implied any acquiescence to the Tenure of Office Act.

These, then, were the bounds within which the General of the Army committed his treachery to the President of the United States. By January, 1868, if not before, Grant had undoubtedly become aware in his rather dull way that he had got himself into a bad scrape, and he was no longer any too particular how he got out of it. And he was dull indeed if he had not begun to suspect that he himself was going to be the next President. He was already receiving a good deal of coaching, and was probably being chided daily for having let himself be drawn into Johnson's schemes for self-vindication in the first place. It may not have been *his* wits that foiled Johnson with a resignation which came too soon for one side of the executive plan and too late for the other, but for all his own political naïveté it could not have failed to occur to him at some point that the more completely he was rid of the business, the better it would be for him. It might be said that Johnson wrestled with Grant's political managers for control of the inert General's scruples, and Johnson lost.[28]

---

[28] The present author is assuming that the version of Johnson (that the General had been guilty of deceiving him) was technically correct. Needless to say, Grant himself never so assumed. Grant's own side of the case rests mainly on the emphasis with which he expressed his desire to Johnson, in their interview of January 11, to leave the War Office. Johnson's side depends on the clarity with which it was understood that Grant would remain pending further developments. Badeau, who saw Grant before and after this interview, says that the General was adamant and that Johnson, who "pleaded and argued," was the indecisive one. This is "indirect" evidence, but then so was everything that followed. Seward's statement indicates that there did not seem to be full clarity of understanding between the two men. At the cabinet showdown, on the other hand, Grant, confronted by an angry President with a roomful of supporters, hardly showed to his best advantage. It is on the basis of this episode, and the subsequent epistolary efforts of the President and his cabinet advisers to describe it, that

At any rate, documentary evidence now seemed to exist showing that Johnson had tried to plot with Grant to break the law, thus providing some solid ground for impeachment. But the members of the Reconstruction Committee, much as they would have loved to strike, reluctantly voted after much searching of soul not to recommend it. They could hardly impeach Johnson without involving Grant, who had, to say the least, bungled his part of the affair. So once again the impeachment drive was stalled, and again the issue was closed, if Johnson would now let it remain *in statu quo*. Said Thaddeus Stevens in disgust: "I shall never bring up this question of impeachment again."[29]

IV. THE FINAL EFFORT: FEBRUARY 21–MAY 26, 1868

Most of Johnson's closest advisers now urged him to ignore Stanton and make no further attempt to remove the barricaded Secretary, who had taken to eating and sleeping in his office at the War Department. But Johnson would have none of this advice. He turned grimly to this general and that, while each fled in dismay from the President's efforts to elevate him to cabinet honors. General Sherman resisted the Presidential entreaties and hastily left town; Johnson subsequently tried to get him back by making him a brevet general in command of a new military department, with headquarters at Washington, created for the occasion. Sherman, in fresh alarm, wired his brother John from St. Louis to have

---

the history of the affair (by DeWitt, Milton, and others) has been written. A more recent biographer of Grant, however, is inclined to dismiss all this evidence as decidedly biased and flimsy, and to assume that Grant's intentions were just what the General said they were. He thinks that Grant, never noted for "courage in battles of words or wars of ideas," simply botched the affair. See William B. Hesseltine, *Ulysses S. Grant, Politician* (New York: Dodd, Mead, 1935), pp. 107–110.

[29] The House Committee on Reconstruction, which had taken charge of the impeachment question, voted 6–3 on February 13 to lay an impeachment resolution on the table. *New York World,* February 14, 1868. The Stevens statement is from an interview with the *World*'s Washington correspondent. Stevens thought that Johnson and Grant were probably both lying to some extent, "though the President has the weight of evidence on his side."

the Senate kill the appointment. Johnson tried the same approach with General George H. Thomas, also with the lure of a brevet general's commission, but the Rock of Chickamauga, now weary of strife, managed to excuse himself from this new call to arms. The President thought of making General Thomas Ewing Secretary of War, but old Thomas, Senior—Johnson's otherwise loyal counselor—would not hear of his son's career being ruined. Even the chief clerk at the War Department, John Potts, could not be persuaded to accept the place. At last the President resurrected General Lorenzo Thomas, an aged dandy full of nonsense, who had been languishing for some time in semiretirement, and put the proposition to him. Thomas received the President's plan with much relish. Upon being told that he was expected to "support the Constitution and the laws," he said that he would. He was accordingly given a letter of authority to assume the duties of office *ad interim* on February 21.[30]

Thomas presented himself to Stanton with his letter on the same day, and Stanton told him he would think it over. The General then left and proceeded to float through the most riotous twenty-four hours of his life. He told half the town how he was going to take office by force the next day; that evening he went off to a masked ball where he waltzed and drank toasts into the small hours; news of the old beau's drunken exploits penetrated even to the darkened executive mansion. Thomas emerged from his bed in the morning to be met by a federal marshal with an arrest warrant which had been sworn out by Stanton during the night; he went and made bail, reported to the White House, and was told to go out and storm the works. But confronted by an adamant Stanton flanked by radical Congressmen, the would-be hero, now weak with hunger, proved unequal to his supreme test. He ended his brief Secretaryship of War (*ad interim*) in a surrender ceremony

[30] Browning, p. 182; T. Ewing to Johnson, October 12, 1867, and January 29, 1868, T. Ewing to W. T. Sherman, January 25, 1868 (Johnson Mss.); Sherman, pp. 425–433; Thorndike, *Sherman Letters,* pp. 300–307; M. A. DeWolfe Howe, ed., *Home Letters of General Sherman* (New York: Scribner's, 1909), pp. 368–374; *Trial,* I, 483–485, 517, 521, 529–530; McPherson, pp. 263, 346; Milton, p. 741 n.; Sioussat, pp. 119–120; *Trial,* pp. 417–418.

which involved a fresh round of guzzling before breakfast, the whisky this time being provided by Stanton himself, who was gracious in victory and still, to all intents and purposes, Secretary of War. A faint war cry from Lorenzo Thomas' home state would later come back to haunt him: "The eyes of Delaware are upon you!"[31]

While the nation's military affairs were suspended amid these light doings, the House of Representatives voted to impeach President Andrew Johnson for high crimes and misdemeanors. At that moment there was very little doubt that the crazed members had the support of a majority of their fellow-citizens.[32]

With all the combustible matter that Johnson had heaped together for them over the past three years, it is understandable that the impeachers could at last imagine—in the blaze set off by this final spark—that they had a perfect case. It is no wonder that a majority could not only desire but fully believe that all would be over in a puff. The eleven articles of impeachment were themselves a kind of hectic mirror of this illusion. The first nine articles, barely distinguishable from one another, all had to do with Johnson's "plot" to violate the Tenure of Office Act; the tenth involved

[31] *Trial*, pp. 211, 221, 223–228, 427–437, 509, 515–516; Milton, p. 506.

[32] *Congressional Globe*, 40th Congress, 2nd Session, pp. 1336–1355, 1358–1369, 1382–1402, Appendix (see Index to Appendix, "Impeachment of the President," for speeches). The resolution for impeachment, presented to the House on February 22 by the Reconstruction Committee, could not be passed, owing to the flood of oratory that it inspired, until the twenty-fourth. Every Republican state convention that met between that time and the end of the trial strongly supported impeachment. See *American Annual Cyclopaedic*, 1868, pp. 384, 493–494, 542, 604, 619–620, 758, 766. In the showers of letters and telegrams which Congressmen received from home, it is typical to find Congress being chided for not having acted sooner: "The people are alarmed . . . by the apparent apathy of Congress"; "Let there be no halting or wavering"; "Security for the future hitherto denied us on grounds of expediency is all that we ask of our Senators"; Congress had redeemed itself at last for "the rather disreputable effort heretofore to dodge or give it [impeachment] the go by." T. Foote to Austin Blair, February 24, 1868 (Blair Mss. Detroit Public Library); N. Ewing to John Covode, February 27, 1868 (Covode Mss. Historical Society of Western Pennsylvania); Frank G. Dounsbery to Charles Sumner, March 5, 1868 (Sumner Mss.); J. Reed to James Garfield, March 7, 1868 (Garfield Mss.).

Johnson's "scandalous harangues"; and the eleventh—which in the trial was voted on first—was an effort to encompass in print everything upon which the President could conceivably be condemned. The longer they were debated, the flimsier they looked. The trial, which has been minutely described in many other places, ended for practical purposes on May 16, 1868. On that day the seven "recusant Senators" (Fessenden, Fowler, Grimes, Henderson, Ross, Trumbull, and Van Winkle), with their votes for acquittal, left the prosecution with one vote short of conviction. The key man, Ross of Kansas, had been in doubt up to the last. When the Senate reconvened on May 26, only two more articles were voted upon before everyone realized that impeachment had been a failure. The "court" thereupon adjourned sine die.[33]

The impeachment was a great act of ill-directed passion, and was supported by little else. It was rather like an immense balloon filled with foul air, the most noisome elements of which were those most active. But as from a balloon, the air began oozing out fairly early. Most people, including the noblest of the recusant Senators, were sick to death of Andrew Johnson and would have given much to see the end of him.[34] But this could be accomplished neither by a popular referendum nor by a legislative vote of "no confidence," though either one would have settled his fate in an instant, and in either event the zeal of Trumbull and Fessenden would have been only too available. But the only form open was that of a judicial trial, and matters had reached such a pass that many men were quite willing to stretch their principles all out of shape, to seize

[33] Under Article I, Sections II, 5 and III, 6, of the Constitution, the House of Representatives prefers the charges (that is, does the impeaching); the Senate sits as a court of impeachment to judge the merits of the case and decide whether to convict or acquit the accused; and if the President of the United States is the accused, the trial is presided over by the Chief Justice of the Supreme Court.

[34] For example, Fessenden frequently expressed his contempt for Johnson in private correspondence, and after the trial wrote to a friend: "It was hard enough to keep down my own strong impulses towards conviction as it was." Shelby Cullom, then a young Congressman, said in his memoirs that Trumbull had originally favored impeachment. While the House vote was being taken on the Articles, Trumbull said to Cullom: "Johnson is an obstruction to the Government and should be removed." Fessenden, *Fessenden*, II, 226; Cullom, p. 154.

upon any form at all that was plausible, and to face their consciences later. "Not a loyal tongue will wag against impeachment," Representative Blair was assured by a constituent from Flint, Michigan; "The people want rest." Yet political principles were one thing, legal principles quite another. The Tenure of Office Act, thanks to the equivocations of a joint conference committee back in February, 1867, was quite unable to bear the intense legal scrutiny to which it was subjected during the trial of Andrew Johnson. The President's counsel, men of the very highest character and ability, showed rather mercilessly how little protection the Act really gave to Lincoln's holdovers, and they argued most effectively that nothing treasonable could be found in the President's effort to test a law which he considered unconstitutional. The Managers of Impeachment, whose composite personality was a curious blend of demagogue and rascal, were not really able to give them much of a battle. More than one observer must have cringed at the spectacle.[35]

The longer the show dragged on under such circumstances, the less ardent became the general desire to continue it. There was great gnashing of teeth when it was over, since many normally honorable men had been committed to seeing the folly out to the end. But there was also considerable secret and not-so-secret relief. *The Nation,* having hoped all along for Johnson's conviction, had at last had enough; it declared, on May 28: "We shall . . . hear no more of impeachment, and we are glad of it."[36]

---

[35] George W. Fish to Austin Blair, March 3, 1868 (Blair Mss.). The Managers of Impeachment—or "prosecuting attorneys"—chosen by the House were Thaddeus Stevens, George S. Boutwell, Benjamin F. Butler, John A. Logan, Thomas Williams, James F. Wilson, and John A. Bingham. The President's counsel were William M. Evarts, Benjamin R. Curtis, Henry Stanbery, and William S. Groesbeck. Evarts, an extremely witty and brilliant lawyer who would later serve as Hayes's Secretary of State, did the bulk of the work for Johnson's case. *The Nation,* despite its desire for Johnson's conviction, conceded that "the Managers were overmastered throughout in learning and ability. There is no use now in passing this over without notice. The contrast was patent to everybody throughout the trial and was a constant subject of comment" (VI [May 21, 1868], 404).

[36] *The Nation,* VI, 421.

All of which suggests still another use for the "balloon" metaphor: the principal function of the impeachment was that of a long-needed psychological blow-off. There were still, after all, certain compensations. The extreme step had, at least, been taken, and the impeachers had come very close; they had failed by only one vote. Meanwhile the people had been rescued from a very questionable act and all its possible consequences; there were not many who really welcomed the thought of Ben Wade as President and Ben Butler as Secretary of State, even for a little while.[37] Legend tells, and quite truthfully, that Fessenden and the others came in for much abuse because of the votes they gave. But it is also true that these men were rewarded, almost from the moment the trial ended, with an audible and growing chorus of praise. *The Nation* was not alone when it affirmed: "We believe, for our part, that the thanks of the country are due to Messrs. Trumbull, Fessenden, Grimes, Henderson, Fowler, Van Winkle, and Ross, not for voting for Johnson's acquittal, but for vindicating . . . the sacred rights of individual conscience."[38] The affair had served, in short, as a catharsis.

[37] Wade, as presiding officer of the Senate, would have become President in the event of Johnson's conviction. He had already made up a list of his cabinet, headed by the name of Benjamin F. Butler as Secretary of State. Badeau, pp. 136–137; Milton, p. 603.

[38] "Happily the great body of the party, certainly all the intelligent portion of it, and all its most influential and respected newspapers, made a determined stand against this amazing burst of folly [the attack on Fessenden and the others], and thus saved the party from damnation. . . ." *Harper's Weekly*, VI (May 21, 1868), 404. The *Chicago Tribune*, referring to Republican newspapers in general, declared on May 20: "While there is no difference of opinion among those journals as to the righteousness of impeachment, neither is there any difference as to the impolicy of rending one's garments over the result, or of . . . reading Senators out of the party who have not been able to vote for the conviction of Johnson." *Harper's Weekly* said: "Whoever has read the opinions of Senators Fessenden, Grimes, and Trumbull, however he may regret the conclusions to which they come, will not deny the ability, the dignity, and the candor with which their views are stated" (XII [June 6, 1868], 354). *Harper's* quoted the Providence *Journal*, *Chicago Tribune*, Boston *Advertiser*, Hartford *Courant*, *Chicago Post*, Bridgeport *Standard*, Cincinnati *Commercial*, and the Union League Club of New York, all to the same effect. *Ibid.*, XII (May 30, 1868), 339. A present-day scholar goes so far as to say that the "martyr" story on the "recusant Senators" was hardly more than a myth from the

Finally, the country had a cheering new object for its attention. Between the first and second votes on impeachment, the Republican national convention had met and nominated Ulysses S. Grant —looked upon everywhere as the man of peace—for the next President. No one could yet foresee, of course, the shoddiness of Grant's own administration, or yet know that it would still require the whole of Grant's two terms to liquidate all the passions and badness engendered by the Johnson regime. But his appearance now, as standard-bearer for the future, was a vast relief. It was miraculous how quickly impeachment was forgotten, as all turned to beam upon the hero.[39] Stanton retired from the War Department; General Schofield, acceptable to all sides, was confirmed as Secretary of War; and the remainder of Andrew Johnson's Presidency passed in relative tranquillity.

---

first. See Ralph J. Roske, "Republican Newspaper Support for the Acquittal of President Johnson," *Tennessee Historical Quarterly,* XI (September 1952), 263–273; and "The Seven Martyrs?" *American Historical Review,* LXIV (January 1959), 323–330.

[39] For example, Nast's June 6 cover for *Harper's* shows a matronly Columbia benignly pinning a medal (the nation's hopes) on a serene and inscrutable Grant. After this time, there is surprisingly little talk of impeachment in the editorial columns. "'Impeachment' is dying out," wrote David E. Bayard to John Covode from Uniontown, Pennsylvania, on June 1. "As Andy has but a short time to serve we can 'stand' him his term out" (Covode Mss. Historical Society of Western Pennsylvania). Later in the summer a friend of Jacob Howard (one of the more radical Senatorial judges) wrote: "Although I would rejoice to see Andrew Johnson deposed it does not strike me now as game worth the candle. These are or were about your views too as I gathered from our last talk. The political situation looks well to me. . . . I believe Grant will really walk over the course." N. G. King to Jacob Howard, September 1, 1868 (Howard Mss. Detroit Public Library).

✪

The Tennessee Epilogue

When he left the White House, a private citizen for the first time in thirty years, Andrew Johnson was driven to the house of his devoted friend, John Coyle, one of the proprietors of the *National Intelligencer*. Mrs. Patterson and her family were visiting the Welles family. They were to stay in Washington two weeks longer to procure the necessary articles to make habitable the Greeneville home to which, despite proposals of European tours, Johnson had decided to return.

In accordance with his promise to the Baltimore committee, the former President left Washington on the morning of March 11, on his visit to that city. A committee of distinguished Marylanders had come to escort him. Upon his arrival, the square around the Camden Station was found to be filled with a great applauding throng. When Johnson descended, a troop of cavalry and a battery of field artillery stood at attention and a great band played. The ex-President entered an open carriage drawn by four gray horses, and the parade began. The streets were lined with men and women and children, cheering, shouting, and waving handkerchiefs and flags.

A little later a great levee was held, and thousands of people waited for hours to shake hands with the Defender of the Constitution. When a number of pretty young ladies stepped up, the President showed a new trait of his character by kissing them one by

Reprinted by permission of Coward-McCann, Inc. from *The Age of Hate* by George F. Milton. Copyright 1930 by Coward-McCann, Inc.; renewed 1958 by Alice Fort Dwight.

one resoundingly on the cheek, while the spectators "seemed to derive as much pleasure from the operation as the ex-President himself."[1]

That evening a great banquet was given, with covers laid for 275. The toast to "Our Guest" expressed Baltimore's admiration of "the patriot statesman . . . the bulwark of equal rights, and the defender and martyr of the Constitution." Johnson gratefully responded. "My deliverance," he concluded, "has been the greatest case of emancipation since the rebellion commenced." The next day he returned to Washington with Maryland's plaudits ringing in his ears.[2]

On March 18 the Johnson party began its homeward journey to Greeneville. In addition to the retiring President, there were Mrs. Johnson, now a frail old lady; Martha Patterson and her husband, whose Senatorial term had ended on the fourth of March; Robert Johnson; and the children. At Lynchburg enthusiastic citizens entertained the party in a manner quite different from that which had marked Johnson's stay there eight years before. At a great reception in his honor, the ex-President said that he was on his way to his home in Tennessee, where he planned to go into retirement, but that he was bearing "the advice of Cato to pray for Rome."[3]

There was also an impromptu reception at Bristol. The special train carrying the party from Bristol to Greeneville had to stop at almost every station along the way so that the people might see and hear the returning warrior. At Limestone, where the crowd shouted that Johnson would have to run for Governor, he remarked to a newspaper correspondent: "Yes, there is a good deal of life in me yet."

Eager to receive its distinguished townsman with proper honors, the Greeneville town council had met on March 17 and passed a resolution that it would go to the station in a body to receive and welcome him, without specific indorsement or repudiation of the

---

[1] Baltimore *Sun,* March 12, 1869.

[2] David Rankin Barbee, Nashville *Banner,* September 1, 1929.

[3] Nashville *Union and American,* March 19, 1869. For the Tennessee newspaper references in this chapter and much of the other material on Johnson's Tennessee epilogue, I am indebted to the Brabson Thesis.

policies of his Presidential career. But the mayor of the town, a petty radical, said that the reception was intended to indorse Johnson's policies, and vetoed the council's resolution![4]

Nonetheless, there was a jollification as the train arrived. Four of Greeneville's prettiest girls—Lulu Evans, Maria Harmon, Bert and Kitty Crawford, all granddaughters of old friends of the statesman—presented him with great bouquets of flowers and led the procession that escorted the Johnson family to the house of a friend. There, from an open porch, addresses of welcome were made to him, and Johnson replied.

"I feel proud," he said, "in coming back among old friends to help them bear the burdens, if I can do nothing to relieve them." Then came a note of warning. "If the Constitution is not wrested from the hands of the usurper, in a few years the government will be gone," he prophesied. And at the last there was a phrase of disillusion: "An old man, weary with the cares of state, has come to lay his bones among you."[5]

Thus, after eight years, Andrew Johnson again took up his abode among the Greene County folk who loved him. With his return to Tennessee, there came much speculation as to what he planned to do. Would he really go into retirement, to live among the bitter memories of his Presidential years, or would he re-enter Tennessee politics?

By frugality and prudent investment, Johnson had accumulated what for those days was considered a substantial fortune. In the spring of 1869, he was worth probably $150,000. He began to improve his Greeneville property, and a little later bought a large brick business building. The rumor grew that he planned to use it either to organize a bank or to reopen a wholesale and retail tailoring establishment. People of the town noted him as he walked down the street, his hands clasped behind his back, a silk beaver hat resting on his head, bent in meditation. Frequently he would take long walks through the woodlands.

Johnson enjoyed this interlude of relaxation, but he had made

[4] Nashville *Union and American,* March 21, 1869.
[5] Letter of H. H. Ingersoll, who was Johnson's host that night, to Colonel Brabson. See also Nashville *Union and American,* March 28, 1869.

up his mind to get back into the fight. Even while beset with Presidential cares, he had commented that, in his case, to live he must be busy. He dreaded the effect of retirement and rest, and he had welcomed the talk of entry into Tennessee politics which came to him two months before he left the White House.[6] A. A. Kyle of Rogersville wrote urging on him the public duty of running for Governor, while Colonel Cooper reported that he found "the people—the masses—more than anxious" for Johnson to enter the race.

Late in March, he intimated to his friends that, while he was out of public life "for the time," he owed all that he was to the people of Tennessee, and if they commanded, he would try to help them lift their burdens. A week later he told a Knoxville audience of five thousand that the measure of his ambition had been satisfied and he sought nothing more, "but in returning to your midst, is it anything unnatural that I should desire to set myself right before you, and not be misunderstood?"

Early in the summer, Johnson made a great tour throughout the state. He went to Knoxville, spent several days there with the richest man in town, and held a levee, making friends with his former secessionist foes.[7] He rode from city to city in a special train, and made many speeches. In these he took pains to set himself right with the Negroes. His objection to Negro suffrage, he declared, had not been that he did not want the Negroes to vote, but that granting suffrage was a state, not a federal function. But his chief theme was that Congress had usurped the functions of the government and had pushed aside the Constitution; under the radicals, it was becoming a vast and remorseless empire. How long would the people bow their necks to despotism?

In June, when he visited Washington to see his son in school there, the ex-President told a *New York Herald* correspondent that Grant did not "understand the philosophy of a single great ques-

---

[6] *New York World,* March 29, 1869.

[7] David R. Barbee to author, Washington, August 10, 1929; this despite Johnson's alleged aversion to rich men. When a principle was not at stake and a vote was, Johnson was not averse to flattery.

tion, and is completely lost in trying to understand his situation. He is mendacious, cunning, and treacherous. He lied to me flagrantly, by God, and I convicted him by my whole Cabinet."[8] While in the capital, a throng of several thousand called upon him, clamored for a speech and cheered him to the echo.

On his return to Tennessee, he continued his exhortations. At first, his Tennessee audiences had received him with deference; now they manifested increasing approval. The Tennessee radicals took alarm and adopted countermeasures. On August 2, at Maryville, they organized a mob to break up a Johnson meeting, and made three charges on the speaker's stand. Unawed by the tumult, the Old Warrior abashed them and forced them back every time. The better element of the state was humiliated at this ruffianly conduct, and vigorously expressed its disapproval.[9]

The occasion for this state-wide appearance of the former President was the pending election of a Governor of Tennessee and the members of the legislature. Late in February, when Brownlow had resigned as Governor to accept Patterson's seat in the Senate, D. W. C. Senter, Speaker of the Senate, had succeeded to the gubernatorial chair. Already unpopular with Tennessee's radical leaders, Senter wanted to be elected to succeed himself. For commissioners of registration he named Republicans who had favored a liberal interpretation of the radical franchise laws. In May his policy was strengthened by a decision of the State Supreme Court that any person with an old election certificate could use it. Thus a great antiradical vote was created in Middle and West Tennessee. Senter had the support of the conservative elements in his campaign. Johnson stumped the state, urging Senter's election and the choice of a conservative legislature. In every speech, he carried the war into Africa by his assaults on the radicals.

The results were the triumph of the Governor over his radical opponent and the election of a conservative legislature. After these unexpected events, the state began to buzz with the possibility that the former President might be elected to the Senate which so lately had tried his impeachment.

---

[8] *New York Herald,* June 27, 1869.
[9] Nashville *Union and American,* August 5, 1869.

Upon this prospect, radicals of the North and the South showed their apprehensions. President Grant told a Tennessee radical that he would regard Johnson's coming to the Senate as "a personal insult" to himself.[10] Boutwell, now Secretary of the Treasury, cried in alarm that Johnson's election "will raise gold from 136 to 200 and thereby endanger the national debt." The radicals tried to inflame the apprehensions of the bondholders, and the report was circulated that a large sum of money had been raised to use in the Tennessee legislature to encompass Johnson's defeat.

To this chorus of attack, the conservative and Democratic papers responded vigorously. "No man in the State," the St. Louis *Republican* declared, "could represent Tennessee with greater ability or usefulness." The Nashville *Union and American* predicted that "he may be thrust into office against his will," and a great demand went up in the state from the common people that their spokesman throw his hat into the ring.

Democrats in Washington were watching the Tennessee situation with keen attention. On August 8 Samuel J. Randall wrote Johnson of "the great joy which has been expressed by your friends . . . over your triumph in Tennessee. I know of no political event of recent years which can compare with it. You have once again fastened your foot upon the necks of your enemies and traducers." But Randall warned him that the radicals were raising money in Washington and through the North "to corrupt the legislature of Tennessee and thus defeat your election as Senator," and suggested that the Tennessean have Edmund Cooper report any evidence of the expenditure of any such fund, so that the Democrats in Congress would expose it.[11]

Tennessee was bitterly divided. It was urged against Johnson that East Tennessee already had one Senator. Others feared that his selection would tie the state to his personal grievance. One

[10] There is another version, given by J. B. Brownlow, the Parson's son, as to Grant's attitude. Brownlow was quoted in the Nashville *Union and American* of September 4, 1869, as saying that Grant had said Johnson would suit him as well as any other Democrat, and had ridiculed the idea that the ex-President would be any special annoyance to his administration. For citation, see Johnson Mss., CLV, No. 25,003.

[11] Johnson Mss., CLV, No. 24,834.

editor hinted that Johnson would give offense to Grant. But the Old Warrior went straight ahead, putting his devoted friend Edmund Cooper, now a State Senator, in charge of his campaign.[12]

The legislature met in October, and on the nineteenth, Cooper put Johnson in nomination. His "reputation as a statesman of broad and comprehensive views and of incomparable integrity and unflinching courage," he said, "is coextensive with the nation itself." On the first ballot, Johnson received eleven votes in the Senate and thirty-two in the House. The fourteen Senators and forty-nine Representatives against him were divided among the number of candidates. On the second and third ballots, Johnson's manager complimented his brother, Henry Cooper, a Senator from Davidson County, by voting for him, but on the next four he returned to Andrew Johnson.

On the eighth ballot, Johnson had lacked but two votes of the necessary number for success. Some of his ambitious and determined friends determined to be "practical," and secure the needed men. They set to work and presently one of them, a former president of the Nashville and Chattanooga Railroad, said: "Mr. President, you will be elected tomorrow." Johnson expressed his doubt. The friend answered that he had secured the necessary two votes.

"How?" Johnson inquired.

"I have to pay $1,000 for each vote," the railroad man replied.

"You will do no such thing," Johnson answered indignantly. "Go and tell those rascals the deal is off."

Upon his friend's demurring that he could not do it, as he was in honor bound to complete the deal, Johnson thundered: "But it is my honor that is involved. If I am elected by those purchased votes, as sure as the Lord lets me live, I will go before the legisla-

[12] At one time Cooper has been one of Johnson's private secretaries. Then he had been a member of the House from Tennessee. Later the President had nominated him Assistant Secretary of the Treasury. In June, 1868, Cooper went to New York to manage Johnson's interests in the Democratic national convention, and had written Johnson from the New York convention that the "ingratitude" which Southern leaders had displayed toward the President "is well calculated to cause one to doubt the honesty and integrity of mere politicians."

ture and expose the fraud and refuse to accept the election."[13]
And Johnson had his way.

On the evening of October 21, one of the roistering young
blades of the town, very much in his cups, staggered into Johnson's
room in the Maxwell House, cursed him wildly, and announced his
intention of cutting the ex-President's throat. The young drunkard
was quickly hustled out of the room, but the story was magnified a
thousand times, and added to the excitement of the packed hotel
lobbies.[14]

That same evening, a secret caucus was held at the City Hotel
by the radicals and the few conservatives who, because of private
bitternesses, were willing to join with anyone to block Johnson's
election. Emerson Etheridge, old-line Whig and Unionist though
he had been, announced that he would support and vote for any
man upon whom they could unite, "even if it were a negro."[15]
Other conservatives who personally hated Johnson expressed similar sentiments. One of the editors of the *Republican Banner,* the
Nashville organ of the radicals, suggested that they center upon
Henry Cooper, in order to attract the vote of the brother of their
candidate, Johnson's friend and manager! The group seized upon
the plan. Edmund Cooper had not been in the caucus and was
much embarrassed and disturbed at its decision, but finally agreed
to the plan. On October 22, a radical nominated Henry Cooper,
and he received fifty-five votes to Johnson's fifty-one, and was thus
duly elected to the Senate of the United States.[16]

Conservatives the country over were regretful over the outcome.
The *New York Herald* suggested that Johnson had fallen between
two fires; the bitter radicals and the equally bitter ex-Confederates

[13] Reeves's statement, quoted in Lloyd P. Stryker, *Andrew Johnson, A
Study in Courage* (New York, 1936), p. 831. Possibly the ex-president of
the railroad referred to was Michael Burns.

[14] Knoxville *Whig,* October 22, 1869, quoted in Knoxville *Journal,*
November 24, 1928.

[15] Nashville *Union and American,* November 1, 1874.

[16] Conversation of Duncan B. Cooper with Colonel Brabson, in Brabson's
Thesis; Nashville *Union and American,* October 23, 1869. Johnson never
forgave either of the Coopers, for the new Senator-Elect was also under
obligation to him, inasmuch as in 1862, while Military Governor, Johnson
had appointed him to a judgeship which he had held for five years.

had combined against him, the former because of his policy of
mercy to the South while President, the latter because of his support of the Union while the war itself was being waged. But it was
not Johnson's Presidential policies which had defeated him, the
Nashville *Union and American* declared. "The members of the
legislature that contributed mostly to his defeat were those who
sustained his policies both during the war and during his presidential term. It was his Democracy that defeated him."[17]

Yet, bitter though he was against the Coopers, Johnson did not
blame all the legislators, for he later gave a great supper to the
Assemblymen, and filed away in his papers the receipted bill from
the Stacy House for $664.00.[18]

During this same session of the legislature, the conservative majority decreed a new constitutional convention. Johnson followed
the sessions with sympathetic attention. The new constitution was
ratified at the polls, and in 1870 went into force. The legislature
immediately repealed the radical election and franchise laws, a
step which the radical North interpreted as the undoing of Reconstruction. Threats were made that federal bayonets would be sent
to Tennessee to insure Negro rights. When Governor Senter's
request for legislation to suppress the Ku Klux Klan was not met,
he asked Congress to reconstruct the state, and the Reconstruction
Committee held a prolonged investigation.

Stirred by these developments, the Speakers of the two Tennessee Houses issued a joint statement claiming that the legislature
had done everything in its power to remove all political distinction
against the Negroes. To the general surprise, Grant did not send
troops into the state. General Forrest announced that the Tennessee Klan had disbanded, and federal interference was avoided.

Early in 1870, it was disclosed that the radical who represented
the First Tennessee District in Congress had sold a West Point
cadetship. In March, the House passed a vote censuring him and
took up the question of whether or not to expel him. But as the
radicals feared that Andrew Johnson would be sent to succeed this

[17] Issue of December 8, 1869.
[18] Johnson Mss., CLV, No. 25,012.

worthy, the motion for expulsion fell short by twelve of the necessary two-thirds vote.[19]

During this year, Johnson remained at Greeneville, and rumors revived that he planned to re-enter business. He spent most of the time in his study, talking to old friends, reading newspapers, and writing letters and articles in defense of his policies. Whenever there was a court day, his house would be filled with friends from the country. His conversational style must have been somewhat difficult. He would state his views and then would demand that his listener "Answer that!"

The former President seemed ever keen to extend the circle of his friendship. Two young lawyers from the North established themselves in Greeneville, and he quickly cultivated them. Another young man, a former colonel in the Confederate Army, came to Greeneville to practice law. Two or three days after he had hung out his shingle, a distinguished gentleman entered his office, saying, "Mr. Reeves, I suppose; my name is Andrew Johnson." He paced up and down the office floor, telling the briefless lawyer that fees would come to him slowly at first. "I have traveled the road of poverty, and have felt its pinch," he continued. "If at any time you shall be in need of some financial help, just call on me, and it will be my pleasure to aid you." Then he said "Good day" and walked out. A little later Reeves was given a place on the *National Union,* Johnson's organ at Greeneville, and was formally appointed secretary to the tailor-statesman.[20] The addition of an ex-Confederate to his staff was a crafty political stroke. Johnson subdued his prejudices to accomplish his great ambition—his vindication by the people of Tennessee.[21]

He was urged to run for Congress from his old district, but refused; he did not think this a great enough vindication. Yet his mind could not keep away from politics and public problems. In the summer and fall of 1870 he made a few speeches, chiefly concerning the onerous nature of the public debt and the villainy

[19] Nashville *Union and American,* March 19, 1870.

[20] Reeves, pp. 826–827.

[21] Reeves's help proved invaluable in defeating the "Confederate Brigadiers." Some shrewd students say that without it Johnson could not have won in 1875.

of Congressional Reconstruction. He predicted that Grant would be re-elected because the majority sentiment against him in the nation could not be consolidated. Thus he kept his views before the people of the state.

In 1872, under a general redistricting bill, Tennessee was accorded an additional member of Congress, and there was some discussion about selecting him from the state at large, rather than from a newly created Congressional district. In May the Nashville *Union and American* announced authoritatively that if such a course was followed, Johnson would be a candidate. His friends became active in his behalf, and Colonel Reeves was dispatched to Nashville.

According to instructions, the night before the Democratic state convention at which the Congressman-at-large would be nominated, Reeves called on the Old Warrior in the latter's favorite room, No. 5, at the Maxwell House. After locking the door, Johnson told his aide of the pressure on him to become a candidate, but that he could not do so, because he had laid plans to run for the Senate to succeed Brownlow in 1875. "I would rather have the vindication of my State," he continued, "by electing me to my old seat in the Senate of the United States than to be monarch of the grandest empire on earth. For this I live, and will never die content without. . . . Go to the convention tomorrow, and if my name is put in nomination promptly withdraw it on my authority."[22]

The ex-President's directions were carried out, and on June 21 General Cheatham, Reeves's old Division Commander, was nominated by acclamation. Horace Maynard was selected by the Radical Republicans.

On his way home, Reeves was amazed to read an announcement from Nashville that Johnson had announced an independent candidacy for Congressman-at-large. The ex-President never explained this sudden change to his Confederate secretary, nor gave him an opportunity to ask about it.[23]

[22] Reeves, p. 832.
[23] Colonel Reeves told the author that the explanation he had arrived at in his own mind was that Johnson had acted under the influence of liquor. He also said that Johnson was not a man easily questioned about his

The announcement aroused furious public discussion. The former secessionists were vitriolic in their denunciation of this candidacy, which they rightly feared would result in Cheatham's defeat. A pamphlet was issued, in which the ex-President was raked fore and aft for all the sins of his career. F. C. Dunnington of Columbia, with Johnson's pardon in his pocket, assailed him as having "betrayed" his state, and quoted the harsh phrases of the first month of the Presidency about "traitors" needing to be "made odious and impoverished." With Johnson, he charged, ambition had become a passion; he had never "passed an eulogy on any living thing, except himself."[24]

But Johnson's friends were equally enthusiastic and combative in his behalf. There was a great demonstration in Nashville late in August. A band of workmen headed a monster procession to the public square, ending in a meeting at which the Old Warrior was formally put into nomination.

This campaign was one of the great political battles of Tennessee, ranking with the forensic combats of James K. Polk and "Lean Jimmy" Jones, Johnson's own tilts with Gustavus A. Henry and Meredith P. Gentry, the more recent War of the Roses between Bob and Alf Taylor, and the Patterson-Carmack joint debate. But the former President was greatly handicapped. Most of the conservative papers had already committed themselves to Cheatham. The chief incident was a great three-cornered debate. The candidates opened at Bristol, and proceeded westward through the state. One meeting of the three aspirants took place in a cedar grove near Lebanon, a little Middle Tennessee college town. Cheatham was no orator. He haltingly read the speech the editor of the Nashville *Union and American* had prepared for him, but the crowd applauded him to the echo. His main theme was that, after twenty-seven years in office, Johnson ought to give him a chance.

---

conduct, that he preserved an air of great dignity even with his intimates, and, in all the six years of Reeves's association with him, never addressed his quasi-secretary except formally as "Mr. Reeves."

[24] *Mr. Dunnington to Ex-President Johnson* (Columbia, Tennessee, September 30, 1872); an extremely rare pamphlet, for photostat of which I am indebted to Mr. David Rankin Barbee of Washington.

Earnest, quiet, deliberate, Johnson spoke without a trace of bombast.[25] His appearance was dignified and courtly, but "while he never ranted, his eyes were ablaze." His words, readily understandable, revealed mastery of the English language and breadth and play of intellect. The impression he made was not of eloquence, but of impressive truth; his chaste, well-chosen language, his homely, apt illustrations, and his remarkable magnetism compelled people to listen to him.

General Cheatham had denounced Johnson with bitterness. The ex-President, while assailing Toombs, Yancey and other Southern leaders who had precipitated secession, was courteous toward Cheatham himself, but minced no words in defending his own support of the Union. He had stood for the Union and the Constitution in 1861 and recanted not a single word. He was still for the Union and the Constitution and therefore was determinedly opposed to the Radical Reconstruction scheme.

A crowd of rowdies kept crying out: "Tell us something about Mrs. Surratt." But having learned a costly lesson in the "swing around the circle," Johnson ignored these shouts from the crowd, and kept to his closely reasoned speech. At the beginning, the great majority of the crowd was unfriendly to him, but upon his conclusion he received a great ovation.

The debate was closed by Horace Maynard, then in the height of his power as an orator; "he wielded the blade of an Aladdin," one who heard him there recounted. Nonetheless, Johnson had the honors of the triangular argument. His sincerity had won the crowd.

Many stories yet linger concerning this famous campaign. A beginning lawer at Jasper was amazed to see the former President toss off a tall tumbler of peach brandy with as much unconcern and with as little perceptible aftereffect as if it had been water.[26] After a speaking engagement in the Sequatchie Valley, Johnson

[25] Foster V. Brown of Chattanooga and General Lillard Thompson of Lebanon, both of whom were in the audience that day, have kindly furnished me memorandums of their recollections and impressions of the speech.
[26] Recollections of Foster V. Brown of Chattanooga to author in conversation.

had himself driven to the Tennessee River, to cross it and catch a train to Chattanooga. When the yawl in which he was being ferried ran aground and he saw the train approaching, the campaigner jumped into the river and waded to the bank.[27] That afternoon he was on hand at old James Hall in Chattanooga to cross swords with his two competitors.

The meeting lasted all afternoon. Cheatham, as usual, was brief in his discussion, and Maynard masterful in his attack on Johnson's administration. But the former President carried off the honors. "His impressive earnestness," an auditor declared, "was penetrating. No competitor indulged in an anecdote but once. Mr. Johnson made the orator ashamed of himself for wasting the time of the people when the momentous issues of their country were under discussion." At the close of the debate, Maynard retired to his hotel "as exhausted as a race horse that had run four miles." But a crowd, with a band of music, appeared to serenade Andrew Johnson, who came out of his hotel, mounted a baggage truck at the Union Depot, and made a touching speech. As he approached, the crowd warmed up and one old Irishman jumped on the truck and took the speaker in his arms, shouting, "It's the same Andy of 1856!"[28]

"Maynard will be elected," Johnson told friends before the vote, "but I have succeeded in breaking up that military ring in Nashville."[29] His prediction was verified. Maynard received 80,000, Cheatham 63,000, and Johnson 37,000 votes. The tailor-statesman was not disappointed, for he had "reduced the rebel brigadiers to the ranks."[30]

In 1873 East Tennessee was visited with a fearful cholera epidemic. Johnson and his family had the means to flee the plague, but this did not seem an example to set and they remained in Greeneville. At length, the ex-President was seized with the

[27] Reeves, p. 833.

[28] Recollections of Colonel W. M. Nixon of Chattanooga, who was in the crowd; communicated to author, May 17, 1929.

[29] James S. Jones, *Andrew Johnson* (Greeneville, Tenn., 1901), pp. 347–349.

[30] Temple, *Notable Men of Tennessee*, p. 142.

cholera. For a while he was at the point of death; after several weeks he rallied, but he never fully recovered his strength.

On June 9, when his infirmities seemed about to overcome him, the stricken statesman gave a last message to his friends. "Approaching death to me is a mere shadow of God's protecting wing," he wrote. "Here I know can no evil come; here I will rest in quiet and peace beyond the reach of calumny's poisoned shaft; the influential, evil and jealous enemies; where treason and traitors in States, where backsliders and hypocrites in the church, can have no place, where the great fact will be realized that God is Truth, and gratitude the highest attribute of man."

Later that year, the famous Johnson-Holt controversy over the case of Mrs. Surratt arose. Holt began it by a long diatribe in the Washington *Chronicle* of August 25. The Judge Advocate General had been so harried by the reports that he had suppressed the recommendation of mercy that he sought to deny the charge. Surprised at this bold declaration, Johnson wrote some of his old associates, including Colonel Moore and Gideon Welles, for their recollections, and in October published a dignified but crushing reply.

The Panic of 1873 was wreaking havoc in the country. Among the banks which failed was the First National Bank of Washington, which at the time had on deposit $73,000 of Johnson's savings. His loss was so generally discussed in the press that he issued a statement that even if the entire amount was lost, his resources would be sufficient to maintain him.[31]

Later that fall, someone asked if he planned to be a candidate for the Senate. "Of course I will," he answered jocularly. "The damned brigadiers having been destroyed, what hinders me from going to the Senate?"[32]

When Johnson started his campaign for the Senate in the fall of 1874, no one thought he had any chance. But he planned very shrewdly. First, he sent Reeves around to check up on the prefer-

[31] On November 10 the bank paid a dividend of 30 per cent; on April 8, 1874, 20 per cent; on April 4, 1875, 10 per cent; and Johnson's estate later was paid in full.
[32] Winston, p. 498.

ences of the new legislators. Then he himself opened a powerful campaign against Governor Neil Brown, one of the candidates for Brownlow's seat, with incidental denunciation of the Coopers. Most of the legislators were divided in their attachment between Governor Brown and General Bate, the latter having a slight advantage.[33]

Johnson was much pleased at Reeves's report. "Brown can't be elected, but he is desperate," he told his aide. "Brown will not let Bate, and Bate, being the stronger of the two, will not let Brown be elected; therefore the two will fight each other instead of fighting me; my plan is working just as I have contrived."[34]

The response to Johnson's "swing around the circle" in the state was also gratifying. He covered Tennessee from Bristol to the Mississippi, and everywhere attacked Brown alone of the Senatorial competitors. In every speech he also denounced the Cooper brothers, this excoriation forming the climax and culmination of his speech. It was a blistering invective. He was scheduled to speak at Columbia, the home of Colonel D. B. Cooper, half brother of the "traitors." Before he reached the town, word came that if he repeated his denunciation there, he would be killed.

On his arrival, he learned that a bitter political enemy had secured the courthouse and was talking against time to keep him out. Thereupon Johnson instructed two young men to find some goods boxes, and put them outside the courthouse—he would speak from them. They placed them under D. B. Cooper's window.

"I have been told," the Old Warrior began his speech, "that if I repeated here today what I said on former occasions, perhaps I would be assassinated. But these two eyes have never yet beheld the man that this heart feared. I have said on former occasions, and I repeat it now, that Jesus Christ had his Judas, Caesar had his Brutus, Charles I had his Cromwell, Washington had his Benedict Arnold, and I have had my Edmund and Henry Cooper."

[33] The Shelby County voters had likewise held an informal referendum on the Senatorship and Johnson had received a large majority. The Memphis members announced that they considered themselves bound by this expression of the voters' will.
[34] Reeves, p. 833.

As he paused, pistols were cocked and trained on Cooper's window. But there was no sign of trouble. Johnson went on with his speech.[35]

The legislature, which met on January 4, 1875, was made up of ninety-two Democrats and eight Republicans. On January 19, it proceeded to the Senatorial election. In addition to Johnson, Brown and Bate, William H. Quarles, William H. Stephens, Edwin H. Ewing, and John H. Savage were put into nomination. On the first ballot, Johnson had ten more votes than any other candidate. A deadlock between Brown and Bate quickly developed, and the feeling between their supporters grew more bitter day by day. As Johnson predicted, each was determined that the other not be named.

The former President stayed in his room at the Maxwell House, listening to reports and impressing all comers with his optimism. But he was not without wile. General Nathan Bedford Forrest had come to Nashville to work in behalf of General Bate. "When the gods arrive, the half-gods depart," Johnson told Forrest. "If the people really wanted to send a Confederate military hero to the Senate," he said, "they would elect Forrest himself, instead of a 'one-horse general.' " Struck by the force of this observation, the Wizard of the Saddle abandoned his efforts for Bate, and went back to Memphis.[36]

After four days of exciting and fruitless voting, Brown, Stephens, and Quarles withdrew, and their strength went to Andrew Johnson. On the forty-fourth ballot, Bate had forty-eight, just one shy of the necessary number; the former President had forty-two. "I may not be elected, but Bate never will be," Johnson declared, on learning this news. "When a man gets that close, and does not get the final one vote necessary, he never will get it."[37] His prophecy proved correct.

Bate withdrew the next day and Brown re-entered. On the fifty-fourth ballot, Johnson secured three new votes in the Senate. He

[35] A. M. Hughes, Nashville *Banner,* December 18, 1927.

[36] Temple, p. 439–442.

[37] Brabson Thesis, quoting conversation with Chancellor John Allison of Nashville.

maintained his strength in the House, and was thus chosen, by a
majority of one, to succeed Parson Brownlow in the Senate of the
United States.[38]

Upon the election, young Alf Taylor, Republican Representative from Carter County, ran from the Capitol to the Maxwell
House, dashed up the steps to Room No. 5, shouted: "Mr. Johnson, you are elected!" and then fell in a faint. The new Senator was
dashing water in his face when the less speedy Reeves arrived. In a
moment N. B. Spears of Marion County, a huge giant of a man,
lumbered in, seized the new Senator by his feet and trotted around
the room with him, dancing and capering with joy. As the news
spread over Nashville, a great crowd assembled at the Maxwell
House to cheer the vindicated statesman.[39]

The night after Johnson's election, a great mass meeting was
held in his honor. George W. Jones, the saddlemaker who had
become the watchdog of the Treasury, and then had followed his
state, presided. It was a great moment when he introduced his
lifelong friend, the tailor who had gone with his nation, to the
throng in his hour of final triumph. The new Senator made a
speech in which he paid tribute to the affectionate perseverance of
his friends. "Look to the legislature," he said, "and see how many
Confederate soldiers supported me. How many Republicans do
you think supported me? . . . There they were all united around
the altar of the country, and gave their decision in favor of me."[40]

Nor did he neglect to thank individual legislators, and to tender
them sound advice. "What I have to say seems very simple and
unimportant," he said to young Benton McMillin, then finishing
his first term in the General Assembly. "But it is of the utmost

[38] Two of the men who changed explained that they did so because their
constituents were overwhelmingly for Johnson. Of those who elected him,
forty-four were Democrats, eight Republicans. Thirty ex-Confederates and
twenty-two ex-Federals voted for him (Nashville *Union and American,*
January 29, 1875). The story of this election would not be complete without
reference to the loyalty with which the Shelby County legislators had kept
their pledge to abide by that county's referendum on the Senatorship. Many
of them were bitterly hostile to Johnson personally, and one, J. Harvey
Mathes, had lost a leg at Chickamauga while serving on Bate's staff.

[39] Reeves, p. 834.

[40] Nashville *Union and American,* January 27, 1875.

importance to one who seeks favor of the public. If you should continue in public life, be sure of one thing . . . that you always strive to keep in touch with and on the side of the *common people.* With them for you, corporations and combinations may organize against you . . . but they will war in vain. . . . Keep the common people on your side and you will win."[41] It was advice from the depths of his heart.

This final triumph caught the attention and aroused the admiration of the country. No "common man," Thurlow Weed wrote the editor of the *New York Tribune,* "could have dug himself out of a pit so deep and so dark as that into which he had fallen."[42] Every mail brought the new Senator congratulations from the whole nation. General Custer wrote delightedly from Fort Lincoln. Groesbeck and Stanbery were almost transported with delight. "I have received so many personal congratulations," wrote the latter, "that I almost began to think I was myself the successful candidate—such a shaking of hands I have not gone through for many a day. . . . There is more real satisfaction in your success than I have known upon the election of any Senator."

In Buffalo, exultant New York Democrats fired one hundred guns in honor of the great triumph. Citizens of Atlanta held a great public meeting on January 30 to pass resolutions of delight. In transmitting them, W. M. Lowry added, "Who knows, my dear sir, but that in the whirl of events you may be the next Democratic candidate for President?" Ex-Governor Joe Brown, now president of the Western and Atlantic Railroad, sent him an annual pass and asked him to visit the Georgia capital. From Chattanooga, D. M. Key wrote of the genuine joy that Johnson's election had given "to all parties, not only in your own State, but throughout the nation."[43]

The newspapers of the country, radical and conservative alike, paid tribute to Johnson's indomitable pluck. The St. Louis *Repub-*

[41] Statement of former Governor McMillin to author, Nashville, March 29, 1928.

[42] *New York Tribune,* January 25, 1875.

[43] Johnson Mss. CLXIII–CLXIV are filled with these and similar expressions of delight over the ex-President's success.

lican termed his election "the most magnificent personal triumph which the history of American politics can show." The Nashville *Union and American* said that he had never been greater than in the moment of his victory. The Cincinnati *Commercial* testified to the common people's abounding faith in him, and *The New York Times* predicted that he would have something to say well worth the nation's hearing. Johnson's "personal integrity was beyond question," said *The Nation,* "and his respect for the law and the Constitution made his Administration a remarkable contrast to that which succeeded it."[44]

President Grant soon called the Senate into extra session to act on a treaty with the ruler of the Sandwich Islands. It was to begin on March 4, and Johnson proceeded to Washington. On March 4 the Senate galleries were packed, and as the new Senator from Tennessee walked down the aisle, thunderous applause burst from them.

The Senate was to organize the next day. Johnson's desk was covered with flowers sent by admirers. A little after noon, the ex-President entered the Senate, his sturdy form clad in old-fashioned broadcloth, and a group quickly formed around him. Edmunds of Vermont, who had voted to impeach him, was addressing the chair. He looked at the group about Johnson, faltered in his speech, "kicked over a lot of old books on his desk, and abruptly sat down." Roscoe Conkling pretended to read a letter, but looked slyly at Johnson from the corner of his eye. Frelinghuysen sank to his knees after a book. Carl Schurz, now a liberal Democrat, stood up. John Sherman at first seemed not to know what to do; then he approached and shook hands. Oliver P. Morton was in a dilemma. First he had supported Johnson and then he had voted to convict him. But the Tennessean magnanimously stretched forth his hand. "He wore the same kindly smile as in times before," Morton later said. "That showed nobility of soul. There are not many men who could have done that!" Boutwell sat at his desk, perhaps meditating on "the hole in the sky" to which seven years before he had proposed that Johnson be consigned. Physically, the former Presi-

[44] *The Nation,* August 5, 1875.

dent had changed less than almost any other Senator on the floor. His hair was somewhat thinned, but the *Herald*'s correspondent noted that there were neither "hard lines, nor deep wrinkles in his face"; his expression, however, showed a mixture of earnestness and sadness.

The clerk began to call the roll for newly elected Senators to take the oath. "Hannibal Hamlin," he called, and Lincoln's first running mate responded. "Andrew Johnson," he continued, and Lincoln's second running mate answered, "Present." Then Johnson's Tennessee colleague—it was Henry Cooper!—came down the aisle, bowed stiffly, and with Senator McCreery of Kentucky escorted the new Senator to the Vice-Presidential desk, where he stood beside Hamlin and Burnside of Rhode Island. Vice-President Henry Wilson of Massachusetts, who, seven years before, as a Senator, had voted not only to convict Johnson of high crimes and misdemeanors, but likewise "for his disqualification from hereafter holding any office under the Constitution he has violated and the government he has dishonored," administered the oath. After he had sworn, the Tennessean turned and shook Hamlin's hand and then that of the Vice-President, to a tumult of applause and cheers. As he went to his seat, a little page stepped up and handed him a bouquet.[45]

Throughout this scene, Johnson bore himself composedly, but to avoid its continuance he retired to the cloakroom, followed there by former enemies eager to shake his hands. "I miss my old friends," he told McCreery, with tears in his eyes, "Bayard, Buckalew, Reverdy Johnson, Fessenden, Fowler, Trumbull, Grimes, Henderson, Ross, all gone, all but yourself." Gone likewise were some of his enemies. Sumner's fine figure was no more to be seen. Ben Wade had been removed by the people of Ohio. Of the thirty-five Senators who voted to convict, only thirteen remained.

There was a good deal of speculation throughout the country as to how Johnson would conduct himself. "I have no wrongs to

---

[45] Brabson Thesis; DeWitt, *Impeachment*, pp. 623–624; *New York Herald*, March 8, 1875; *New York World*, March 6, 1875; Crook, *Through Five Administrations*, p. 150; Stryker, pp. 809–810; Winston, pp. 503–505.

redress but my country's," he told a correspondent. "My election settled all personal injuries ever inflicted. I come now to deal only with present issues."[46] When the *Tribune's* correspondent commented that his two rooms on the second floor of the old Willard were not as commodious as his former home on the Avenue,[47] the Old Warrior answered, with a twinkle in his eye, "But they are more comfortable."

A day or so after he had taken the oath, Johnson sent for his old friend Crook to come to see him. He wanted to know where in his scrapbooks he would find the notices about Grant. "You remember where you pasted them in," he said to his old attaché; "I don't." Crook turned the pages, put in the proper markings, and rose to go.

Then the ex-President unburdened himself. "Crook, I have come back to the Senate with two purposes," he said. "One is to do what I can to punish the Southern brigadiers. They led the South into Secession, and they never have had their deserts." Crook asked what was the other. "The other is to make a speech against Grant, and I am going to make it this session."[48]

Sure enough, his one speech during the special session of the Senate was on Grant. He made it on March 22, in connection with a resolution which Grant men had introduced into the Senate to approve that President's action in using federal troops to prop up the unspeakable Kellogg's villainous administration in Louisiana. Announcement had been made that the Tennessean planned to speak, and the galleries were filled with people eager to hear him turn the tables upon Grant. The subject was fruitful, for it is doubtful if any of the Southern carnivals of corruption which masqueraded as governments were more shameless than that in Louisiana. The crowning outrage—thus far—had come when Grant presumed to ignore the verdict of a state, and to place by force an expelled adventurer in the Governor's chair.

"The President of the United States assumes to take command of the state and assign these people a governor," the indignant

---

[46] Nashville *Union and American,* March 11, 1875.
[47] *New York Tribune,* March 8, 1875.
[48] Crook, pp. 151–152.

Senator from Tennessee proclaimed. He read Grant's weak excuse that the election at which Kellogg had been displaced was "a gigantic fraud." If such were the case, Johnson commented, both candidates were disqualified. But the truth was that "the President finds a usurper in power, and he takes it upon himself to make the Government of the United States a party to his usurpation. . . . Is not this monstrous in a free Government?"

The Constitution had been trampled under foot so often that no one knew whither things were drifting. "Is Louisiana a commonwealth as it now stands? Or is her government maintained by military power, and that through the President of the United States? Is it his government?" He urged the Senate to defeat the resolution for Grant's endorsement, and in its place to make him the Catonian answer: "Bid him disband his legions; return the commonwealth to liberty." These alarums of Southern outrages, he hinted, were planned so that "in the midst of the war cry," Grant could "triumphantly ride into the Presidency for a third presidential term." "And when this is done," he shouted, "farewell to the liberties of the country." The galleries broke forth into wild applause, which was repeated when he asked, "How far off is empire? How far off is military despotism?"

His conclusion had the ring of his speeches on the eve of Sumter: "Give me the Constitution of my country unimpaired. . . . In the language of Webster, let this Union be preserved 'now and forever, one and inseparable.' Let us stand equals in the Union, all upon equality. Let peace and Union be restored to the land. May God bless this people, and God save the Constitution."

It was Johnson's last great public speech. Two days later the Senate adjourned, and he returned to his home in Tennessee. He stayed at Greeneville for several weeks, seeming particularly happy with Martha Patterson and her children. On July 28, he set out to visit his other daughter, Mary Stover, who was living in Carter County, about two miles from Elizabethton.

On the train from Greeneville to Carter's Station, the ex-President talked with Alf Taylor, who found him "never more interesting." Captain W. E. McElwee of Harriman, another old friend who was on the train, elicited from Johnson this retrospecting:

"More than a hundred times I said to myself: What course may I pursue so that the calm and great historian will say one hundred years from now, 'He pursued the right course'?" McElwee remembered that Johnson had termed Stanton the "Marat of American politics" and had explained that he was not assassinated by Charlotte Corday, "but had cut his damned throat from ear to ear." It was kept out of the public press, Johnson continued, but Stanton had cultivated his vindictive anger until "his reason was dethroned."[49]

When Johnson alighted at Carter's Station, his daughter's buggy had not arrived, and young Selden Nelson, son of his counsel in the impeachment, procured him a horse.[50] He had not ridden far when the Stover buggy met him, and he reached his daughter's farm about an hour before noon.

Johnson had often said that, when he died, he hoped and expected to go "all at once and nothing first."[51] His hope came true. After lunch that day, his granddaughter, Lillie Stover, walked to his room with him. As she was going out, she heard a heavy thud; Johnson had fallen on the carpet. It was a stroke of paralysis. As he lay in bed the next day, he talked of the days of long ago, of his tailor shop, political campaigns, the battles of ante-bellum Tennessee. Another stroke followed, and he became unconscious. He lingered on, until at two thirty on the morning of July 31, Andrew Johnson died.

The Stover house was filled with mourners, plain people from the hills. Early Sunday morning, the family set out for Greeneville with the body. The town was draped in black. The old tailor shop was hung with mourning. With difficulty a suitable casket was secured for the body; the silver plate upon it was engraved: "Andrew Johnson, Seventeenth President of the United States." "When I die," he had said several years before, "I desire no better winding sheet than the Stars and Stripes, and no softer pillow than

[49] McElwee statement is in Tennessee State Library, quoted in Chattanooga *News,* May 21, 1923.
[50] Statement of the late Selden Nelson to author. Nelson remembered how well Johnson looked that morning and derided the possibility of there being any truth to the canard that he had been intoxicated the night before.
[51] *New York World,* March 29, 1869.

the Constitution of my country." Remembering, his friends wrapped him in a fine new flag with thirty-seven stars, while they placed his worn and much thumbed copy of the Constitution beneath his head.

Knoxville, Nashville, and Memphis each asked the privilege of affording burial to the departed statesman. But his family denied them all; in Greene County's soil he should be laid to rest. He had himself selected the spot for his burial, a cone-shaped hill about half a mile from his home. With his own hands he had planted there a willow from his yard, the offshoot of the tree brought from Napoleon's St. Helena tomb.[52]

All Tennessee and much of America was represented at the funeral. The procession, more than half a mile in length, included the great and the humble, the statesmen from the national capital, and the unkempt mourners from the hills. Blackstone McDannell walked at the head of the coffin, and the procession slowly made its way through the little town to the chosen hillock.

After the sonorous phrases of its burial, a Masonic choir chanted the requiem, a bugler sounded taps, and Andrew Johnson was at rest.[53]

Among those who attended the funeral was a boy of seventeen, a young printer on the Knoxville *Chronicle* named Adolph Ochs, on his first news story. He had telegraphed to several papers seeking the assignment to "cover" the obsequies, and Henry Watterson's Louisville *Courier-Journal* had ordered 250 words. About a year later, when young Ochs, now a reporter for the Knoxville *Tribune,* revisited Greeneville, he found that Johnson's grave had not been marked. After the publication of his story telling of this, his paper received a letter from Mrs. Patterson, explaining the reason for the delay. The Master Tailors' Association of the United States, she wrote, had asked the privilege of erecting the monument to the

[52] Brabson Thesis.
[53] Winston, pp. 507–509; Brabson Thesis; Stryker, pp. 822, 823, 824. Johnson's first Masonic degrees had been conferred by Greeneville Lodge, No. 119. He later was passed and raised, and became a Royal Arch Mason and a Knight Templar. See Greeneville, Tennessee, *Democrat-Sun,* December 23, 1929.

nation's only tailor-President, and the family had agreed. But the association had been slow in carrying out its plan.

Soon thereafter, the Pattersons themselves undertook the erection of an appropriate monument.[54] A few months later it was unveiled with fitting ceremony, and Andrew Johnson's lifelong friend, George W. Jones, made the chief address.

There, in the friendly soil of his beloved Greene County, rests Andrew Johnson, his head cushioned on the worn copy of the Constitution, his body wrapped in the Stars and Stripes. Carved on the simple shaft above him are the words: "His faith in the people never wavered."

[54] Statement of Adolph S. Ochs, to author, Chattanooga, May 16, 1929.

Bibliographical Note

The Introduction to this volume, being principally concerned with the mode and quality of changing thought on Andrew Johnson, hardly constitutes a full guide to the literature. For this, the reader is referred to the following essays, which combine virtues both historiographic and bibliographic: Willard Hays, "Andrew Johnson's Reputation," *East Tennessee Historical Society Publications,* Nos. 31 (1959), pp. 1–31, and 32 (1960), pp. 18–50; Albert Castel, "Andrew Johnson: His Historiographical Rise and Fall," *Mid-America,* XLV (July 1963), 175–184; and Carmen Anthony Notaro, "History of the Biographic Treatment of Andrew Johnson in the Twentieth Century," *Tennessee Historical Quarterly,* XXIV (Summer 1965), 143–155.

The items that follow are—with a few exceptions—works discussed or mentioned in the introductory essay.

Henry Wilson, *History of the Rise and Fall of the Slave Power in America,* 3 vols. (Boston: J. R. Osgood, 1872–1877); James G. Blaine, *Twenty Years of Congress: From Lincoln to Garfield,* 2 vols. (Norwich, Conn.: Henry Bill, 1884); George S. Boutwell, *Reminiscences of Sixty Years in Public Affairs,* 2 vols. (New York: McClure, Phillips, 1902); Carl Schurz, *The Reminiscences of Carl Schurz,* 3 vols. (Garden City: Doubleday, Page, 1913); Hugh McCulloch, *Men and Measures of Half a Century: Sketches and Comments* (New York: Scribner's, 1888); John T. Morse, ed., *Diary of Gideon Welles, Secretary of the Navy under Lincoln and Johnson,* 3 vols. (Boston: Houghton, Mifflin, 1911). These are all reminiscences written by Johnson's contemporaries.

David M. DeWitt, *The Impeachment and Trial of Andrew Johnson*

. . . (New York: Macmillan, 1903); William A. Dunning, *Reconstruction, Political and Economic* (New York: Harper's, 1907); James Ford Rhodes, *History of the United States* . . . (New York: Macmillan, 1893–1922), V–VI; James Schouler, "President Johnson and Posterity," *Bookman*, XXXIV (January 1912), 498–504, and *History of the Reconstruction Period, 1865–1877* (New York: Dodd, Mead, 1913); Benjamin B. Kendrick, *The Journal of the Joint Committee of Fifteen on Reconstruction* (New York: Columbia University Press, 1914); Clifton R. Hall, *Andrew Johnson, Military Governor of Tennessee* (Princeton: Princeton University Press, 1916); and Ellis P. Oberholtzer, *A History of the United States Since the Civil War* (New York: Macmillan, 1917–1937), I–II, are works by professional historians, together representing the trend of historical thought on Johnson prior to World War I. The quotation in the Introduction from J. G. de Roulhac Hamilton is in "The Southern Policy of Andrew Johnson," *State Literary and Historical Association of North Carolina Proceedings* (1915), p. 80; that from Lawrence H. Gipson is in "The Statesmanship of President Johnson: A Study of the Presidential Reconstruction Policy," *Mississippi Valley Historical Review*, II (December 1915), 382.

Two works typical of the 1920's are Don C. Seitz, *The Dreadful Decade* (Indianapolis: Bobbs-Merrill, 1926) and Claude G. Bowers, *The Tragic Era: The Revolution after Lincoln* (Boston: Houghton, Mifflin, 1929).

Three biographies, published in successive years, are Robert W. Winston, *Andrew Johnson, Plebeian and Patriot* (New York: Henry Holt, 1928); Lloyd Paul Stryker, *Andrew Johnson, A Study in Courage* (New York: Macmillan, 1929); and George F. Milton, *The Age of Hate: Andrew Johnson and the Radicals* (New York: Coward, McCann, 1930).

Howard K. Beale, *The Critical Year: A Study of Andrew Johnson and Reconstruction* (New York: Harcourt, Brace, 1930), defends Johnson, but, in stressing economic factors, does so on somewhat different grounds from those of his predecessors; James G. Randall, *The Civil War and Reconstruction* (Boston: D. C. Heath, 1937), proceeds on established lines. W. E. B. Du Bois, *Black Reconstruction in America* (New York: Harcourt, Brace, 1935) and James S. Allen, *Reconstruction: The Battle for Democracy* (New York: International Publishers, 1937) are Marxist studies.

The "revisionist" essays mentioned are T. Harry Williams, "An

Analysis of Some Reconstruction Attitudes," *Journal of Southern History,* XII (November 1946), 469–486; Howard K. Beale, "On Rewriting Reconstruction History," *American Historical Review,* XLV (July 1940), 807–827; and David Donald, "Why They Impeached Andrew Johnson," *American Heritage,* VIII (December 1956), 21–25, 102–103.

Works published since 1960 include Eric L. McKitrick, *Andrew Johnson and Reconstruction* (Chicago: University of Chicago Press, 1960); Harold M. Hyman, "Johnson, Stanton, and Grant: A Reconsideration of the Army's Role in the Events Leading to Impeachment," *American Historical Review,* LXVI (October 1960), 85–100; John Hope Franklin, *Reconstruction after the Civil War* (Chicago: University of Chicago Press, 1961); H. M. Hyman and Benjamin Thomas, *Stanton: The Life and Times of Lincoln's Secretary of War* (New York: Knopf, 1962); LaWanda and John H. Cox, *Politics, Principle, and Prejudice, 1865–1866* (New York: Free Press, 1963); W. R. Brock, *An American Crisis: Congress and Reconstruction, 1865–1867* (New York: St. Martin's, 1963); and Kenneth M. Stampp, *The Era of Reconstruction, 1865–1877* (New York: Knopf, 1965). James G. Randall and David Donald, *The Civil War and Reconstruction* (Boston: D. C. Heath, 1961) is the revision, incorporating recent scholarship, of a work originally published in 1937. Two popular accounts which reflect older attitudes on Johnson and Reconstruction, and are thus exceptions to the interpretive trend discussed in the introductory essay, are Milton Lomask, *Andrew Johnson: President on Trial* (New York: Straus & Cudahy, 1960); and Lately Thomas, *The First President Johnson: The Three Lives of the Seventeenth President of the United States of America* (New York: Morrow, 1968). Leroy P. Graf and Ralph W. Haskins, eds., *The Papers of Andrew Johnson* (Knoxville: University of Tennessee Press, 1967–   ), I, is the first volume in what will be the definitive edition of Johnson source materials.

Contributors

HOWARD K. BEALE (1899–1959) taught at the University of North Carolina and was Professor of History at the University of Wisconsin from 1948 until his death. In addition to his *Critical Year* he wrote *Theodore Roosevelt and the Rise of America to World Power* (1956), which was part of a projected major biography of Roosevelt.

LAWANDA C. COX, born in 1909, and her husband, JOHN H. COX, born in 1907, collaborated to write *Politics, Principle, and Prejudice,* together with other monographic essays on the Reconstruction era. Mrs. Cox is Professor of History at Hunter College. Mr. Cox has taught at the College of the City of New York since 1941.

CLIFTON R. HALL (1884–1945) taught American history at Princeton University for thirty-five years. He was an authority on Theodore Roosevelt and had partially completed a biography of Roosevelt at the time of his death.

GEORGE F. MILTON (1894–1955) was a newspaper editor, historian, and economist who served in several government posts in the administrations of Franklin D. Roosevelt. He published numerous works, among them *The Eve of Conflict: Stephen A. Douglas and the Needless War* (1934), *The American Civil War* (1941), *Abraham Lincoln and the Fifth Column* (1942), and *The Use of Presidential Power, 1789–1943* (1944).

KENNETH M. STAMPP, born in 1912, is Morrison Professor of History at the Berkeley campus of the University of California. He has been a Commonwealth Fund lecturer at the University of London and Harmsworth Professor of American History at Oxford. A leading student of American slavery and the Civil War era, Professor Stampp has written *The Era of Reconstruction, 1865–1877* (1965), *The Peculiar Institution* (1956), *And the War Came* (1950), and *Indiana Politics during the Civil War* (1949).

OLIVER P. TEMPLE (1820–1907) was active in Tennessee politics for most of his life, and had the distinction of making the first Union speech in the state after the election of Abraham Lincoln. He knew Andrew Johnson personally. His published works include *East Tennessee and the Civil War* (1899) and *Union Leaders of East Tennessee* (1903).

ROBERT W. WINSTON (1860–1944) was a lifelong participant in the political and cultural affairs of his native North Carolina. A lawyer by training, he re-entered college at the age of sixty to prepare himself "to interpret the New South to the Nation and the Nation to the New South." Besides his *Andrew Johnson, Plebeian and Patriot* (1928), his writings include *The Life of Jefferson Davis* (1930) and *Robert E. Lee* (1934).

ERIC L. McKITRICK, born in Michigan in 1919, holds three degrees from Columbia University, where he is now Professor of History. Mr. McKitrick has taught at the University of Chicago and Douglass College, Rutgers University, and has been the recipient of numerous awards, including fellowships from the Rockefeller Foundation, the Social Science Research Council, and the National Endowment for Humanities. A specialist in nineteenth-century American history, Professor McKitrick won the Dunning Prize of the American Historical Association with his first book, *Andrew Johnson and Reconstruction* (1960). He has since published *Slavery Defended: The Views of the Old South* and is now at work on a book about the age of Washington and Jefferson.

✪

AÏDA DiPACE DONALD holds degrees from Barnard and Columbia and a Ph.D. from the University of Rochester. A former member of the History Department at Columbia, Mrs. Donald has been a Fulbright Fellow at Oxford and the recipient of an A.A.U.W. fellowship. She has published *John F. Kennedy and the New Frontier* and *Diary of Charles Francis Adams.*